The ABCs of
Windows NT
Workstation 4

The ABCs of
Windows® NT®
Workstation 4

Charlie Russel

SYBEX®

San Francisco – Paris – Düsseldorf – Soest

Associate Publisher: Gary Masters
Acquisitions Manager: Kristine Plachy
Developmental Editor: Sherry Schmitt
Editor: Lee Ann Pickrell
Technical Editor: Rob Sanfilippo
Book Design Director: Catalin Dulfu
Book Designer: Design Site, Tracy Dean
Desktop Publisher: Jimmie Young
Production Coordinator: Kimberley Askew-Qasem
Indexer: Ted Laux
Cover Designer: Design Site
Cover Photographer: Eric Meola
Cover Illustrator: Jack D. Myers

Screen reproductions produced with Collage Complete.

Collage Complete is a trademark of Inner Media Inc.

SYBEX is a registered trademark of SYBEX Inc.

TRADEMARKS: SYBEX has attempted throughout this book to distinguish proprietary trademarks from descriptive terms by following the capitalization style used by the manufacturer.

Every effort has been made to supply complete and accurate information. However, SYBEX assumes no responsibility for its use, nor for any infringement of the intellectual property rights of third parties which would result from such use.

Library of Congress Card Number: 96-69915
ISBN: 0-7821-1999-9

Manufactured in the United States of America

10 9 8 7 6 5 4 3 2 1

Acknowledgments

Lots of people made contributions to this book, and I appreciate them all. Thanks especially to

Linda L. Gaus, who added much to the manuscript;

Lee Ann Pickrell, who edited the manuscript and improved it in a thousand different ways. Her price is above rubies;

Ted Laux, whose indexes add so much to a book's usability. Always glad to have him on the team.

I also want to thank Carrie Lavine and Richard Mills for their contributions to the original ABCs concept. And Sherry Schmitt for her work on this book in particular.

I also appreciate the input of technical editor Rob Sanfilippo, production coordinator Kim Askew-Qasem, and desktop publisher Jimmie Young.

This book, like all that preceded, exists because of a vote of confidence first cast by Dianne King and Rudy Langer. Thanks.

Contents at a Glance

Table of Contents

Introduction

Thousands of new networks are being constructed in businesses and institutions every year. The benefits of being able to share equipment and information are obvious for these organizations. In addition, many of these networks will need to be connected to other networks—usually through the Internet.

A big percentage of those new networks are going to be based on the technology of Microsoft Windows NT 4. The operating systems of Windows NT Server and Windows NT Workstation provide what these networks need—efficiency, security, stability, and the tools to build both Internet and intranet connections.

This book is your guide to understanding and fine-tuning NT Workstation for your own needs.

Who Is This Book For?

This book is written for the person coming to the world of Windows NT Workstation for the first time. Perhaps you've worked on a network before but never on a machine running NT Workstation. Maybe networks are all new to you, but the new interface, imported from Windows 95, is no stranger. It's even possible that both computers and networks are completely new to you, and you're not crazy about either one—you just have a job to do. It doesn't matter because this book can answer all your questions. (Except those about the meaning of life—wrong book.)

I make occasional references to earlier versions of Windows NT Workstation, but previous knowledge of Windows is definitely *not* required. In addition, networking experience isn't necessary because everything you need to know about being a network computer user is in this book.

What We Think You Know

This book doesn't assume you have a lot of computer knowledge. But I do pretty much take for granted that you've used a computer with a mouse (or some other pointing device) before. So I don't explain what it means to click a button or select something from a menu.

Beyond that, however, most things are explained; because even if you know what a window looks like, many of the window's elements, such as the Minimize and Maximize buttons, have a new look in NT Workstation 4. So you'll see lots of illustrations and plenty of explanations as we go along.

I presume you are a reasonably intelligent person, so I don't talk to you as if you're a dummy because lots of smart people don't know much about computers.

Also assumed is that you want to get going with Windows NT Workstation as soon as possible. You can read just the chapters about subjects that interest you and come back to the others when you're ready—though I recommend not skipping Chapters 1 and 2 because they give you some basic facts about NT Workstation that'll help make you NT-competent much more quickly.

What's in This Book?

Inside you'll see nineteen chapters plus a glossary. I arranged the chapters so the first seven or eight are the basic stuff that you'll need to know to move around in NT Workstation. The rest of the chapters are also easy to use, but some will interest you more than others, so feel free to dip into them as questions come up. Here's how the chapters break down.

Chapter 1: What's New about NT Workstation 4?

A short chapter on the things that make NT Workstation different from what has come before. Includes simple definitions of the terms you might hear tossed around, such as networks, multitasking, and multithreading, plus a summation of the new features that make NT Workstation useful and efficient.

You'll also find a list of the hardware requirements for installing and running NT Workstation.

Chapter 2: First Things First (or Second in This Case)

A chapter you shouldn't skip because it includes tips and instructions on using two key elements of the new NT Workstation interface: shortcuts and the new powers of the mouse. Once you get the hang of using these, you're well on your way to navigating around NT Workstation 4 with no difficulty.

Chapter 3: Getting Started

Deals with the Desktop you see on first entering NT Workstation. What the elements are and how to make them work for you. You'll see how to log on, use the Start button, and set the look of your screen.

Chapter 4: Making and Taking Shortcuts

More on those wonderful tools—shortcuts. In fact, everything you'll probably ever need to know about making and using them.

Chapter 5: New Mouse Powers

Details of what the mouse can do now and how you can configure it to do even more. Settings for your mouse and using mouse pointers of many types, including animated ones!

Chapter 6: Exploring

The abilities of the Explorer are described here. This chapter includes how to change window views and navigate through your hard drive's contents. For the nostalgic, there are instructions on how to find and use File Manager.

Chapter 7: Files and Folders

Here's where you'll find the basics on moving, copying, renaming, and deleting files and folders. There's also a section on the new search tool called Find, which can search your computer as well as other computers on the network. If you're new to long file names, this chapter covers their benefits as well as their limitations.

Chapter 8: Networks Are for Sharing

This chapter covers the ways you can find and use resources on other computers. You'll learn how to read and use files others have made as well as how to share your own files and folders. This is also where you'll find information on finding and using networked printers.

Chapter 9: Running Programs

All the different ways you can run programs in NT Workstation are in this chapter. Choose the method that works best for you. If you like the look of Program Manager, you can even find that, too.

Chapter 10: The Recycle Bin

New to NT Workstation, the Recycle Bin lets you decide the exact margin of safety you want for deleted files. This chapter tells you the easy way to approach setting up Recycle Bin.

Chapter 11: Using the Command Prompt

NT Workstation will run all your DOS programs *better* and *faster* than old DOS. Even games can be tamed with the proper settings, and this chapter tells you how.

Chapter 12: Hardware Made Easy

Windows NT Workstation isn't plug-and-play, but it's not exactly plug-and-*pray* either. Hardware installation is considerably easier than it used to be. With the aid of this chapter you can install a modem, sound card, and printer with ease. You'll also find information on how to troubleshoot any ornery hardware.

Chapter 13: Sights and Sounds

This chapter describes all the really cool multimedia features that come with NT Workstation, including new sound and video capabilities. You'll see how easy it is to record and play back your own sound files and use the CD player to listen to your favorite music.

Chapter 14: In the Control Panel

Here's where you'll find explanations for all the icons in the Control Panel. Find out what they mean and how to make them work.

Chapter 15: Administrative Tools for Non-administrators

Early on in your use of NT Workstation, you'll see a menu called Administrative Tools. This chapter tells you what each tool does and which are actually useful.

Chapter 16: Communicating within Your Network

Communication is what a network's all about. In this chapter, you'll get the basics of the new intranet tool, Peer Web Services, plus more ordinary connection tools like Microsoft Mail and Chat.

Chapter 17: Communicating with the Wider World

Here's where you'll find out about the Exchange Messaging Service and the Internet Explorer—ways to connect to computers within your network and to the larger world of the Internet. This chapter also covers Remote Access, the tool for connecting to your network over a telephone or other communications channel.

Chapter 18: A Bushel of Applets

This chapter has simple instructions on how to extract the maximum in benefit from the many programs included with NT Workstation, such as the Calculator, Phone Dialer, HyperTerminal, Paint, and more.

Chapter 19: Protecting Your Data and Workstation

Safety First is the motto—or at least no later than second. For your peace of mind, NT Workstation comes with a backup program, a tool for configuring an uninterruptible power supply, and a means for making an Emergency Repair Disk. All are covered in this chapter, where you'll also find some advice on protecting your computer against viruses.

Glossary

Computers—and networks especially—are surrounded by masses of incomprehensible acronyms and jargon. This glossary contains simple definitions of dozens of these terms. Keep this book handy, and you can sneak a peak when you're perplexed.

What You'll See

At various points in the text you'll see boxes like these:

NOTE These are Notes. They usually represent alternative ways to accomplish a task or some additional information that needs to be highlighted.

TIP These are tips—quicker and smarter ways to accomplish a task.

WARNING   Alas, there are a few of these warnings, too. Most are placed next to features that may not work as described. This usually happens because network configurations can be wildly divergent.

What's Next

Now it's time to flip the page and get started. I'd be delighted to hear from you if you find the book useful or even if you find it's missing something you'd like to see included in a future edition. My E-mail address is *charlie@scribes.com,* and I promise all messages will be welcome.

Chapter 1

WHAT'S NEW ABOUT NT WORKSTATION 4?

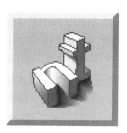

- **What is a network?**
- **Why choose NT Workstation?**
- **Workstation's new features**
- **Why being on a network is different**

Windows NT 4 is a big step forward for the already popular Windows NT network operating system. Windows NT, in previous versions, has long had the advantages of security and multitasking, but now it also has the Windows 95 easy-to-use interface plus plenty of new features and improvements to old ones.

Windows NT actually consists of *two* operating systems: Windows NT Server and Windows NT Workstation. NT Server is an operating system for the computers that administer your network. Windows NT Server looks just like Windows NT Workstation; except, it has numerous tools for providing services to users and keeping the network operating smoothly.

NT Workstation is also a very powerful operating system, but it's designed to work *with* the network (not control it). NT Workstation has remarkable capabilities that make it ideal for designers, software developers, serious number crunchers, and others who demand a lot from the computer on their desktop. NT Workstation is not the only operating system that works on a Windows NT network, but it is the most seamless and the easiest for a network administrator to install and configure.

As an operating system, NT Workstation 4 is designed to be *discoverable.* This means that as you potter about, you can find many of the features and shortcuts all by yourself. Most of us, however, have work to do and lives to live, so we don't have endless hours in which to discover the best, shortest, and easiest way to do things. This book will give you a quick start on how to use the features of NT Workstation 4 to your best advantage.

It's not at all necessary to learn a bunch of technical stuff to use NT Workstation, but a little information about the basics goes a long way toward making the whole system more understandable and accessible.

In this chapter, we'll talk a bit about networks and then review some of the features found in Windows NT Workstation. At the end of the chapter is a list of the hardware necessary for a successful Windows NT Workstation installation.

What Is a Network?

If you've ever made a phone call or used a bank ATM, you've already experienced using a network. After all, a network is simply a collection of computers and peripheral devices that can share files and other resources. The connection can be a cable, a telephone line, or even a wireless channel.

Your bank's ATM consists of hardware and software connected to central computers that know, among other things, how much money you have in your account. When you call cross country or just across town, telephone company software connects your phone through multiple switching devices to the phone you're calling. It's something we do every day without any thought as to the complicated processes behind the scenes.

Why Windows NT Workstation?

Computers on a Windows NT network can be running many different operating systems including

- MS-DOS
- Windows 3.1
- Windows for Workgroups
- Windows 95
- OS/2
- UNIX

So why would a network administrator select NT Workstation? It's not cheap, and it requires some pretty heavy-duty hardware to run at its best. It's because NT Workstation provides a combination of features not otherwise available: mainly multitasking and multithreading combined with excellent security. Here's what it means in real life.

Multitasking and Multithreading

The simplest way to explain *multitasking* is to say it's what you're doing when you're running more than one application at a time. The need to get information from various sources and many applications means multitasking has become an increasingly desirable and perhaps even a necessary feature of an operating system. Where would we be if we couldn't run our word processor and spreadsheet at the same time?

Multitasking is a bit of a misnomer. The processor in your computer can't really do more than one thing at a time. It actually switches very rapidly among processes. However, many *applications* can actually multitask. For example, you can import images into a graphics program while recalculating a spreadsheet and downloading your e-mail.

Multitasking has been going on for a long time, starting with Windows 3.1. What Windows NT adds to the mix is *threading*, also called *multithreading*. This means that when two or more programs are competing for the processor's time, NT creates a thread. Each thread is a small portion of a program's activity. The thread gets its own scheduling priority and processor time but is easier to create and manage than a full, separate process. Threads slip through the processor more quickly and don't collide in unseemly ways (the cause of many program crashes in environments like Windows 3.1 and Windows 95, where programs can multitask, but not multithread).

This is all very nice, but in the end what does this mean for the user? The short version is this: much better performance in the form of speed and reliability.

Security

The other feature NT Workstation 4 has over other operating systems is security. Its extensive security features ensure that the appropriate people (usually the system administrator and others with administrative responsibilities) have complete control over who gets access to which resources. With networks being only as strong as their weakest link, a secure operating system is key.

Reliability

One more reason NT Workstation stands head and shoulders above many other operating systems is its reliability. Some operating systems may crash under the influence of a badly-behaved program, but not NT Workstation 4. A program may crash (and they *will* do that), but on NT Workstation, you can close the program, and the operating system soldiers on unaffected. This is essential when you're running databases or other systems that your business depends on.

So What *Is* New in NT Workstation 4?

NT Workstation 4 offers many new features that previous versions of NT Workstation didn't have. Some are merely cosmetic while others truly add a new and improved degree of functionality.

Simple User Interface

The Desktop that greets you when NT Workstation 4 starts is free of clutter and has an obvious entry point, the Start button. The Desktop is an actual working area that you can customize to your heart's content. Chapter 3 provides a quick introduction to the Desktop elements and how to use them.

A Smarter Mouse

The mouse in NT Workstation 4 is more than a handy point-and-click device. Not only is NT Workstation 4 noticeably more "mousy" than previous operating systems, but the mouse also has many more functions. For answers to all your mouse questions, see Chapters 2 and 5.

Taskbar

Part of the clean and efficient look of the Desktop is the Taskbar where the Start button rests. The Taskbar is the home for icons representing all your open programs. A single-click on a program icon will bring that program to the top of your display, so no matter how many programs you have running, the one you need is immediately at hand. Chapter 3 has more on using the Taskbar.

Almost Infinite Configurability

You can design and arrange your Desktop and menus, within some limits, to suit your preferences. Chapters 2 and 4 tell you more about shortcuts, one of the really valuable tools you'll use to customize your setup.

Run Programs from the Command Prompt

Almost any DOS program can be run while you're still running NT Workstation 4. And even the most resource-hungry DOS program can be set up to run without having to reboot your machine. Chapter 11 explains how to use the Command Prompt to your best advantage.

Easier Hardware Installation

While it's not quite up to the plug-and-play standard set by Windows 95, NT Workstation 4 represents a big step toward hardware installation without tears. Installing new hardware is covered in Chapter 12.

Sight and Sound

Multimedia capabilities of considerable power are also included in NT Workstation 4. Want to play music CDs, view video clips, or record your own sound files? All are possible with the right equipment and NT Workstation 4. See Chapter 13 for more information.

Peer Web Services

On a network with Internet Information Server, you can make your own personal Web pages for information you want to share. See Chapter 16 for more on doing your own Web publishing.

Internet Explorer

Surf both the Internet *and* the intranet, your network's internal Web. Internet Explorer lets you create shortcuts to the Web sites you need. The Internet Explorer and how to use it are described in Chapter 17.

Exchange

Microsoft Exchange is the solution to centralizing all your messaging operations. Chapter 17 tells you how to set it up.

Networking versus Going It Solo

On a network, what you do often affects others, so if you have a strong strain of rugged individualism, there will be times you'll need to restrain it. Someone may be using that printer you need *right now,* or someone else's monster file transfer may slow down the network at the worst possible time. However, the benefits of networking will become clear to you pretty quickly. Now everyone can use that fancy new color printer (well, eventually), and messaging systems can spare you the nonstop flow of paper memos (most of which are instantly lost).

When your computer is connected to a network, you can share resources—drives, folders, or printers, just to name a few things—quickly and easily. You can set up your own workgroups, so all members of a project team can share files and stay informed.

Be aware, however, that every network—and every network administrator—is different, so your computer may not always do the things this book describes. If something doesn't work, the system administrator may have set network permissions in such a way that whatever it is you're trying to do is off-limits (usually for a good reason, I might add!). Whenever you encounter questions that seem to be network-specific, the best advice is to consult he or she who knows all: the system administrator.

If your NT Workstation isn't connected to a network, you won't be able to take advantage of shared resources, and some things you'll see may look a little different than the examples you'll see in this book. Don't be too upset by this—regardless of the slight differences in appearance—most things will work just the same.

Hardware Requirements

Windows NT Workstation 4 is a powerful operating system; therefore, it requires some pretty heavy-duty hardware. In this section, I'll list the minimal hardware requirements, along with some notes on optimal equipment.

Processor
32-bit x86-based microprocessor, 80486/25 or higher; Intel Pentium; or RISC-based microprocessor, such as MIPS R4x00, Digital Alpha AXP, or Power PC. The 80486/25 is Microsoft's minimum, but a 40846/66 is a much more realistic minimum.

Monitor
VGA or higher resolution monitor.

Hard drive
At least 118MB free hard drive space on the partition that will contain the NT Workstation system files, though you may need as much as 125MB to do a successful installation. On a RISC-based system at least 149MB must be free on the partition where the system files will be.

Other drives
For x86-based computers, you need a 3½ floppy drive plus a CD-ROM drive. If installation is done over a network, neither of these is required.

Memory
For x86-based computers, the absolute minimum is 12MB of RAM. However, with less than 16MB, the machine is not useful. Generally, I'd recommend 32MB.

Mouse
A mouse or other pointing device isn't, strictly speaking, required, but it's hard to imagine using this interface without one.

Network card
A network interface card is needed to use Windows NT Workstation on a network.

NOTE A key element to using NT Workstation successfully is to use hardware from the Hardware Compatibility List (HCL) that comes with the software. Hardware not on the HCL can often be made to work, but if something goes wrong, Microsoft will blame the hardware and send you to the hardware manufacturer—who may or may not be responsive.

Next Step

And these are only a few of the features that make NT Workstation 4 special and that you'll find easy to master with the help of this book. In the next chapter, we cut straight to the chase and tell you a couple of important skills and concepts that will give you a head start on using NT Workstation 4. In fact, it's not too much of an exaggeration to say that after Chapter 2, you'll be well equipped to start your own explorations. However, if you also read the rest of the book, you can save yourself some considerable discovery time.

Chapter 2

FIRST THINGS FIRST (OR SECOND IN THIS CASE)

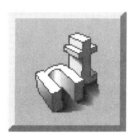

FEATURING

- **New powers for your mouse**
- **A short look at shortcuts**

I'm going to break with tradition and tell you some very important skills up front and not dole it out in dribs and drabs in a dozen places in the back of the book. Of course, this isn't everything that's important—there's lots more than can fit in a single chapter. That's why there's a whole book. But if you read no more than this chapter, you'll still have a head start on making NT Workstation work for you.

The Mighty Mouse

The first thing to understand is that the key to using NT Workstation efficiently is right there on your Desktop—namely, your mouse or trackball. NT Workstation is very mousy when compared to other high-powered operating systems. In fact, you scarcely have to touch the keyboard at all for most basic operations.

> **NOTE** For the dyed-in-the-wool keyboard user, there is a list of the things you can do from the keyboard in Chapter 4.

But your old familiar mouse works quite differently now in two important ways.

Mouse Trick #1:

First, the right mouse button is used *everywhere*. In fact, it's not too much of an exaggeration to say that you can place the pointer almost anywhere, press the right mouse button and something will happen. Usually, you'll see a *pop-up* menu like the ones shown here:

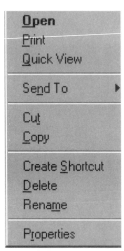 

The contents of the menu will vary depending on whether you're pointing at a file, a *folder* (NT Workstation's term for a directory), an NT Workstation element, or an icon representing hardware of some type.

Then there are those occasions when you're looking at a dialog box full of settings—most of which you don't understand. Place your pointer on the text and click the right mouse button. If you see a "What's This?" box like the one shown here, you can click on it and get a window of explanation. Usually it's good information too, so always try that first.

Mouse Trick #2:

Here's another way the mouse behaves differently. To open a menu, you click only once on the menu title. Slide the mouse pointer to the item you want to select and (only then) click one more time.

Holding the mouse button down as you move the pointer is limited to those times you're actually dragging and dropping an object. However, there's different behavior depending on whether you're using the left or right mouse button.

Click and Drag Object with	Location	Result
Left mouse button	Within a drive	Object is moved
Left mouse button	Across drives	Object is copied
Right mouse button	Anywhere	Menu allowing choice between moving the object, copying the object, or creating a shortcut

As you can see from the above list, the right mouse button is by far the easiest to use. The left mouse button requires you to remember where the object is relative to your hard drive(s). If you get in the habit of using the right mouse button, you can be saved from that silliness.

Throughout this book a *click* refers to pressing the left mouse button and a *right-click* to pressing the right button. (Unless you're using a left-handed mouse, in which case everything is reversed!)

You'll be using the mouse a lot in NT Workstation, so you might as well start practicing now.

> **NOTE** In NT Workstation, the mouse has even more skills that you can read about in Chapter 5.

Shortcuts

If you're to use your NT Workstation Desktop as a workplace, you want to be able to organize everything you need in one place and be able to access it instantly. And even if documents aren't involved—as in, say, using a calculator or phone dialer—you'd like to have immediate access to necessary programs without searching for them.

Shortcuts are one of the leading benefits of NT Workstation, and yet they're not an *obvious* feature like multitasking or long file names. That's why shortcuts are mentioned here, so you can learn a little about what they are and the part they play in NT Workstation.

A *shortcut* is a little file that acts as a pointer to a document or a folder or a program. For example, a shortcut lets you have as many "copies" of your printer as you want—in as many locations as you want. Of course, a shortcut to the printer isn't really a copy of the printer, just a pointer. With shortcuts you can have your word processor in as many locations as necessary and only use a little hard disk space for each instance. Another advantage of shortcuts is that when you're done with one, you can delete it with impunity. Deleting the shortcut has no effect on the original object.

Shortcuts are identifiable by the little arrow in the lower-left corner of the icon.

When created they'll also have a label: "Shortcut to..." followed by the name of the object. Shortcuts can be renamed to make the label more manageable.

The Create Shortcut option is available:

- On objects' pop-up menus
- From various drop-down menus
- On the Desktop (see Figure 2.1)

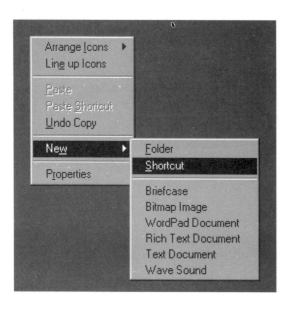

FIGURE 2.1:
The Create Shortcut command can be found on many menus, including the one that pops up when you right-click on the Desktop.

For more on shortcuts and their many talents, see Chapter 4, where you'll find information on how to make the most of these useful tools.

Next Step

Now that you've been introduced to the basic concepts that make a difference from day one, in the next chapter you'll get an introduction to the Desktop elements you first see when you log on to NT Workstation.

Chapter 3

GETTING STARTED

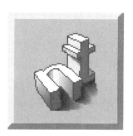

FEATURING

- **Using the Start button**
- **Getting help when you need it**
- **Main features of the Desktop**
- **Setting the Desktop's look**

In this chapter, we'll do a quick tour of the screen you see when you first start NT Workstation. There'll be a description of what you see and how to get more information on each item. Of course, everything can't be covered in detail here, so there are frequent references to later chapters—but I'll try not to bounce around any more than necessary.

NOTE On a network, the person closest to God is the system administrator. The system administrator has many powers denied to mere mortals. As a result, your Desktop and menus may be configured differently than I describe here. If a feature doesn't appear to be working properly, it may be because of an error or it may be because the system administrator made it work that way. There are times when your only choice is to *ask*.

Logging On

Logging on to NT Workstation is a snap—just press Ctrl+Alt+Delete and you should see a dialog box requesting your username and password. Type the appropriate information in each box, click OK, and you're in. If you've made a typo, you'll see a warning about how NT Workstation couldn't log you on, but never fear—as they say—try, try again. Retype your username and password, click OK, and you're ready to begin your adventures.

On a network, there'll be a third box in the Logon window labeled Domain. You can probably leave that alone; if you're supposed to log on to another domain, other than the default one, your system administrator will let you know.

NOTE When you log on to the computer the very first time, you may well be asked to supply a new password. In fact, requests from the system for new passwords may come at regular intervals. There's no point in trying to fight this—the system administrator has done it on purpose to make the system more secure.

Start Menu

The opening screen in NT Workstation is a mostly blank Desktop with a Taskbar at the bottom of the screen and two or more icons in the upper-left corner. Fortunately, there's a clear signal where to begin in the form of the Start button in the lower-left corner.

Click once on the Start button to open a menu of choices. Initially there will be only a few basic items, but they're enough to get you going. Starting from the top, here's what you'll see.

Programs Slide the mouse pointer to Programs and you'll get a cascading menu that includes pointers to Accessories and Startup as well as to the Command Prompt, Microsoft Exchange (that's the mail program described in Chapter 17), and to the Explorer (talked about here and in Chapter 6, among other places).

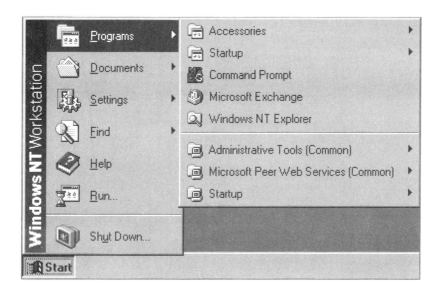

You can add programs to the Start menu and change what's on the Programs menu quite easily. Take a look at Chapter 9 for the steps to do just that.

Documents NT Workstation remembers the files you recently worked on and puts them on this menu. To clear the Documents menu:
1. Right-click on the Taskbar and select Properties.
2. Select Start Menu Programs.
3. Under the Documents menu, click on the Clear button.

This will clear the Documents list completely. To delete only some of the documents in the folder, see "Deleting from the Documents Folder" in Chapter 7.

Settings Branching off this item, you'll find the Control Panel, the Printers folder, and another way to get at the Taskbar settings. For information on elements in the Control Panel, see Chapter 14. Others you can find by checking the index. Printers and their settings are covered in Chapter 12. Using shared printers on the network is covered in Chapter 8.

Find This is a neat program that will let you search for files or even a particular piece of text. Chapter 7 has more on using Find to search for almost anything. You can search your whole computer or just a particular drive. On a network, you can search for a particular computer by name.

Select Find and then Files or Folders to open this window.

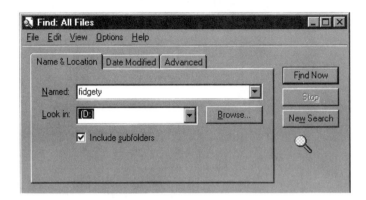

As you can see from the tabs, you can search by name and location and by the date modified. The Advanced tab has an option for searching for a particular word or phrase. The menus include options to make your search case sensitive or to save the results of a search.

The really nice thing about Find is that once you locate the file you want, you can just double-click on the file to open it or you can drag it to another location. In other words, the file or list of files displayed at the end of a search is "live," and you can act on it accordingly.

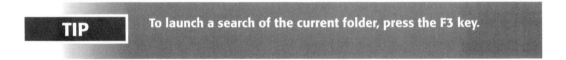

TIP To launch a search of the current folder, press the F3 key.

Help The Help files in NT Workstation are much improved over those in the past. They're a lot more searchable, for one thing. When you first select Help, you'll get a window like the one shown in Figure 3.1.

The Contents and Index tabs are pretty straightforward. However, a nice new feature is on the Find tab. Using Find you can search all or part of the Help files for a particular word or phrase. This can be really nice when you know the term you want but haven't a clue as to what the authors of the documentation might have filed it under.

FIGURE 3.1:
Getting help

The first time you use this tool, NT Workstation builds a database of Help files for future searching. You choose from one of three options:

Minimize Database Size   With this option you don't get every single Help file but all the ones likely to have useful information.

Maximize Search Capabilities   This means every Help file is included. It's the most thorough approach, but it's slower to set up and may also make searches a little slower depending on your processor and hard drive speeds.

Customize Search Capabilities   Select this option and you can decide which Help files go into the database.

After the database is built you can use the Find tab to make very sophisticated searches.

Run   Those who love the command line will find succor here. Select Run and you can type in the name of any program you want to launch. You'll have to include the path, but if you like this kind of hands-on operation, you won't mind at all.

You can also use the Browse button on the Run dialog box to look around for the program you want. And if you click on the downward arrow, you get a drop-down list of all the recent programs you've run from this box.

> **NOTE** When you type in the path to run some Windows 3.1 programs, you may find that they're not completely happy in the NT environment. In that case, return to the Run box and check the box next to Run in Separate Memory Space. That will keep the Windows 3.1 programs from bumping into one another.

Taskbar

The Taskbar starts out at the bottom of your screen. Every open program (or folder) will have a button on the Taskbar. This is extremely handy because it means you don't have to close windows or move them aside to find other ones. Click on the button, and the corresponding open item will become active.

You can change the Taskbar's location. Just click on it and drag it to the top or to either side of the screen. To make it wider or taller, position the mouse pointer at the edge of the Taskbar and when you see a double-headed arrow, click and drag the border to where you want it.

Make the Taskbar Disappear

If you have a smallish monitor, you may want the Taskbar to disappear except when you need it. To try this look, take these steps:

1. Click on the Start button and select Settings ➤ Taskbar.
2. On the Taskbar Option page put a check mark next to Auto Hide.
3. If you want to be able to get at the Taskbar even when you're running a program full-screen, select Always on Top as well.

Now when you move the mouse pointer away from the Taskbar, the Taskbar will fade away. Move the mouse pointer back, and the Taskbar pops up.

My Computer

This icon is on every NT Workstation Desktop. Double-click on it to see icons for all your drives, plus folders for the Control Panel, Printers, and Dial-Up Networking (assuming it's installed). This isn't the only way to get at your drives—maybe not even the easiest way—but some people definitely prefer it to using Explorer.

My Computer and the Explorer are essentially the same thing. (Chapter 6 is all about the Explorer.) This may not be apparent at first because My Computer opens as a single pane with the Large Icons view selected. But if you right-click on the My Computer icon and select Explore from the pop-up menu, you'll see that the two are the same.

One important difference is that My Computer cannot be deleted or even removed from your Desktop. So it's always handy for making changes to settings:

- Double-click on the My Computer icon and select Options from the View menu. On the Folder tab, you can select whether you want single-window or separate-window browsing. Single window means that as you go from folder to subfolder to sub-subfolder, only one window is open at a time. Separate window means that the parent folders also stay open.

Single-window browsing is probably preferable unless you have a very large monitor. On the average monitor, having every double-click open a new window (with all the old ones remaining) can turn your Desktop into a crowded mess very quickly.

The My Computer folder is discussed again in Chapter 6.

> **NOTE** If the name My Computer is just too, too cute for your tastes, right-click on the icon and select Rename from the menu. Type in a new name that's less annoying.

Recycle Bin

The Recycle Bin, as you might imagine, is where old deleted files go to die.

Despite the name, the deleted files aren't recycled unless you rescue them from the bin before they're deleted permanently. Nevertheless, the Recycle Bin gives you a nice margin of safety that wasn't available in previous versions of NT Workstation (unless you had another program that provided it). Now when you delete a file you have days or even weeks (depending on how you set things up) to change your mind and retrieve it.

Chapter 10 is all about the Recycle Bin, how to configure and use it to your best advantage. In the meantime, here are two important facts about the Recycle Bin:

- The Recycle Bin icon cannot be renamed or deleted.
- Files that are deleted using DOS programs or any program that's not part of NT Workstation are not sent to the Recycle Bin. They're just deleted. Be careful.

NOTE   Other icons that may be on your Desktop, depending on the installation, include the Inbox and a globe labeled Internet Explorer. These are covered in Chapter 17.

Briefcase

Those of you who work with multiple computers and have trouble keeping your files synchronized will be glad to know that NT Workstation has a solution for you: the Briefcase. You should find the icon for this handy applet on your Desktop after you've installed NT Workstation; if you don't, it's quite easy to create another instance of it. You'll get the gory details about how the Briefcase works in Chapter 18.

Properties Sheets

In previous versions of NT Workstation or in Windows 3.11, finding out how to change the settings for something was a real pain. Depending on whether it was a file or a program or a piece of hardware, you had to memorize where critical settings were found. This is all changed in NT 4 Workstation, so now there's only one rule to remember:

- Right-click on the object and select Properties.

When you select Properties, you open what's called a Properties sheet. Properties sheets vary, of course. Some types of files will have multiple pages in the Properties sheet, others will have only one page and very few options. Figure 3.2 shows a Properties sheet for a simple text file.

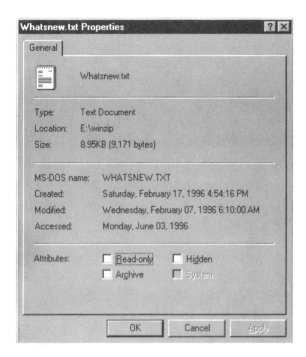

FIGURE 3.2:
A Properties sheet for a text file

Properties sheets are valuable repositories of information about files, programs, and devices. So when you find yourself with a program or a piece of hardware that isn't working the way you want it to, refer to the rule above. As a matter of fact, you might apply that rule to just about every aspect of NT Workstation. When you want to know more about *anything* in NT Workstation, right-click on it and see what appears.

How to use Properties sheets is discussed in later chapters. For example, the Properties sheets for the Command Prompt are covered in Chapter 11, Properties sheets for printers are covered in Chapter 12, and Properties sheets for other objects are covered in their respective chapters.

Desktop Settings

The default NT Workstation screen is not one likely to induce little cries of joy unless you're a total neat freak, and then you won't want to change a thing. However, most of us will find it a tad boring. But you can have it as plain or fancy as you want.

Remember you can use the entire area of your monitor's screen in NT Workstation. You can have many folders, a few, or none on the Desktop. You can have all your programs on menus that fold out of the Start button's menus, or you can have program icons on the Desktop where you can open them with a double-click.

Even better, you can have colors, fonts, and Desktop wallpaper of many types. Here's how to get at all the settings that affect the Desktop.

Move the pointer to a blank spot (of which there's a muchness) and click the right mouse button. Select Properties from the pop-up menu and you're there (see Figure 3.3).

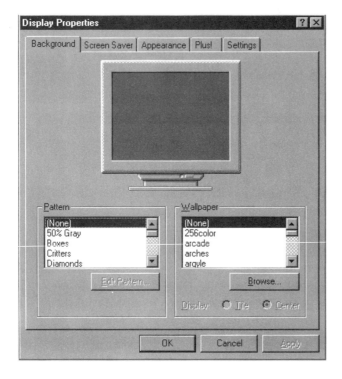

FIGURE 3.3:
The first tab of the Display Properties dialog box

Each tab covers one aspect of the display. Next, we'll explore the contents of the individual tabs.

Background

Here you set the wallpaper and background pattern much like the Desktop settings in previous versions of NT Workstation. Use the Browse button to locate files you can use as wallpaper.

Any files that are bitmaps (.BMP) or device-independent bitmaps (.DIB) can be used as wallpaper.

> **TIP** The Apply button lets you see how a setting will work without having to close the Display Properties dialog box.

Screen Saver

If you're using screen savers—either the ones that come with NT Workstation or some other package—you can adjust the settings on this page. All the installed screen savers are in the Screen Saver drop-down list.

Click on the Preview button to get a full-screen view of the selected screen saver. Move your mouse or press any key on the keyboard to return to Display Properties.

Appearance

This page is also similar to Desktop settings in previous versions of NT Workstation. Use one of the many color combinations listed under Schemes or make your own.

Click on any of the elements in the window at the top of the Appearance page and a description appears in the Item box. Change the size or color or both. If there's a font that can be changed, the current one will show in the Font box.

Settings

Of all the pages in the Display Properties, this page has the most going on (see Figure 3.4). Here's where you can change how your screen actually looks (as well as see what NT Workstation knows about your display hardware).

Changing Resolutions

Displays are described in terms of their resolution—that's the number of dots on the screen and the number of colors that can be displayed at the same time. The resolutions you can choose using the slider under Desktop Area are determined by the hardware you have. You can't make your monitor and video card display more than is built into them.

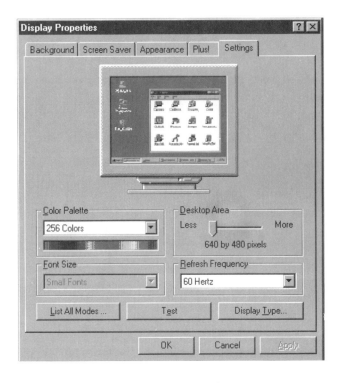

FIGURE 3.4:
Information about your display

Here are the most likely possibilities:

640 x 480   A standard VGA display that's 640 pixels wide by 480 pixels high.

800 x 600   A typical SVGA display (super VGA).

1024 x 768   This is the upper limit of SVGA and the beginning of more advanced systems such as 8514/A and XGA. This is a very fine (that is, non-grainy) resolution, but if your monitor is 15 inches or smaller, you'd better have very good eyes.

1280 x 1024   A very fine resolution but one that requires a large monitor. Even with a 17-inch screen, you'll need good eyes.

You'll notice as you move the slider toward higher resolutions that the number of colors displayed in the Color Palette box changes. As resolution numbers go up, color numbers have to go down because they're both competing for the same video memory.

That's why, if you want the most realistic color represented on your screen, you'll need a video card (also called a display adapter) with 4 or more megabytes of its own memory.

Resolution choices are based on what you like to look at—constrained by the capabilities of your monitor and video card. At the lowest resolution, you may not be able to see all the elements of some programs, so try the next higher resolution. At the highest resolutions, screen elements are very small, so you may want to try Large Fonts from the Font Size box. That will make the captions on the Desktop easier to see.

Most of the time you'll have to reboot to see the effect these changes have.

NOTE   If you change your screen resolution, you may end up with some very peculiar arrangements of your icons. They may be way too far apart or so close together that they're difficult to use. The Appearance page has controls for the spacing of icons. Pull down the Item drop-down list and select one of the Icon Spacing choices. You can also select Icon and change both the size of your icons and their font. However, I strongly recommend that you make note of the original settings because it's fairly easy to make a hash of your Desktop and not remember where you started.

List All Modes

Click the List All Modes button to see all the possible combinations for your hardware's display (shown in Figure 3.5). Any setting in this list should be acceptable to your display adapter (video card). Select one, and then click the Test button on the Settings page, and you'll find out immediately if it'll work.

Changing the Display Type

Also on the Settings tab is a button labeled Display Type. This is used when you're changing either your display adapter (video card) or monitor. (Or if you want to use a different video driver besides the one NT Workstation is currently using.)

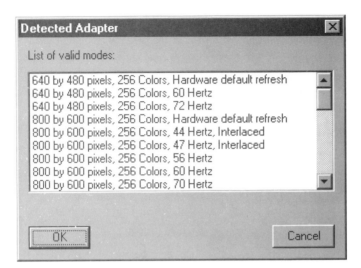

FIGURE 3.5:
All the resolutions available to your hardware are shown in this window.

Click on the Display Type button and you'll see a window like the one in Figure 3.6. To change either the adapter or the monitor, click on the Change button and follow the instructions.

FIGURE 3.6:
Information about your video system

NOTE If you happen to have the Plus! for Windows 95 package (as you might if you're running NT Workstation on a dual-boot machine), there will also be a Properties sheet tab for Plus!, which lists various visual enhancements that Plus! provides. Choices that are grayed-out are not available because your hardware can't deliver them.

Next Step

Now that you've been at least casually introduced to NT Workstation, we'll move to specifics. In the next chapter, you'll find everything you need to know about the tools known as *shortcuts*—which will probably become indispensable very quickly.

Chapter 4

MAKING AND TAKING SHORTCUTS

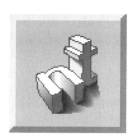

Shortcuts introduce a new level of convenience and customization to NT Workstation. They're meant to be easy ways to get at all the things on your computer or network: documents, applications, folders, printers, and so on. So they're most likely to be placed on your Desktop, on the Start menu, or in the Send To folder. In this chapter, we'll cover all the ways to make and modify a shortcut and how to place the shortcuts you want in the places you want them to be.

A shortcut is identified by the small arrow in the lower-left corner of the icon (see Figure 4.1). The arrow isn't just there to be cute. It's important to know (particularly before a deletion) whether something is a shortcut or a real object. You can delete shortcuts at will. You're not deleting anything that you can't recreate in a second or two. But if you delete an actual program or other file, you'll have to rummage around in the Recycle Bin to retrieve it. (And if it's a while before you notice it's missing, the Recycle Bin may have been emptied in the meantime and the object is *gone*.)

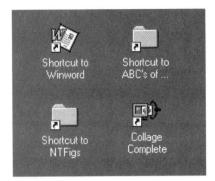

FIGURE 4.1:
Shortcuts can be indentified by the arrow in the lower-left corner of the icon.

NOTE   **Configuring and using the Recycle Bin is covered in Chapter 10.**

Here's an example. I have a folder on my hard drive called *ABCs of Win NT Workstation.* On my Desktop, I have a shortcut to that folder.

If I delete the shortcut folder on my Desktop, the folder on the hard drive remains untouched. If I want to create a shortcut to that folder at any time in the future, I find the folder in Explorer, right-click on it, drag it to the Desktop (or to some other location), and select Create Shortcut Here when I release the mouse button.

If I delete the folder on the hard drive—and under some rare circumstances if I move the folder—the shortcut is still there but there's nothing for it to point to. Then when I click on the shortcut, I get a dialog box like the one shown in Figure 4.2.

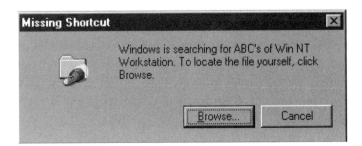

FIGURE 4.2:
Windows NT looks for the target of a shortcut that points to a deleted folder or file.

You'll find the Create Shortcut option in a lot of places, including:
- On objects' pop-up menus (see Figure 4.3)
- On various drop-down menus
- On the desktop pop-up menu as New ➤ Shortcut

FIGURE 4.3:
Create Shortcut is an option
almost every time you
right-click on an object.

Shortcuts are an excellent tool for configuring your Desktop to suit you. You can make shortcuts to folders, to programs, and to individual files. Arrange them any way you want on the Desktop, inside other folders, or on the Start menu.

NOTE

In previous versions of NT Workstation, the term *shortcut* always referred to a keyboard shortcut—in other words, a combination of keys that would produce some action on screen. But now we have shortcuts meaning *pointers*. In this book, *shortcut* will always mean a pointer, and *keyboard shortcut* will be used when a key combination is meant. A list of keyboard shortcuts, which are officially known as *accelerator keys,* is included later in this chapter.

How to Make a Shortcut

Shortcuts are pointers to objects. So you need to either find the object you want to point to or be able to tell the system where the original object is located. The easiest way to make a shortcut to a program is to right-click on the Start button and select Explore. The contents of your Start menu, including the Programs folder, will be in the right pane of the window that opens. Click your way down through the tree until you find the program you want.

You can also open Explorer and similarly find the program. Explorer (or My Computer) is where you'll need to look to find drives, printers, or folders when you want to make shortcuts to them. Explorer (or My Computer) will also be needed for a DOS program, a shared file on the network, or any program that doesn't manage to install itself off the Start menu.

With the Original in View

To make a shortcut when you have the original object in view inside the Explorer or My Computer, follow these steps:

1. Point to the object and click on it once with the right mouse button.
2. Holding the button down, drag the object to the Desktop.
3. When you release the mouse button, you'll see a menu like the one below.
4. Select Create Shortcut(s) Here.

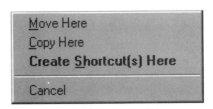

Here's a shortcut to the Word for Windows program on the Desktop. This shortcut, when double-clicked, will open the Word for Windows program.

> **NOTE** If you use the method of right-clicking on the Start button described above, you'll be using a shortcut to make another shortcut, without having to go back to the original object. Just right-click on the shortcut and select Create Shortcut from the menu that opens.

Cut and Paste a Shortcut

Another way to make a shortcut is to right-click on the program or file, and select Create Shortcut from the pop-up menu. A shortcut to the object you clicked on will appear in the same folder. You can then move the shortcut by right-clicking on it and selecting Cut from the menu. Then right-click where you want the shortcut to be and choose Paste. (Or you can drag it from the folder and drop it in a new location.)

To Absent Objects

If the original object isn't handy or you don't want to go find it, you can still create a shortcut as follows:

1. Right-click on the Desktop and select New ➢ Shortcut.
2. In the dialog box that opens, type in the location and name of the original object. If you don't know the path (and who ever does?), click on the Browse button.
3. Using the Browse window, mouse around until you find the file or object you want to link to. You may have to change the Files of Type item in the Browse window to read All Files. Highlight the file with the mouse (the name will appear in the File name box) and click on Open.
4. The Command line box will now contain the name and location of the object. Click on Next and accept or change the name for the shortcut.
5. Click on Finish, and the shortcut appears on your Desktop.

Renaming a Shortcut

When you create a new shortcut, the system always gives it a name that starts with "Shortcut to" and then names the object the shortcut is pointing to. To rename the shortcut, you can right-click on the icon and select Rename from the menu that opens.

Type in the name you want. Click on a blank spot on the Desktop when you're through.

You can also rename a shortcut (or most other icons for that matter) by clicking once on the name, waiting a second or two, and clicking again. That'll highlight the name, and you can edit it as you wish.

Choosing a Name

When you rename a shortcut, take full advantage of long file names to give it a name that's meaningful to you. No need to get carried away, but you might as well call a folder **March Budget Reports** rather than MARBUDGT, as you might have previously. Certain characters aren't allowed in shortcut names: / \ < > | : " ? * (but you ought to be able to live without those few).

TIP

Sometimes a shortcut with a long name ends up truncated with an ellipsis (. . .) showing something's missing. You can force the display of the whole name by right-clicking on the Desktop and selecting Properties. Click on the Appearance page. In the Item drop-down list, select Icon Spacing (Horizontal), and experiment with the spacing. Increase the horizontal spacing by a few pixels. Click Apply, and see how your shortcut looks. Keep trying until it looks right to you and then select OK.

Starting a Program When NT Workstation Starts

You may have programs you want to have started and ready to run when you start NT Workstation—for example, your calendar or other applications that you want to be able to launch immediately. NT Workstation includes a Startup folder for such programs. To put a shortcut in the Startup folder, follow these steps:

1. Right-click on the Start button and select Open or Explore from the pop-up menu.
2. Double-click on Programs and then Startup.
3. Drag shortcuts to the programs you want launched into the Startup folder. If you want to leave the original shortcut where it is, drag with the right mouse button and choose Copy Here from the menu that pops up when you release the button.

To specify how you want the programs to look when NT Workstation starts:

1. Right-click on the shortcut and select Properties.
2. Click on the Shortcut tab.
3. In the Run window select Minimized (or Normal window or Maximized).
4. Click on OK when you're done.

A minimized program will be on the Taskbar after the system starts. A Maximized selection will cause the program to appear full-screen. Normal will be whatever the normal-sized window was for that program before the last time you exited from it.

Putting Shortcuts Where You Want Them

Obviously, the point of shortcuts is to save time and energy. Merely placing a bunch of shortcuts on your Desktop may help you or it may not. So here are a number of other ways shortcuts can be made useful.

Putting a Start Menu Item on the Desktop

As you've seen, when you click on the Start menu and follow the Programs arrow, you get a hierarchical display of all the programs installed on your system. All those menu items are just representations of shortcuts. To find them and put the ones you want on your Desktop, you'll need to (if you'll pardon the expression) go Exploring.

1. Right-click on the Start button and select Open or Explore.
2. Double-click on the Programs icon.
3. Find the programs you want here, or you may have to go down another level by double-clicking on one of the folders.
4. Right-click on the shortcut you want and drag it to the Desktop, selecting Create Shortcut Here from the menu that opens when you release the mouse button.

Adding a Program to the Start Menu

You undoubtedly have some programs that you'd like to get at without having to go through the menus or without searching around the Desktop. To add a program to the top of the Start menu, just click on a shortcut, drag it to the Start button, and drop it on top. Then when you click on the Start button, the program will be instantly available (as shown in Figure 4.4).

FIGURE 4.4:
Add your favorite programs to the top of the Start menu for quick access.

Remove programs from the Start menu by selecting Start ➢ Settings ➢ Taskbar. Click on the Start Menu Programs tab and then on the Remove button. Highlight the program you want to remove and then click on the Remove button.

As you can see in Figure 4.5, you can also use this page to add programs to the Start menu, though it requires more steps than the simple drag-and-drop method.

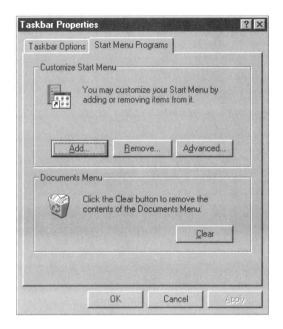

FIGURE 4.5:
You can use the Taskbar Properties dialog box to add and remove programs from the Start menu as well as to clear the Documents menu.

This page is also where you can clear the Documents menu that branches off from the Start menu.

NOTE For clearing the Documents menu selectively, see Chapter 7.

Adding a Shortcut to *Send To*

When you right-click on most things in NT Workstation, one of the choices on the menu is Send To. By default, the Send To menu includes shortcuts to your floppy drive (or drives), the Briefcase, and also may include (depending on your installation) shortcuts to mail recipients.

To add a shortcut to Send To, follow these steps:

1. Click on the Start button and select Programs ➤ Windows NT Explorer.
2. In the Explorer, find your Windows NT folder in the left pane and double-click on it.

3. Under the Profiles folder, find the Default User folder and double-click.
4. Under the Default User folder, find the Send To folder and click.
5. Use the right mouse button to drag and drop shortcuts into this folder to add them to the Send To menu.

You may have to open a second instance of the Explorer to get at other folders if the shortcuts you want are not on the Desktop. Or you can use Copy and Paste on the right-mouse-button menu.

NOTE When you use Send To, you're actually doing the equivalent of drag and drop. The item you've highlighted will be dropped on the selection you make in Send To.

Shortcut Settings

Every shortcut has a Properties sheet that you can get at by right-clicking on the shortcut icon and selecting Properties from the pop-up menu (shown in Figure 4.6).

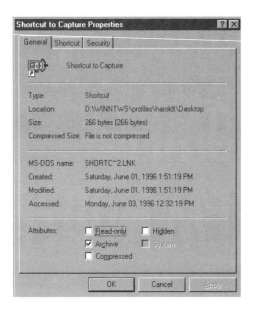

FIGURE 4.6:
Shortcut properties

You'll see three tabs for pages that are described in the next sections.

General

The General tab isn't much different from the general tabs on other dialog boxes: just the file type, size, and location (of the shortcut, not the original file). There's also handy information on when the file was created, changed, and last accessed—handy to whom, I can't imagine.

Shortcut

This page is actually useful, allowing you to find the original file that the shortcut points to as well as other settings.

Finding the Original File

Click on the Find Target button to find out just where the shortcut is pointing. When you click on this button, a window opens into the folder containing the application or file the shortcut is for.

Changing a Shortcut's Icon

Shortcuts to programs will display the icon associated with that program. However, shortcuts to folders and documents are pretty dull. In any case, you can change the icon for a shortcut by following these steps:

1. Right-click on the icon and select Properties from the pop-up menu.
2. Select the Shortcut tab and click on the Change Icon button.
3. If it's a shortcut to an application that includes its own assortment of icons, you can select one.
4. If your shortcut is to an object that doesn't include icons, you'll be shown the default icon file, SHELL32.DLL. Highlight an icon from the file (see Figure 4.7) or use the Browse button to look in other files (WINNT\SYSTEM32\MORICONS.DLL has a bunch).

NOTE To view .DLL files, open the Explorer and select Options from the View menu. On the View tab, select Show All Files and click OK.

5. Click on OK twice and the new icon will be displayed.

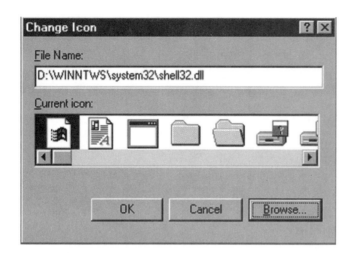

FIGURE 4.7:
Selecting a different icon
for a shortcut

Many icons are available from icon libraries that are distributed as shareware. Icons are often included in executable files, so if you have a shortcut to an application (a file with an .EXE extension) you can pick from those icons as well.

Keying to a Shortcut

If you're fond of opening certain applications with keystrokes, you can still do so in NT Workstation—with some limitations. At the end of this chapter, you'll find a list of the keyboard shortcuts used to move around the screen; however, you can also set up a key combination to open a shortcut to a program or folder.

1. Right-click on the shortcut and select Properties.
2. On the Shortcut page, click in the Shortcut key field.
3. Type in a letter, and Windows will add Ctrl+Alt. (So if you enter a W, the keyboard combination will be Ctrl+Alt+W.)
4. Click on OK when you're finished.

To remove a keyboard shortcut, you need to click in the Shortcut key field and press the Backspace key.

It's best to limit keyboard shortcuts to just a few programs or folders because these shortcuts have precedence in NT Workstation. So if you define a keyboard combination that's also used in a program, that program loses the ability to use the key combination.

Security

There will be a Security page on the shortcut's Properties page only if the shortcut is on a drive that's been formatted with the NT file system, NTFS, because NTFS includes security features, and FAT (the file system used by DOS, Windows 3.*x*, and Windows 95) does not.

The meanings of the buttons are as follows:

Permissions

Files you create (including shortcuts) belong to you. You can grant others permission to access them or not. See Chapter 8 for information on permissions.

Auditing

This has to do with the network keeping track of events surrounding a particular file. Users don't usually have access to this function.

Ownership

When you create a file, you own it. If you don't grant permission for others to use it, they can't. Only an administrator can take ownership of a file.

> **NOTE** None of these settings matter very much when it comes to shortcuts, but they are important when dealing with files. See Chapter 8 for the details.

When the Linked Object Is Moved or Renamed

As I've said, the shortcut is only a pointer to the original object—a pretty smart pointer, but with limitations. If you move the original object, the shortcut can almost always find it. (It may take a few seconds the first time for the search to be made.) Even renaming the original object doesn't thwart NT Workstation.

However, if you move the original object to a different drive or both move and rename the original object, the system will offer you a chance to browse for the original object. If that doesn't appeal to you, just let the search continue. NT Workstation will come up with a suggestion.

If the proposed solution is correct, click on Yes. If it's not, select No. Click on the shortcut with the right mouse button and select Properties. On the Shortcut page, provide the correct path for the shortcut.

WARNING Shortcuts to DOS programs will not be so forgiving. So if you move your game to another drive or rename a batch file, plan on making new shortcuts.

Shortcuts to Other Places

Shortcuts quickly become a normal way of accessing files and programs on your own computer, but they're a much more powerful tool than you'd suspect at first.

DOS Programs

Shortcuts to DOS programs are made in the same way as other shortcuts. Find the program file in the Explorer and do a right-mouse drag to the Desktop. The Properties pages for a DOS program are more complex to allow for individual configuration of older programs.

Disk Drives

Right-click on a disk drive in the Explorer or My Computer and drag it to the Desktop to create a shortcut to the contents of a drive. When you click on the shortcut, you'll see its contents almost instantly—it's much quicker than opening the entire Explorer.

Other Computers

You can put a shortcut to another computer—or part of it—on the Desktop. It can be a computer you're connected to on a network or even a computer you connect to using Dial-Up Networking. Just use Network Neighborhood to find the computer or part of it or even a single file, right-click on it and drag it to your Desktop (or another folder), and create a shortcut there.

HyperTerminal Connections

After you've used HyperTerminal to make a connection, you can drag the connection out of the folder onto your Desktop. Double-click on it, and the call will be made.

NOTE HyperTerminal is an applet that comes with NT Workstation and is described in Chapter 18.

In E-mail and Other Documents

Shortcuts can even be dropped into your e-mail or other documents. This still has limited use, but if you're communicating with someone who's also using the Internet Explorer you can make a shortcut of any Web site and drop the shortcut into an Exchange message. When the message is received at the other end, the recipient merely has to double-click on the shortcut. Internet Explorer will open with the Web site loaded.

TIP To make a shortcut to a Web site, just right-click on any spot where your pointer has turned into a hand. Select Copy Shortcut. Move your mouse pointer to your Desktop, or to the e-mail message, or to wherever you want it to go. Right-click and select Paste Shortcut.

As you can see, shortcuts are a valuable tool now and have even more potential in the future. As you experiment, you'll find even more ways to use shortcuts that are specific to your needs and work habits.

Keyboard Shortcuts

Even though NT Workstation 4 is much more mousy than earlier versions of NT Workstation, you can still do practically everything from the keyboard. Of course, you probably can't be bothered memorizing all these keyboard combinations, but you may want to consider a few for your memory bank (the one in your head) particularly if there are actions you do repeatedly that you find the mouse too clumsy for.

The following list includes the most useful (and in many cases, undocumented) keyboard shortcuts.

Key	Action
F1	Help.
F2	Rename the file or folder that's highlighted.
F3	Open Find.
F4	Open the drop-down list in the Toolbar. Press F4 a second time, and the drop-down list will close.
F5	Refresh the view in the active window.
Tab or F6	Each time you press this key, the focus will move from the drop-down window in the Toolbar to the left pane to the right pane and back again.
F10 or Alt	Put the focus on the menu bar. To move between menus, use the left ← and right → arrow keys. The ↓ key will open the menu.
Backspace	Move up one level in the folder hierarchy.
Alt+Esc	Switch between open applications. Hold down the Alt key, and each press of Esc will take you to another application. Applications on the Taskbar, once highlighted, can be activated by then clicking on Enter once or twice.
Alt+Tab	Open files and folders (see Figure 4.8 at the end of this table). Hold down the Alt key and press Tab to move the cursor from item to item.
Alt+Shift+Tab	Move the cursor through the open items in the opposite direction from Alt+Tab.
Ctrl+Esc	Open the Start menu.
Alt+F4	Close the current application. If no application is open, will activate the Shut Down window.
Alt+Spacebar	Open the Control Menu (same as clicking on the icon at the extreme upper-left corner of the application or folder window).
Spacebar	Toggle the choice.

Key	Action
Tab	Move the selection cursor to the next choice in a folder or dialog box.
Shift+Tab	Move the selection cursor in the opposite direction from Tab.
Alt+PrintScreen	Copy the active window to the Clipboard.

NOTE The Clipboard mentioned above is a special place in memory and not a specific application. However, there is a Clipboard Viewer (available under Accessories) that can see whatever you copy. In addition, there may be a Clipbook Viewer on your networked machine. See Chapter 18 for more on both.

FIGURE 4.8:
Using Alt+Tab to switch among active programs and folders

Next Step

Now that you've been introduced in detail to shortcuts, we'll cover some of the new strengths that NT Workstation gives to the mouse (or whatever pointing device you use).

Chapter 5

NEW MOUSE POWERS

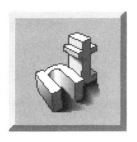

- **Understanding double- and single-click**
- **Right-clicks and left-clicks**
- **Setting up your mouse**
- **Changing pointers**

The Windows user interface has always depended on a mouse or other pointing device and with NT Workstation that reliance is even more pronounced. You can still do most things from the keyboard (Chapter 4 has a whole list of key combinations), but everything is much easier when you're using a mouse. Fewer steps are required, and you don't have to memorize anything, as you do when you use the keyboard a lot.

NOTE In this chapter the term *mouse* is used, but all devices that perform point-and-click actions (such as trackballs and pens) are included.

Everywhere you go in NT Workstation, you can click with the mouse to produce an action—whether it's opening a file or just getting helpful information. In this chapter, we'll discuss how the mouse works and how you can customize most functions for your own use.

Double- or Single-Click

It's not always easy in NT Workstation to know whether to double- or single-click the mouse button. The *double-click* (two rapid clicks in succession) with the left mouse button serves to open icons on the Desktop. If the icon represents a program, the program is started. If the icon represents a folder, the folder expands into a window on the Desktop so you can see and get at what's inside.

A single-click with the left mouse button serves to highlight the item clicked on. So if you're choosing a file in the Explorer or other folder with the idea of moving it or acting on it in some other way—other than opening it—a single-click will do the job.

NT Workstation 4 attempts to reduce the number of clicks needed by making use of the right mouse button. Use the right mouse button to click on a file or folder, and you have an array of choices on the menu that pops up. The top choice on this menu is usually Open, so you can open a program or file or folder with the right mouse button as easily as double-clicking with the left. Other functions are just as direct.

The Right Mouse Button

You can right-click on everything on the Desktop as well as the Desktop itself. As mentioned in Chapter 2, a right-click almost anywhere will provide some helpful result. All the programs that come with NT Workstation 4 as well as programs written specifically for NT Workstation 4 will use the right mouse button extensively. Bear in mind that programs written for earlier versions of NT Workstation will not use the right mouse button in the same way, though quite a few have some right—mouse button functionality built-in.

Right-Click on a File

Right-click on a file and you're presented with a menu of multiple options, including opening the file with its associated program.

If the file is of a registered file type, you can get still another option. Hold down the Shift key while right-clicking and you get Open With—an option that lets you open the file with a different application.

A number of programs will add other entries to the right mouse button menu. For example, the archiving program WinZip puts the item Add to Zip on the menu so you can select files to be added to an archive. Or if the program Quick View is available and associated with the file, Quick View will be on the menu to give you a look at the contents of the file without actually opening it.

Right-Click on a Folder

The menu that opens when you right-click on a folder is similar to the one for a file.

If you choose Open, you'll see the contents of the folder. Explore does much the same thing, except the folder will be shown in Explorer view—two panes with the left one showing the folder and its placement on the hard drive and the right pane detailing the folder's contents.

Right-click on a folder and select Find. The Find program will open ready to search in that folder. (There's more on using Find in Chapter 7.)

Right-Click on the Start Button

Place your pointer on the Start button and right-click to bring up three choices:

Open Opens the Start Menu folder. This is the folder that contains the programs you've dropped on the Start menu as well as another folder called Programs that contains all the shortcuts that make up the Programs menu that cascades off the Start menu.

Explore Opens the Start Menu folder but in the Explorer view.

Find Finds a file in the Start Menu folder (this is a shortcut).

The first two choices on the menu are quick ways to get at the items on the Programs menu, so you can move a program up a level or two or remove one from the menu entirely. If you choose Open, the view is of a single window. If you choose Explore, the window that opens will have two panes, the left one showing the folder and its place in the file system, the right pane showing the files inside whatever folder is chosen on the left. When you double-click on a folder, another window opens showing the contents. If you choose Find, you'll see the Find dialog box, into which you can type the name of the file(s) you'd like to find.

Right-Click on the Taskbar

When you right-click on a blank spot on the Taskbar a menu pops up with options to
- Cascade the windows that are currently open on the Desktop
- Tile the open windows horizontally
- Tile the open windows vertically
- Minimize all the open windows to the Taskbar
- Run the Task Manager
- Access the Taskbar properties

Right-Click on Icons on the Taskbar

Open programs and folders will each have an icon on the Taskbar. Right-click on the icon, and, if the item isn't open on the Desktop, you'll get the option to Restore (in other words, open a window on the Desktop), Maximize (restore it to full screen), or Close.

For items that have a window open on the Desktop, a left-click on the icon will bring that window to the front. A right-click will bring the window to the front plus open the same menu.

Move and Size are keyboard options. Select one of them, and you can move the window or change its size using the arrow keys or by dragging the mouse until you single-click.

Right-click on other icons in the far right corner of the Taskbar, and you'll get a chance to adjust the date and time or adjust the volume on your sound card. Other icons may appear in this section of the Taskbar depending on the hardware and software installed. As in other places, just try the right-click and see what you get!

Right-Click on My Computer

Right-click on the My Computer icon on the Desktop and you have the option of opening My Computer in a regular window or in Explorer view. You can also connect or disconnect network drives, find files, or open the Properties sheets for your system.

On the same menu are options for renaming the My Computer icon and for creating a shortcut to My Computer. There's considerably more about My Computer in Chapter 6.

Mouse Settings

Because the mouse (or other pointing device) is used so much in NT Workstation, it's important to have it set up comfortably. To change how your mouse operates, settings are available in the Mouse icon in the Control Panel. To access the Control Panel, click Start ➤ Settings ➤ Control Panel. The icons are arranged in alphabetical order, so look for Mouse around the middle of the Control Panel window.

Right- or Left-Handed

To change your right-handed mouse to a left-handed one, double-click on the Mouse icon in the Control Panel. On the Buttons page, click on the left-handed button to swap left and right mouse buttons. On a three-button mouse, these are the two outside buttons.

Double-Click Speed

You can adjust the amount of time allowed between two mouse-clicks for them to be counted as a double-click. Open the Mouse icon in the Control Panel. On the Buttons page, move the slider under Double-Click Speed toward Slow or Fast. Double-click in the Test area to try out a different setting, and then follow these steps:

Pointer Speed

As you move the pointer around the Desktop, perhaps you find you have to move the device too much to get a small result on the screen. Or vice versa, you move the mouse just a little, and the pointer moves way too far. To adjust this, double-click on the Mouse icon in the Control Panel.

1. Select the Motion tab.
2. Move the slider under Pointer Speed one notch to the left or the right.
3. Click on the Apply button and try the new setting.
4. Repeat until you have a speed you like and click on OK.

Mouse Pointers

NT Workstation 4 comes with an assortment of new mouse pointers, so you can choose ones you like. You'll probably find them a big improvement on the default pointers. A few of the pointers included with NT Workstation 4 are animated, and many more animated cursors come with the Plus! for Windows 95 package.

Animated cursors are also on their way to becoming the kind of cottage industry that icons were with earlier versions of Windows. Animated cursors can be downloaded from many online services and are also distributed as shareware.

> **NOTE** Your display must be set to at least 256 colors for the animated cursors to work. To check your settings, open the Display icon in the Control Panel, and click on the Settings button. The color palette must be set for 256 colors, High Color, or True Color.

Figure 5.1 shows the Pointers page under Mouse Properties. These default pointers are described in the table that follows. Once you understand what each pointer represents, you're better able to select appropriate substitutes. For example, you wouldn't want an animated pointer for Text Select because the animation would make it very difficult to make a precise selection.

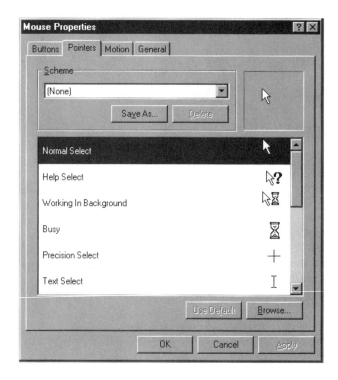

FIGURE 5.1:
The selection of mouse pointers

Pointer	What It Does
Normal Select	The normal pointer for selecting items.
Help Select	Click on the ? button, and move the pointer to the area you want information about, and click again.
Working in Background	Something is going on in the background, but you can often move to another area and do something else.
Busy	Just hang in there. Windows NT Workstation or an application is doing something and can't be disturbed.
Precision Select	Cross-hairs for very careful selection.

Pointer	What It Does
Text Select	The I-beam that's seen in word processors and used to select text.
Handwriting	When you're using a handwriting input device.
Unavailable	Sorry, you can't drag a file to this location because either the area is unacceptable or the application won't accept drag and drop.
Resizing	Cursors that appear when you're moving a window border.
Move	Select Move from the system menu or a right-click menu and you'll get this cursor, allowing you to move the window using the arrow keys.
Alternate Select	Used in the FreeCell card game. Probably other uses to come.

Changing Pointers

You can change one or more pointers and even have more than one set of pointers that you can switch among. To change one or more pointers on your system, follow these steps:

1. Double-click on the Mouse icon in the Control Panel and select the Pointers tab.
2. In the middle of the dialog box, you'll see a display of the pointers with their function. Highlight a pointer you want to change, and click on the Browse button.
3. The window shown in Figure 5.2 will open. When you click on a selection (files with the .ANI extension are animated), it will be displayed in the Preview box.
4. Click on the Open button when you have selected the one you want.

If you accumulate a large number of animated cursors, you may want to gather them together in a folder inside the Cursors folder.

TIP The animated cursors that come with Plus! (which those of you who are using Windows 95 and NT Workstation dual-boot machines may have handy) are located in the Program Files\Plus!\Themes folder. Copy them over rather than moving them. If you move them, your Plus! themes may not work properly.

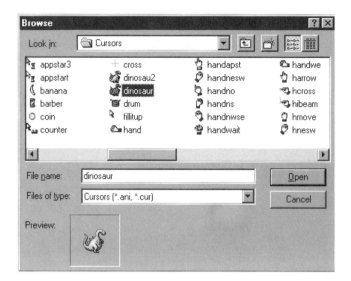

FIGURE 5.2:
Previewing the cursors

To save a selection of pointers as a set, click on the Save As button and enter a name for the scheme. After you save it, the set will be listed in the Scheme drop-down list, and you can select it any time.

Next Step

Now that you're acquainted with all the mouse functions, in the next chapter we move on to some important Desktop elements, namely the Explorer and the icon called My Computer. You'll see how, with some variations, these two elements are really much the same. Which one you use will depend on which one you like best.

Chapter 6

EXPLORING

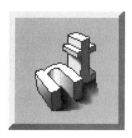

- **Defining Explorer and making it work**
- **Turning file extensions on and off**
- **Connecting files to programs**
- **Using File Manager**
- **Settings in the My Computer folder**

NT Workstation is set up so you can get at most things in more than one way. This is initially a little confusing because you may think you're looking at different places—when only the view has changed. In this chapter, we'll talk about the Explorer and the My Computer icon and the differences between what they offer.

What Is the Explorer?

The Explorer is the heir to the File Manager in previous versions of NT Workstation. It's the main tool for viewing the files and folders on your hard drive. Everything you see in the My Computer window is also in the Explorer.

> **NOTE** **Most of the programs you'll be using will be launched by shortcuts, either from the Start menu or from the Desktop, but you'll still need to use the Explorer to find the objects you want to create shortcuts *to*.**

When you install a program on your computer, the program's folders are placed on the hard drive—usually in the form of a main folder and *subfolders* (folders inside the main folder). Sometimes there are even sub-subfolders. Figure 6.1 shows an open Explorer window with the hierarchy of folders shown on the left. If you look closely, you can see that one of the folders in the left column is shown as "open." The contents of that folder are displayed in the right-hand pane. You use the scroll bars on either side to move up and down through the listing.

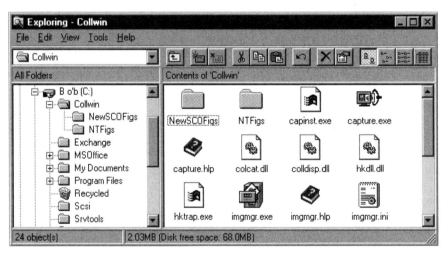

FIGURE 6.1: An Explorer Window with View set to Large Icons and with file extensions on

In the left pane, folders may have either a plus or minus sign next to them. A plus sign means there are subfolders—click directly on the plus sign to expand the view. When expanded, the plus sign turns into a minus sign.

To open the Explorer, click on the Start button and select Programs ➢ Windows NT Explorer.

Understanding Explorer

Slide the scroll bar for the left pane all the way to the top. Note that the hard drive C: and the floppy drives A: and B: are shown connected to My Computer by dotted lines. This indicates their connection to My Computer. But even further up is the top folder called Desktop.

In the Explorer's terms, the Desktop is the top of the hierarchy (see Figure 6.2) with My Computer and all its pieces connected to it.

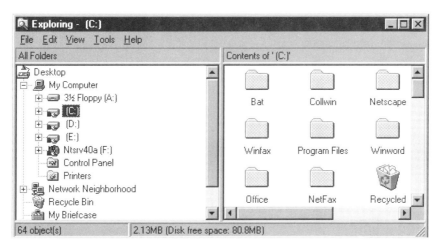

FIGURE 6.2: How the Explorer sees your system

The dotted lines show the connections, like in a flow chart. Lines that come from the bottom of an icon and connect horizontally to other icons indicate that the destination items are contained inside the object represented by the top icon. For example, you can see that the floppy drive A: and drive C: are all part of My Computer. Inside drive C: are numerous folders. The ones with plus signs next to them have subfolders (click on the plus sign to see them). Folders without plus signs have no other folders contained within them.

Looking further down the "tree" in the left pane (Figure 6.2), you can see that the Network Neighborhood is connected to the Desktop on the same level as My Computer. And why not? Other computers on the network are equivalent to your machine. The Recycle Bin is also on the same level—it spans all drives and can't be moved or deleted.

Special folders, such as the Control Panel and the folder for printers, are displayed on the same level as the disk drives, so they're easier to find.

Folders you have placed directly on the Desktop will also show up in the left pane. Shortcuts to folders aren't in the left pane because shortcuts are only pointers to the actual folders. The original folders are found along with other folders on your hard drive. To see the shortcuts that are on your Desktop, click on the Desktop icon in the left pane. The shortcuts will then be displayed—along with the rest of the stuff on the Desktop—in the right pane.

> **NOTE**   Other items that don't show in the left pane are the Inbox for Microsoft Exchange and any individual files that are on the Desktop. All these are visible in Explorer's right pane when you click on the Desktop icon in the left pane.

Exploring a Folder

Right-click on any folder—including My Computer or Network Neighborhood—and select Explore. The folder will open in Explorer view, with the hierarchy of folders shown in the left pane and the content of an open folder shown in the right pane.

Making a Shortcut to Explorer

To put Explorer at the top of your Start menu, open Explorer and find the file called EXPLORER.EXE in your Windows NT folder. Drag and drop it on the Start button.

Similarly, you can put Explorer on your Desktop. Right-click on EXPLORER.EXE and drag it to the Desktop. When you release the mouse button, select Create Shortcut(s) here.

Making a Shortcut to the Desktop

Try as you may, you can't drag the Desktop icon from the Explorer's left pane and create a shortcut that way. But you can create a shortcut to the Desktop following these steps:

1. Click on the WinNT folder in the Explorer.
2. In the WinNT folder, find the Profiles folder and double-click.
3. In the Profiles folder, find the folder with *your* user account name on it and double-click.
4. In the right pane, right-click on the Desktop folder and drag it to the Desktop.
5. Release the right mouse button and select Create Shortcut(s) Here.

Or, instead of dragging it to the Desktop, drag and drop on the Start button to put the Desktop folder on the top of your Start menu.

When opened, this shortcut will contain all the folders and files and other icons on your Desktop—except the system-type folders like My Computer and Recycle Bin.

NOTE   For obvious reasons, you can't get at someone else's Desktop, but it's also possible that you won't be able to access your own Desktop folder. This will happen only if you have been assigned a mandatory Desktop—one that you can't make permanent changes to. The only one who can change this is the system administrator.

Opening Two Explorers

If you're moving around a number of files or folders, it's simpler if you can have two instances of the Explorer open. It's certainly easy enough to have more than one Explorer window open. All you have to do is select Explore whenever you right-click on a folder.

To arrange the Explorer windows so you can access them easily, right-click on the Taskbar and select Tile Windows Horizontally or Tile Windows Vertically. Figure 6.3 shows three instances of Explorer tiled horizontally.

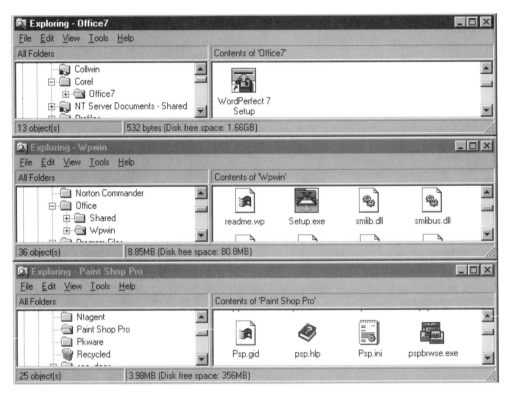

FIGURE 6.3: Tile Explorer windows so you can move between them easily.

Explorer Navigation

As mentioned before, when you see a plus sign next to an icon in the Explorer, it means that at least one subfolder is inside. Click on the plus sign to expand the view. Click on a minus sign and the subfolders will be collapsed inside the main folder. You can slide the scroll boxes to view items that are outside the pane view.

> **TIP**
> Scroll boxes are *proportionate* in NT Workstation. That is, the scroll box shows how much of the window's contents is being displayed. A scroll box that fills half the bar tells you that you're looking at half of what there is to see (in that particular window).

There are several ways to get at folder contents using your mouse:
- Click on a folder in the left pane of the Explorer and the contents are displayed in the right pane.
- Right-click on a folder in the left pane and select Open. A new window will open on the Desktop, displaying the contents of the folder you clicked on.
- Double-click on a folder in the left pane and you expand that branch and display the folder contents in the right pane.

The Toolbar

The Toolbar in the Explorer is a standardization of a visual device that's been used in many Windows and Windows NT applications. It's a collection of icons that provide quick access to the functions on the menus. Position the mouse pointer over a button and a small window opens telling you what the button does. The Toolbar is not on by default, so you'll need to select Toolbar from the View menu for it to be visible.

From left to right, the functions on the Toolbar are
- Move to another folder by selecting it from this drop-down list.
- Move up one level in the folder hierarchy.
- Map a network drive. In other words, assign a letter to a drive on another computer on the network, so your computer can access it.
- Disconnect a network drive (un-map it).
- Cut the highlighted item(s).
- Copy the highlighted item(s).
- Paste what you've just cut or copied.
- Undo the last operation.
- Delete the highlighted item(s).
- View the Properties sheet for the highlighted item.

- Change the view to Large Icons.
- Change the view to Small Icons.
- Change the view to a list.
- Change the view to a list with details about file size, date, and so forth.

Other Tools and Buttons

The Explorer, like the other folder windows, has a number of additional tools and buttons—many of them new in NT Workstation 4.

Minimize, Maximize, and Restore

The Minimize and Maximize/Restore buttons have new icons, and a Close button has been added.

 Click on the rightmost button in the upper right-hand corner of a window and the window will close. The button on the left will minimize the window to the Taskbar. The middle button maximizes the window.

 If the window is already at its maximum size, the middle button will restore the window to its normal size.

Sizing Handles

The odd little graphic effect in the bottom-right corner of some windows is called a sizing handle.

 Click and drag a sizing handle to change the size of a window. An NT Workstation window without a sizing handle can't be resized. Application windows can be resized as they always have been—by dragging a corner or border.

Sort Buttons

A folder that's being displayed in the form of a detailed list will have several sort buttons at the top of the display.

Name	Size	Type	Modified

Click on a button to get the following results:

Name   Contents will be sorted in alphabetical order. A second click will sort the files in *reverse* alphabetical order.

Size   Files will be sorted in order of their ascending size. A second click will reverse the size order.

Type Files will be sorted alphabetically by type with folders first, then files. A second click will reverse the order.

Modified Files will be sorted by the date they were last changed—most recent to oldest. A second click will reverse the order.

All of the above sort methods are also available on the View menu under Arrange Icons.

Setting How the Icons Look

The contents of folders can be viewed as large icons, small icons, a list, or a detailed list. Pull down the View menu in any folder window to try out different looks.

If you use large or small icons, you can select View ➢ Arrange Icons and toggle Auto Arrange on or off. Remove the check mark from in front of Auto Arrange and you can drag the icons around inside the folder. With Auto Arrange selected, the icons snap to an invisible grid and can't be moved about arbitrarily.

If you turn off Auto Arrange and have moved your folder icons every which way until you've made a mess, you can select Line Up Icons from the View menu, and the file icons all snap to an invisible grid.

File Extensions

If you've ever used any version of DOS or Windows prior to Windows 95, you're very familiar with the file-naming conventions used. A file name could have a maximum of eight characters plus a three-character extension. This has historically been one of the more irritating facts about using a PC. Not because naming a file is especially hard—but because six months later you're probably going to have a hard time remembering what CZMLHTL.DOC is all about.

With NT, long file names are permitted, so you can give that file you made a name like **Letter to Hotel in Cozumel**.

By default, NT Workstation hides most file extensions. If NT Workstation knows what program *made* the file, the extension doesn't need to be seen. All you have to do is click on the file, and NT Workstation will open the associated application.

Seeing Extensions

If you want the file extensions displayed, follow these steps:

1. Select Options from the View menu.

2. On the View page, remove the check from in front of Hide File Extensions for Known File Types.

3. Click on OK.

Note that the reference is to all known (or *registered*) file types. If NT Workstation doesn't know what program is associated with a particular file extension, the extension will continue to be displayed whether or not this check box is checked.

Seeing All Files

NT Workstation also hides from normal view a whole assortment of files, including system files and various kinds of device drivers. These are hidden for two reasons. First, most users don't need to see these files, and they just clutter up the Desktop. Secondly, if you were to accidentally change or delete one of these files, it could cause a particular program—or even your whole system—not to work.

However, there's certainly no harm in displaying them, so if you really want to see all the files on your system, you can do so easily. Just select Option from the View menu, and on the View page of the Properties sheet (Figure 6.4), select Show All Files.

Unfortunately, there's no way to pick and choose among the files that are designated as hidden. Either all the preset hidden file types are displayed or none of those types are.

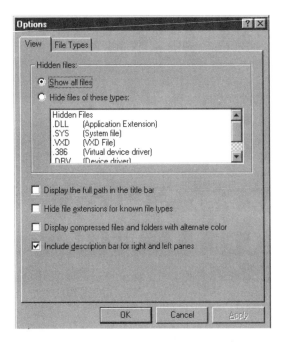

FIGURE 6.4:
Hidden files can be un-hidden using the View menu.

Associating Files with Programs

NT Workstation does a pretty good job of determining which files go with which programs. Once NT Workstation knows that a certain type of file is associated with a particular program, you can click on *any* file with that extension and cause the program to open.

> **NOTE** *Associating* **a file type with a program is the same as** *registering* **it. So when NT Workstation talks about registered file types, the reference is also to associated files.**

Making a New Association

Most of the time, merely installing a program is enough to teach NT Workstation which files go with that program, but not always. If a file is of a registered type, when you right-click on it, the first option on the menu is Open. If it's not registered, the first option will be Open With. Select Open With and you can select from the list of applications as shown in Figure 6.5.

FIGURE 6.5:
Choosing an application for an unregistered file type

If you want to have all your files of a particular type always open with a particular application, you need to tell NT Workstation about it.

To register a file type, follow these steps:

1. Open Explorer, and from the View menu, select Options.

2. Select File Types and click on New Type.

3. In the Description of Type box, enter how you want this type of file to be shown in windows that display in Details view. This is for your information, so you can describe it in any way you choose.

4. In the Associated Extension box, enter the three letters that make up this file type's extension (see Figure 6.6). These three letters *are* important because all files with the same extension will display a particular icon and be acted on in the same way as far as the operating system is concerned.

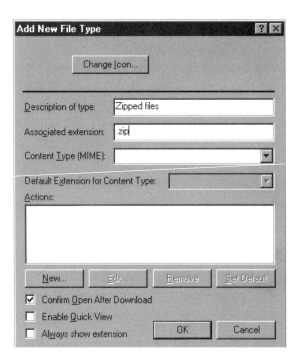

FIGURE 6.6:
Fill in a description of the file type and the file extension.

5. Click on the New button. In the New Action dialog box, type in the action you want performed when you double-click on files of this type and the application used to perform the action (see Figure 6.7).

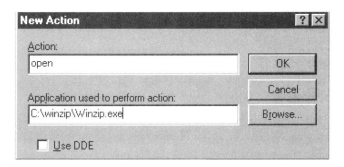

FIGURE 6.7:
Designate the action you want taken and the program that will do it.

NOTE   Chances are, you'll want the program to open the file. That is, the program will start and then load the file that you've double-clicked.

6. Use the Browse button to find the exact location of the application you want used. Click on OK.
7. Back in the Add New File Type dialog box, you can click on the Change Icon button to select a different icon for the associated files. Figure 6.8 shows the finished dialog box. Click on Close when you're done.

FIGURE 6.8:
With this arrangement, double-clicking any file with the .ZIP extension will open the associated program WINZIP.EXE.

One File Type, Multiple Programs

Most file types are associated with a single program—but there are exceptions. For example, when confronted with bitmapped files (extension .BMP) you may want to open some in Microsoft Paint, others in Collage Plus, still others in PaintShop Pro, or another program.

To have multiple associations, follow these steps, substituting the file types and programs you want to use:

1. Open Explorer and from the View menu, select Options.

2. Click on the File Types tab. In the Registered File Types dialog box, find the file type you want to add another association for and highlight it.

3. Click on the Edit button. (Figure 6.9 shows the default actions for text documents [.TXT].) If you double-click on a .TXT file, it will open (the action shown in bold type). The Print action is available from the right-click menu.

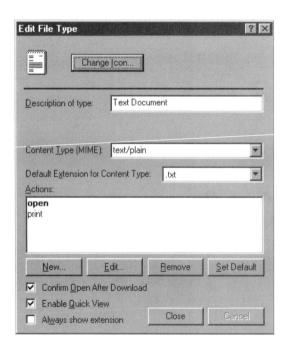

FIGURE 6.9:
Default actions for documents with the .TXT extension

4. Click on the New button to add an action. In the New Action dialog box, enter the action you want performed as well as the application to perform the action. In Figure 6.10 we're adding the option to open the file in Word for Windows.

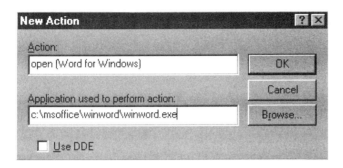

FIGURE 6.10:
Adding Open (Word for Windows) as an association for text files

5. Click on OK. Back in the Edit File Type dialog box, all the actions will be listed. The item in bold will be the default (double-click) action. To change the default, highlight the one you want and click on the Set Default button. Click on OK again when you've finished.

Figure 6.11 shows the results of the above steps. Now a right-click on a text file gives the additional option of opening the file in Word for Windows.

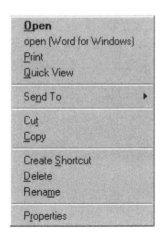

FIGURE 6.11:
A right mouse-click on a .TXT file now produces a menu with an additional option—Open (Word for Windows).

You can clutter up your right-click menu with as many associations as you want.

Changing Associations

To change an association between a file type and a program, follow these steps:

1. Open the Explorer and select Options from the View menu.
2. Under Registered File Types, highlight the type you want to change and click on the Edit button.

3. Highlight the Action you want to change.
4. Click on Edit to make a change, and make the change in the Editing Action dialog box.
5. When you're finished, select OK, then keep closing dialog boxes until you're back on the Desktop.

Deleting Associations

To delete an association, open the Explorer and select Options from the View menu. Under Registered File Types, highlight the file type you want to unregister and click on Remove.

Using File Manager

If you're a convert from a previous version of NT Workstation, you're probably missing File Manager about now. Fortunately, it's still included with NT Workstation.

To open File Manager, open Explorer, open the WinNT folder, and then open the System32 folder. Inside, you'll see a file called WINFILE (or WINFILE.EXE if you have the display extensions turned on). Double-click on WINFILE and the File Manager will open.

You can create shortcuts to the File Manager, so they can be available in areas where you're likely to need them. File Manager is often faster than the Explorer, and if you're migrating from NT Workstation 3.5x, it's certainly more familiar ground. Be aware though, right-clicking to access a menu doesn't work in File Manager.

My Computer

When you first set up NT Workstation, there'll be several icons on the left side of your screen. The number will vary, depending on the options you (or the administrator) chose when installing. One of them—in fact, the first one—is called My Computer. Double-click on it and you'll see a window like the one shown in Figure 6.12. It may not be exactly the same because computers vary.

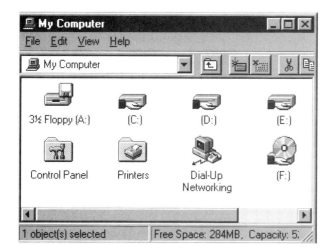

FIGURE 6.12:
The My Computer folder

The items displayed in the window are symbols for the physical contents of your computer, including the floppy drives, hard drives, and CD-ROM drives. There'll also be a folder labeled Printers and one for the Control Panel.

NOTE Because so many settings are accessed through the Control Panel, it makes sense for them to be available in a variety of locations: on the Start menu, in My Computer, and in Explorer. Plus you can make shortcuts to the Control Panel and put them wherever you like.

Click once on a drive and the disk's capacity and free space appear in the status bar at the bottom of the window. Double-click on one of the icons and a window will open displaying the contents. For example, double-click on the hard drive labeled C: and you'll see all the folders contained on the C: drive.

My Computer's Properties

Right-click on the My Computer icon and select Properties. There's a great deal of information to be found in these Properties sheets. If you've got a dual-boot machine (running NT Workstation and Windows 95, for example), the Startup/Shutdown page is of particular interest (see Figure 6.13). Here's where you can see a list of the operating systems installed on your computer. To change the default operating system, click on one of the systems listed here.

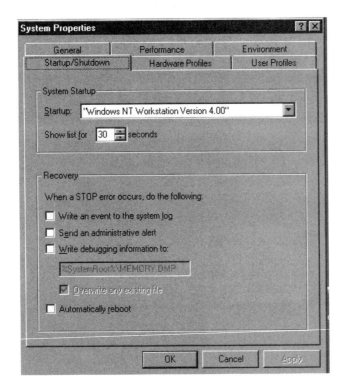

FIGURE 6.13:
The Startup/Shutdown page lets you change the default operating system.

The General page provides you with valuable information about your computer, such as which processor is inside it and how much memory it has. There are a number of other settings on the System Properties pages—particularly under the Performance page—that you may want to take a look at. Most of these settings *never* need to be changed, but you should know where they are.

Disk Properties

Right-click on one of the disk drives and select Properties. You'll get a Properties sheet (see Figure 6.14) that reports the used space and free space in detail. You can also supply a name (what the dialog box calls a *Label*) for the hard drive.

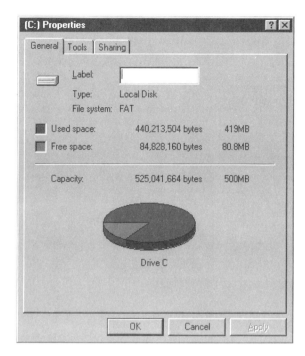

FIGURE 6.14:
The Properties sheet for a hard drive

The Tools tab will let you check the disk for errors, back it up, or defragment it. There's more on these tools in Chapter 19. If you're on a network, the Sharing tab lets you share this drive with others on the network.

One Window or Many

Click on the View menu and select Options in a window (like My Computer), and you can choose from two ways to open folders:

Separate Window   With this choice, every double-click on a folder will open a new window, leaving all previous windows open. This will fill up your screen pretty quickly, but it will give you a clear indication of where you are and how you got there.

Single Window   This means that as you double-click through multiple layers of folders, the contents of the current folder fill the window.

You can experiment to see which one you prefer.

> **TIP**
>
> Select the Single Window option and you'll be able to make some view settings permanent. Using Single Window Browse, if you select (let's say) Large Icons for the parent window, all the child windows will also display Large Icons. For another parent window, another view setting can be selected, and all the subfolders will retain that setting.

Reducing Multiple Window Clutter

It's possible to keep the clutter to a minimum using the Multiple Window option. Open folder windows until you get to the one you want. Then hold down the Shift key, and click on the Close box of the parent folder of the folder you want left open. This will close all windows leading down to the current folder.

Changing to Single Window on the Spot

If you like the Multiple Window option most of the time, you can switch to a single window on occasion. Instead of a simple double-click on a folder to open a new window, hold down the Ctrl key as you double-click. This will open the contents of the double-clicked folder in the current window.

Changing a Folder to Explorer View

Hold down the Shift key as you double-click on a folder and the folder will open in the Explorer view. Make sure the focus is on the folder you want to open this way; otherwise NT Workstation will open all the folders between where you clicked and the folder where the focus actually was.

In a folder where none of the objects are highlighted, the focus is on the object with a dotted line around the name. If an item is highlighted, that's the focus object. Every open folder has an item that is the focus.

Next Step

In the next chapter, we'll continue some of the themes of this one, except we'll go into more detail about the nuts and bolts of moving, selecting, and manipulating files on your system.

Chapter

7

FILES AND FOLDERS

- **Making selections**
- **Making new files and folders**
- **Moving, copying, and deleting files and folders**
- **Undoing a mistake**
- **Using long file names**
- **Formatting and copying floppy disks**
- **Locating anything with the Find command**

In this chapter, we'll continue some of the discussion from Chapter 6 with an emphasis on the basics of making and manipulating files and folders, and getting them organized in ways you find comfortable.

Selecting Files and Folders

A single file or folder is selected by clicking on it once. As soon as you click, you'll see that the object is highlighted. You can do this with the left mouse button and then move or rename or copy the object as described later in this chapter. Or you can click on the object with the right mouse button, and a menu will open with possible actions.

Selecting Everything

To select a bunch of files or folders, open the window where the objects in question are, and then click on the Edit menu and click on Select All. Everything in the window will be highlighted. Right-click on one of the highlighted icons (see Figure 7.1) and choose the action you want to take from the pop-up menu.

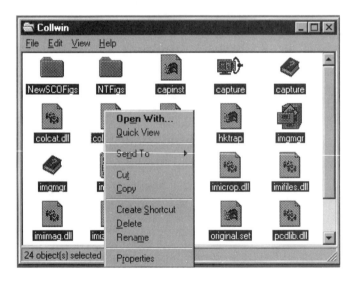

FIGURE 7.1:
All the files are selected and the right mouse menu lets you choose what you want to do with them.

Selecting Some but Not All

There are lots of ways to select some of the objects in a window. The easiest way often depends on how you have the files and folders displayed.

If you have large icons displayed, you might want to simply lasso the items in question. Right-click on an area near the first item, and, holding the mouse button down, draw a line around the icons you want to select. When you're finished drawing the box, the icons will be highlighted, and the pop-up menu will appear, giving you a choice of actions. Figure 7.2 shows some icons selected in just this way.

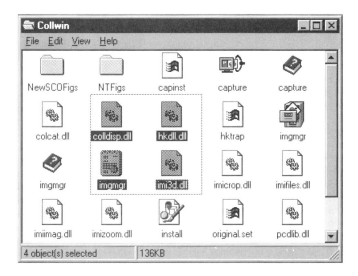

FIGURE 7.2:
Some icons captured by lassoing

You can also draw the box and drag the icons using the left mouse button. But when you release the button, you won't get the pop-up menu you'd get with the right mouse button.

If you have the icons displayed as a list or in the details view, it's probably easier to select them using Ctrl+click. Hold down the Ctrl key while clicking on the items you want.

If you want all the files in a series, click on the first one, then hold down the Shift key while clicking on the last one. All the objects in between the two clicks will be selected.

Making a New Folder

Folders are the NT Workstation equivalent of directories in NT Workstation 3.5x , Windows 3.x, and DOS. There are differences in that NT Workstation folders can contain shortcuts, can be shortcuts to *real* folders in other locations, and can be placed right on the Desktop.

On the Desktop

To create a new folder on the Desktop, right-click on the Desktop in some unoccupied space and select New ➤ Folder from the menu. A folder like the one below will appear with the cursor already placed for you to type in a name.

 This folder is actually located on your hard drive in your very own Desktop folder (you'll find this Desktop folder if you open the WinNT folder, then the Profiles folder, and then the folder with your username). Figure 7.3 shows this new folder as it appears in Explorer.

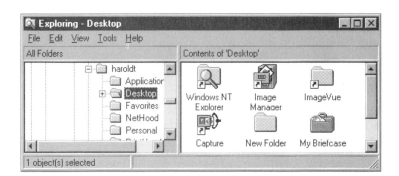

FIGURE 7.3:
The new folder on the Desktop can also be seen in the Explorer.

NOTE If you can't see the Desktop folder, it's because Hide Files of These Types is checked under View ➤ Options ➤ View. Select Show All Files instead and the Desktop folder will appear in Explorer.

Inside Another Folder

To make a folder inside another folder, for example in Explorer, follow these steps:

1. Open Explorer. Use the scroll bars to locate the folder where you want to place the new folder.
2. Expand the existing folder by double-clicking on it.
3. Move your pointer to a blank spot in the right pane and click once with the right mouse button.
4. Select New ➤ Folder from the menu.
5. Type in the name for the new folder.

You can do this with a folder on the Desktop. Just open the folder where you want to place the new folder, and right-click once in a blank spot inside the open window.

Folder Properties

Since everything else has Properties sheets, it should come as no surprise that folders do too. Right-click on a folder and select Properties from the menu. You'll see a dialog box like the one shown in Figure 7.4.

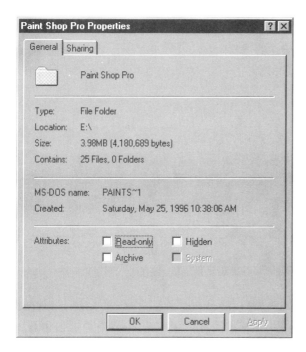

FIGURE 7.4:
Folder Properties

General Page

The General page provides information about the folder, including its size and the number of files and other folders to be found inside. As with Properties sheets for individual files, there are also check boxes for setting attributes:

Read-only   Set this attribute and the folder cannot be written to. This is not a security measure except in that it makes it harder to accidentally change something. A determined person can easily figure out how to change this attribute.

Archive   A check in this box means a folder has been backed up by a program that sets the archive bit. It does not indicate whether the contents of the folder are backed up or not.

Hidden   Folders and files that are hidden will disappear from the NT Workstation interface. They'll still work as usual but just won't be visible to the Explorer or other programs.

System   System files are required by NT Workstation. You don't want to delete them. In any case, a whole folder cannot be designated as System, so this box is always grayed out when you're looking at a folder.

TIP   To change a file or folder from hidden to visible, go to View ➤ Options on a window's toolbar and select Show All Files. Find the file you want to change and open its Properties page so you can change the Hidden attribute.

Sharing Page

You can share your folder with others on the network by selecting the Sharing page and then clicking on the Permissions button. You can give another user or group of users no access, read-only access, read-write (change) access, or, if you're feeling daring, full control. On this page, you can also specify exactly which user or groups of users should have which type of access to a particular drive or file. Don't worry if the Sharing page doesn't make much sense to you yet—we'll give you the lowdown on shared resources in Chapter 8.

Making a New File

As long as you're using older software, not specifically made for NT Workstation 4, you'll probably make new files as you always have: by opening the application and selecting New from the File menu. However, a number of applications do place themselves on a New File menu, and you can make new files from there.

On the Desktop

To create a new file on the Desktop, right-click on the Desktop in some unoccupied space and select New from the menu. Select the type of file you want to make. A file like the one below will appear with the cursor already placed for you to type in a name.

This file is located on your hard drive in your very own Desktop folder, which you'll find if you open the WinNT folder, then the Profiles folder, then the folder with your user account name. Figure 7.5 shows this new file as it appears in Explorer.

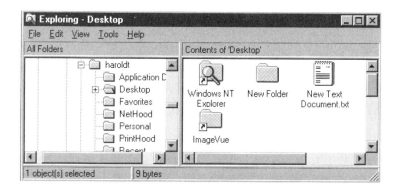

FIGURE 7.5:
The new file on the Desktop can also be seen in the Explorer.

TIP   If you can't see the Desktop folder, it's because Hide Files of These Types is checked under View ➤ Options ➤ View. Select Show All Files instead and the Desktop folder appears.

Inside Another Folder

To make a file inside another folder, for example in Explorer, open the folder that'll be the outside folder. Right-click on a blank spot and select New from the pop-up menu. Then select the type of file from the list and type in the name for the new file.

File Properties

As a rule, most Properties sheets for files are a single page like the one shown in Figure 7.6. It will include some information about the file's location, size, and creation date. There will also be boxes for setting and removing attributes as described previously under "Folder Properties."

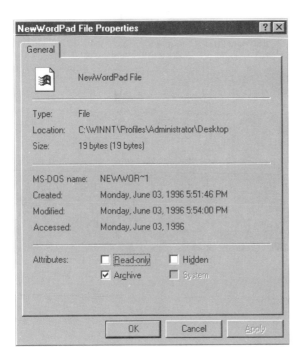

FIGURE 7.6:
A Properties sheet for a specific file

A few programs include other pages on the Properties sheets for files. For example, Word for Windows files include a page of statistics about the file and another page of summary information about the file. As more programs are written specifically for NT Workstation 4, this trend toward including ever more data on the Properties sheets is bound to continue.

Moving and Copying Files and Folders

There are at least three different methods for moving and copying files or folders. You can adopt one method and use it all the time, or you can pick and choose from the various methods, depending on the circumstances.

Move or Copy Using Right Drag and Drop

This is my personal favorite because it requires a minimum of thought:
1. Locate the file or folder using the Explorer or My Computer.
2. Click on the file or folder using the right mouse button.
3. Hold the button down and drag the object to its new location.
4. Release the mouse button and choose Move or Copy from the pop-up menu.

For the shortest distance between two points, you may want to open a second instance of the Explorer, so you can drag and drop directly. Or you can move or copy the object to the Desktop, and then open the destination folder or drive and drag the object a second time.

Move or Copy Using Left Drag and Drop

This method requires a bit more mental attention because when you use the left mouse button to drag and drop, the result is a move only if the source and destination are on the same hard drive. If they are on different drives, the result will be a copy.

 If you're dragging a *program* file (one with the extension .EXE or .COM), NT Workstation will create a shortcut to the original file at the destination. You can tell that a shortcut is going to be made because a shortcut arrow can be seen in the transparent icon that you're dragging.

You can force a move to happen by pressing and holding the Shift key before you release the left mouse button.

TIP If you decide while dragging to cancel the move or copy, just hit the Esc key before you release the mouse button. This stops the drag but leaves the files or folders highlighted.

NOTE There are a few objects, such as disk icons, that you can't move or copy. If you try to, you'll get a message informing you of this fact and asking if you want a shortcut instead.

Move or Copy Using Cut/Copy and Paste

Using the right mouse button menu to move or copy files and folders is very efficient because you don't have to have both source and destination available at the same time.

To move or copy a file, follow these steps:

1. Locate the file or folder you want to move or copy, using My Computer or the Explorer.
2. Right-click on the object and select Cut (to move) or Copy from the pop-up menu.
3. Find the destination folder and open it.
4. Right-click on a blank spot inside the folder and select Paste from the pop-up menu.

Deleting Files and Folders

The easiest way to delete a file or folder is to click on it once with the right mouse button and select Delete from the pop-up menu. Or you can click on the object with the left mouse button and then press the Del key on your keyboard.

Another method is to drag and drop the object on the Recycle Bin icon. A plus of this method is that you won't be asked to confirm that you want to delete the file.

In any of the above methods, the Recycle Bin protects the user from over-hasty deletions because the data is not instantly deleted but can be retrieved from the Recycle Bin if you later decide you want it back. There's much more on the Recycle Bin in Chapter 10.

TIP   To delete a file or folder without sending it to the Recycle Bin, press the Shift key while selecting Delete from the pop-up menu or while pressing the Del key.

Renaming Files and Folders

There are two easy ways to change the name of a file or folder:
- You can click on the name twice (with about a second between each click), and the name will be highlighted so you can type in a new one.
- You can right-click once on the file and select Rename from the pop-up menu.

Unfortunately, there's no provision for renaming a group of files in one swoop.

The Undo Command

When you move, copy, or rename something, the command to undo that action gets added to a stack maintained by NT Workstation. The stack is built up as you move, copy, and rename. The most recent action is on top.

To undo the most recent action that hasn't been undone, you can click on the Undo button on the window's toolbar, or you can right-click on the Desktop or in a free area of a folder, and the Undo command will be on the pop-up menu.

The unwieldy thing about Undo is that it's a big and global stack. You can merrily undo dozens of commands, and you may not be able to see where the Undo is taking place and just what moves and copies and renames are being undone—particularly if you've been working in a variety of folders. So it's best to use Undo quickly and to do it in the folder where you performed the original action. That way you can see the results of Undo.

TIP If you don't remember what you did last, and therefore don't know what Undo will undo, rest your mouse pointer on the Undo button, and the pop-up help will tell you whether it was a move, copy, or rename.

Long File Names

One of the most attractive features in NT Workstation 4 is the ability to give files and folders long file names. However, you don't want to get carried away because the full path, including folder and subfolder names, can't exceed 258 characters.

File names can include spaces as well as characters you couldn't use before like the comma, semicolon, equals sign (=), and square brackets ([]). The following characters are still not allowed in either file or folder names:

\ / * < > : ? " |

File and folder names can also have both upper- and lowercase letters, and the system will preserve them (for display purposes). When you type in the name, you don't have to remember whether you capitalized some part of it or not. NT Workstation will find it as long as the spelling is correct.

NOTE Passwords in NT Workstation are case-sensitive—as they are everywhere.

Long File Names in DOS

The Command prompt (DOS) commands that come with NT Workstation know how to handle long file names. Figure 7.7 shows some files as they appear in an open window in NT Workstation.

FIGURE 7.7:
The Newsletter
folder on the Desktop

Figure 7.8 shows those same items in a Command Prompt window.

```
Command Prompt                                          _ □ ×

Directory of D:\winntws\profiles\janea\desktop\newsletter

07/13/96   01:27p        <DIR>          .
07/13/96   01:27p        <DIR>          ..
07/13/96   01:16p                   708 November Finances.txt
07/13/96   01:17p                 2,274 October Newsletter.rtf
07/13/96   01:13p               308,278 Picture for Newsletter.bmp
                 5 File(s)         311,260 bytes
                            805,384,704 bytes free

D:\winntws\profiles\janea\desktop\newsletter>
```

FIGURE 7.8: The same objects displayed in a Command Prompt window

As you can see, the long file names are preserved even though you're running from the Command Prompt.

NOTE

Note that in Figure 7.8, the path to the Desktop is not as straightforward as it is in DOS. This is because every user who can log onto this machine has his or her own Desktop configuration saved in the Profiles folder inside the Windows NT Workstation 4 folder. Changes you make to your Desktop are made automatically, but the actual Desktop folder is buried deep.

Limitations of Long File Names

Unless you're running all NT Workstation programs (and few of us are), the long file names will be truncated under certain circumstances. For example, if you've made a file in WordPad called **Luisa's Party Invitation** and then want to open it in Word for Windows 6 on, let's say, a computer running Windows 3.11 (even if it's on the network), you'll see the file name has changed to "luisas~1."

After you modify and save the file, though, and return to WordPad, the long name will still be intact.

Similarly if you copy some files to a diskette and take those files to a computer running DOS or Windows 3.x, you can edit the files on the floppy disk, and, when you return to the NT Workstation 4 machine, the long file names will be intact. However, if you copy those files to the other machine's hard drive and edit them, later copying them back to the floppy, when you return to your NT Workstation 4 machine, the long names will be replaced by short names.

Dealing with Floppy Disks

Floppy disks remain part of the computing arsenal even for people on networks. Sooner or later, you have to put something on a floppy or take it off (by deleting or formatting). NT Workstation includes tools to do all the floppy tasks, though some may not work exactly as you expect.

NOTE You may not even have a floppy drive on your workstation. One of the big challenges of a network is maintaining security. Floppy drives are an easy way to sneak software onto a network that shouldn't be there or to copy off information that the Powers That Be do not want copied.

Formatting a Floppy

To format a floppy disk, put the disk in the drive and follow these steps:

1. Open Explorer.
2. Use the scroll bars to move up to the point where you can see your floppy drive in the left window.

3. Right-click on the floppy drive and select Format.

4. The dialog box shown in Figure 7.9 will open. Make sure the choices selected are the ones you want. If not, change them.

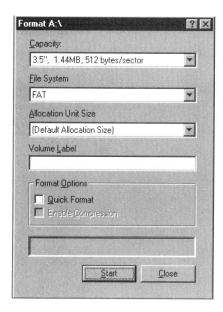

FIGURE 7.9:
The dialog box that opens
to format a floppy disk

5. Click on the Start button. When the formatting is complete (you'll see a progress bar at the bottom of the window), click on the Close button.

> **TIP** Make sure you right-click on the floppy drive. If the contents of the floppy are displayed in the right panel of the Explorer, you won't be allowed to format it because NT Workstation will see the floppy as "in use." This is true even if the floppy has no files on it.

Copying a Floppy

To make an exact copy of a floppy disk, put the floppy in the drive and follow these steps:

1. Open Explorer.

2. Use the scroll bars to move up to the point where you can see your floppy drive in the left window.

3. Right-click on the floppy drive and select Copy Disk.

4. If you have more than one floppy drive, you can specify the Copy From drive and Copy To drive before you click on Start. With only one floppy drive, just click on Start.

The system will read the entire disk then prompt you to insert the disk you want to copy to.

Copying Files to a Floppy

There are two approaches to copying folders or files to a floppy disk, depending on whether the material to be copied is smaller or larger than the capacity of a single floppy.

When the material you want to copy will fit on a single floppy, the process is easy. Put the floppy disk in the drive and use one of these approaches:

- Highlight the file or folder, and then right-click, select Send To ➣ and then select the specific floppy drive.
- Drag and drop the items to the floppy drive icon in the Explorer or My Computer.
- If you have a shortcut to a floppy drive on your desktop or in a folder, drag and drop the items there.

You may even find other ways over time!

Using Find

NT Workstation comes with a very sophisticated file-finding tool that makes it possible to find almost anything on your hard disk, even if you know very little about the file you're searching for.

When You Know the Name

To find a file or folder when you know the name (or part of it), follow these steps:

1. Click on the Start button, slide the pointer to Find, and then click on Files or Folders.

2. Type in the file name, either whole or in part. Unlike previous Find tools, you don't need to know how the file begins or ends. For example, a search for files with *log* in their names, yielded the results shown in Figure 7.10.

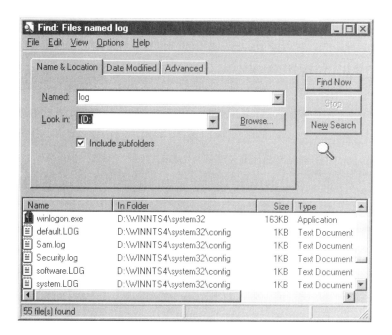

FIGURE 7.10:
Searching with only part of the name

3. The Look In box tells the program where to search. If you haven't a clue, use the drop-down list or the Browse button to select My Computer, and the program will look everywhere on your system.

4. Click on Find Now to start the search.

NOTE The criteria or results of file and folder searches can be saved by selecting Save Search from the File Menu. If you've also selected Save Results from the Option menu, the results of the search are saved as well. The Find window will be saved in the form of an icon on your Desktop. Double-click on the icon to open the Find window with the search criteria and the results displayed.

When You Know Something Else

And then there are the times when you don't know *any* part of the file name. If you have an idea of when the file was last worked on, you can use the Date Modified tab in the Find dialog box. You can specify a search between specific days or just look for files created or modified during previous months or days.

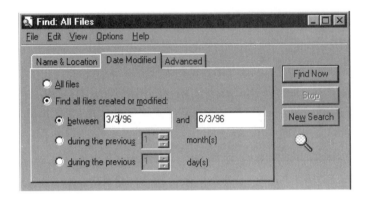

Maybe all you know is that the document you want is a letter written in WordPad and that it was addressed to a branch office in Poughkeepsie. Click on the Advanced tab, select the file type from the drop-down window, and enter **Poughkeepsie** in the Containing text box.

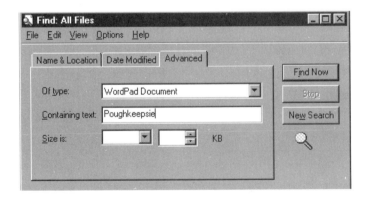

Searches can be based on even skimpier information. You can have the program search All Files and Folders (look in the Of Type drop-down list) for files containing a certain word or phrase. Of course, the more information you can tell the program, the faster the search will be.

TIP

Once you find the file you want, you can drag it to the Desktop or into another folder. You can double-click on program files to open the program. If a file is associated with a program (as discussed in Chapter 6), double-click on the file and the program will open with the file loaded.

Finding a Computer on the Network

You can use Find to locate a particular computer on your network. Again, you don't have to know the entire name of the computer. Just click on the Start button, slide the pointer to Find, and select Computer. Type in what you know of the name and click on the Find Now button. Figure 7.11 shows the result of a search for computers with "rci" in their names.

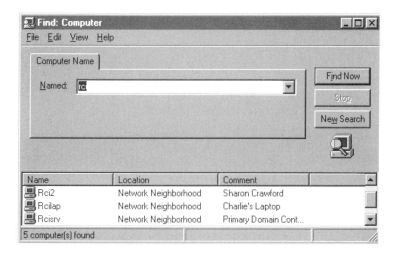

FIGURE 7.11:
A search for computers with "rci" in their names

TIP   To change the way found objects are displayed, right-click in the window where the items are displayed, select View from the pop-up menu, and choose the look you want.

Next Step

Now that we've learned how to navigate the Desktop and handle files, we'll move on in the next chapter to shared resources—files, folders, applications, hardware—and how to make them work easily.

Chapter 8

NETWORKS ARE FOR SHARING

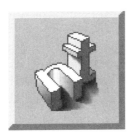

- **Sharing files, folders, and drives**
- **Opening and saving files on other computers**
- **Mapping a drive**
- **Granting permissions**
- **Using networked printers**

Like everything in life, networking has advantages and disadvantages. The biggest advantage of networking is it can improve efficiency by allowing the sharing of resources (files, folders, and printers, just to name a few). The biggest disadvantage of networking is it can introduce security problems—once shared files and folders exist on a networked computer, proper care must be taken to ensure that access to them is limited to appropriate individuals.

Luckily for you and your system administrator, NT Workstation is designed to be granular—that is, it allows you to specify precisely which file(s), folder(s), and/or printer(s) you'd like to share. Thus, NT Workstation gives you all the advantages of networking with few (if any) of its disadvantages. In this chapter, you'll learn how to manage shared resources in order to maximize efficiency and minimize security problems.

Using Network Neighborhood

The Network Neighborhood icon on the NT Workstation Desktop is your key to finding and using shared files, folders, printers, and whatever else is available on the network. It's the best place to start when looking around for resources you can tap.

Looking Around

Double-click on the Network Neighborhood icon and you should see something that resembles Figure 8.1.

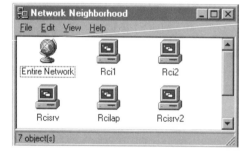

FIGURE 8.1:
Checking out the neigborhood

You should now see icons for all the computers currently connected (and running) on your network. Sometimes you may to need to double-click on the Entire Network icon to get the big picture because large networks are often organized into units called *domains,* like the ones shown in Figure 8.2.

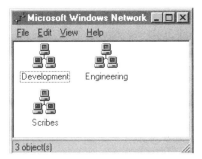

FIGURE 8.2:
On larger networks,
the computers are often
organized into domains.

NOTE Domains, if you'll pardon the expression, are the domain of the network administrator. Even if your network administrator uses this organizational method, you may be able to see only some or none of the other domains.

What Am I Looking At?

When you double-click on a computer in Network Neighborhood, you're only going to see what's being *shared.* Sometimes only folders are shared; sometimes it's the whole hard drive. Figure 8.3 shows some shared folders and a networked printer.

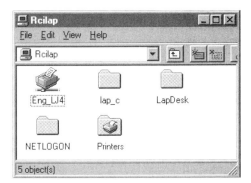

FIGURE 8.3:
What you can see on another
computer is (usually)
what you can use.

The drive (or a folder or even a single file) can be shared with everybody or with some people and not with others. When a drive is shared, for example, it just means other people have permission to access that computer and use whatever's on that drive.

It all depends on how your network is set up. Some networks are quite open, having only a few folders that are not public. Other networks, where security is a big issue, will have strict limits on what you can see.

Figure 8.4 shows a computer with all the drives shared, and Figure 8.5 shows one with basically nothing shared.

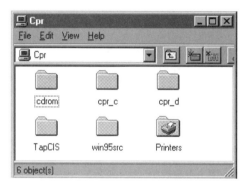

FIGURE 8.4:
This computer has nothing to hide (though the labels on the objects could be a little more informative).

FIGURE 8.5:
And here's a computer with a very secretive attitude.

The NETLOGON folder is part of system administration and is probably empty. The Printers folder won't have anything in it that you don't see in your own Printers folder.

NOTE
Permissions, rights, and sharing are terms that are often used interchangeably in the NT world, though they do have somewhat different meanings. For you to use a file or printer that isn't on your computer, the resource must be *shared,* and you must be granted *permission* on that shared resource. For you to be able to perform some specific action like backing up files or shutting down the network, the administrator must give you the *right* to do so. There's more on permissions and sharing later in this chapter.

Opening Files on Other Computers

To open a file (or folder) on another computer, just double-click on Network Neighborhood, find the computer you want, double-click on it, and just keep clicking until you find the file you want.

If this sounds like a big pain, it is. When you don't have to do this very often, it's probably OK. But if you need to get at this file several times a day, or even several times a week, all this clicking gets old real fast.

TIP
More network language: *local* files or printers are on your computer; *remote* files or printers are on another computer.

A Quick Return to a Remote File

Once you find a file—maybe four or five folders deep—on another computer, you can make a shortcut to the file, so the next time you want it, you won't have to do all that spelunking to get it.

Here's an example showing a file called Rutabaga Plantings. Let's say this file is on another computer, but you need to look at it frequently.

1. Double-click on Network Neighborhood.
2. In the window that opens, double-click on the computer where the file is located. This will give you a view of the computer's available folders. In this case, the file is in a folder called Vegetable Files.
3. Double-click the Vegetable Files folder to see Rutabaga Plantings.
4. Right click on the file, and, while holding that right mouse button down, drag the file to your Desktop. When you release the right mouse button, a little menu pops open.

5. Click Create Shortcut(s) Here on the menu.

Presto, you have a shortcut that you can double-click, and the file will open immediately—if you have the right program on your computer.

All this assumes you actually have *permission* to use this file.

> **TIP**
>
> **If you're trying to open an Excel file, as in the rutabaga plantings example, you have to be able to run Excel for the file to open. That goes for all the files you see. You'll need whatever program goes with the file to open the file.**

To save changes to the file, just select Save from the program's File menu. It doesn't matter whether you're working from a shortcut or directly from the file, the program knows where the file came from and will save it back to its original spot.

Saving a New File to Another Computer

When you make up a brand new file or folder and you want to save it to another computer on your network, the steps are the reverse of the steps you take to open a file on another computer.

Choose Save As from the program's File menu, and start all that clicking through the Network Neighborhood (Figure 8.6) to the computer, to that computer's drives and folders, to the location you want.

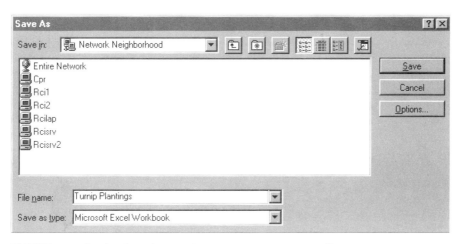

FIGURE 8.6: Starting the trek to another computer to save a new file

When you get to the folder where you want to save the file, type in a name for the file in the File Name box, and click once on the Save button. That's all there is to it.

This method is the best way *only* when you don't have to do it too often. If you need frequent access to another computer, try one of the methods in the next section.

Making Regular Visits Easier

When you find yourself making repeated visits to the same location on another computer, there are several ways you can cut down on all that digging through layers of folders each time. You can make a shortcut to a computer, to a computer's hard drive, or to a folder—all quite easily. Or you can *map* a network drive, so it looks and acts as if it were one of your local drives.

Making a Shortcut to a Computer

Making a shortcut to someone else's computer is a snap. Just double-click on Network Neighborhood and find the computer. Right click on the computer. Hold that right button down, and drag the computer's icon out of the window and to the Desktop.

Release the mouse button and select Create Shortcut(s) Here from the menu that pops up (Figure 8.7).

FIGURE 8.7:
Making a shortcut
to a computer

Double-click on the shortcut as a quick way to get at the contents of the computer. Keep the shortcut on your Desktop or drag it into a folder somewhere.

TIP Shortcuts to folders, printers, hard drives, and practically anything else can be made the same way.

Mapping a Network Drive

When you open the Explorer or the My Computer icon, you see a list of the hard drives on your computer—plus a few other things depending on what's installed. If you want, you can make any shared drive or folder on another computer appear just as if it were a drive on *your* computer.

TIP A *mapped* drive is even better than a shortcut in one important respect: if you're using older programs, they're not going to recognize things like Network Neighborhood and will flat out refuse to open or save files to anywhere other than your own computer. Map a drive, and the program cooperates because now the drive on the other computer appears (to the program at least) to be on your computer.

Here's how it's done:

1. Double-click on Network Neighborhood and find the folder or drive you want to show as one of your local drives.

2. Right click on the object and select Map Network Drive from the menu. The next dialog box that appears (Figure 8.8) has three adjustable entries:

    Drive This is the letter that the new drive will be assigned on your computer. It's usually the next one in the alphabet after your current ones.

    Connect As In the Connect As field, you can specify an account different than the logged on account to connect to the drive.

    Reconnect at Logon Check this box, and every time you logon to your computer, the connection will be made to the computer where this drive physically resides.

FIGURE 8.8:
Mapping a network drive
to my machine

3. Click OK when you're done. Open Explorer or My Computer and take a look. Figure 8.9 shows how the drive being mapped in Figure 8.8 ended up looking.

FIGURE 8.9:
After being mapped,
the drive on the other computer is listed
among your own—
and you can use it just
as if it were your own.

Disconnecting from Shared Drives or Folders

To get rid of a mapped drive or directory, you can highlight it and right-click. Select Disconnect from the pop-up menu.

Or, if you're working in the Explorer, click the Disconnect Net Drive icon on the Toolbar. From the list that appears, select the mapped drive you want to disconnect from and click OK.

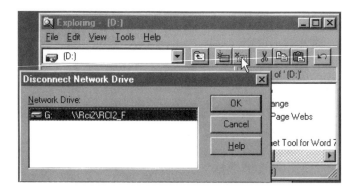

When you disconnect a mapped drive, you're just removing it from the list of drives shown on your computer. It has no other effect on the drive. You can always go back and re-map it if you need to.

Getting the Administrator to Do It

The administrator of the network can share another computer's folder or files *for* you. In fact, that may have already happened.

The administrator can map drives for you, too. This may be necessary because on many networks, users can't map their own drives for security reasons.

Sharing Drives and Folders on Your Computer

Sharing drives and folders on your computer is not difficult. However, there are rules about what you can share. After determining whether you have the right to share an object, the way you specify permissions depends on how your computer's hard drive is formatted.

What You're Allowed to Share

By default, unless you created the file or folder, you will not be able to set any permissions for it. To control permissions for files and folders that you didn't create or to share *any* drive, you will need to be granted that right by the network administrator.

If you *didn't* make the file or folder, you may be able to read it or change it but not be able to delete it or change the rules about who *else* can get at it. Some files you won't even be able to *see;* others you may be able to treat as if they were your own—it all depends on the files and what the system administrator has seen fit to let you do.

However, when you make a new folder or a file, you are designated—as far as the network's concerned—as the *owner* of the new object. As the owner, you have full control over the object. You can make it available to everyone or keep it completely private. By default, the administrator has permission to use the object, but as the owner, you can remove even the administrator's permission.

However, an administrator *can* force the issue by "taking ownership" of the file or folder in question. But they can't do it without you knowing. If the administrator takes ownership, he or she can't give it back—so if your files no longer show you as the owner, you know what happened.

> **NOTE**
>
> **As the owner of your files, you can indeed keep them from anyone. However, it's not wise to exercise this right without some judgment. You don't want to "privatize" files that others need to use.**

Setting Permissions

There are a variety of different types of access that can be granted, though most are not used in everyday life. The following table explains what some of these mean.

Type of Access	What It Means
No Access	Has no access at all.
List	Can view folders and file names but has no access to the files.
Read	Can view a shared resource but can't change its contents. Can also run applications but not change them.
Add	User or group can add files and subfolders but can't access any files.
Add & Read	Has Read and Add access.
Change	Has Read and Add access, plus can change data in files, delete files, and delete the folder.
Full Control	Has Change access, as well as the ability to change permissions and to take ownership.

In most cases, a networked NT Workstation will have its hard drive formatted as NTFS because of the superior security features NTFS offers. To set the permissions for a file or folder you've made, follow these steps:

1. Open Explorer and find the object.
2. Right click on the file or folder and select Properties from the pop-up menu.
3. Click the Security tab and then the Permissions button. This will open the dialog box shown in Figure 8.10.

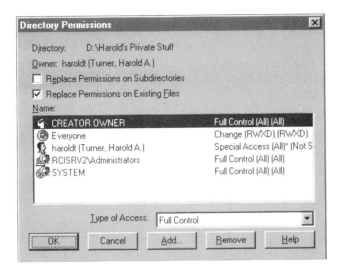

FIGURE 8.10:
Directory Permissions
dialog box

As you can see in Figure 8.10, a whole lot of folks seem to have access to this folder. If you highlight each of them in turn, you can see just what kind of access they have.

NOTE In Figure 8.10, the Directory Permissions dialog box shows both Owner and haroldt as having access; even though, at the moment, they are one and the same. This means that ownership of the folder could change without Harold losing his access.

Removing Permission

Removing someone from the permissions list is easy: just highlight the name and click the Remove button.

WARNING Before you start experimenting with permission removal, make a test folder with a test file inside. Experiment on this folder so you don't back yourself into a corner with a valuable file. You can always go to the administrator if you mess up badly, but that's sooo embarrassing.

Adding Permission

To add an individual or a group to the list of those in the Directory Permissions dialog box, click the Add button and follow these steps:

1. In the Add Users and Groups dialog box (Figure 8.11) you can choose to grant permission to a group or to individual users or both:
   - To add a whole group, highlight the group name and click the Add button.
   - To add some members of a group, highlight the group and click Members. Select the members you want to add and click the Add button.
   - To add individuals, click the Show Users button and scroll down the Names list. Highlight the names you want and click Add.

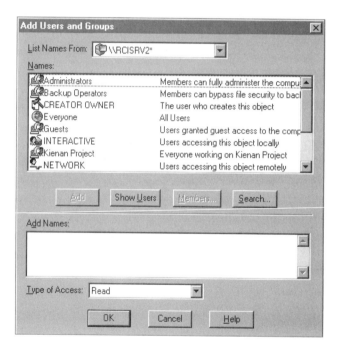

FIGURE 8.11:
Selecting the groups or individual users you want to grant permission to

2. When you have everyone you want in the Add Names box, click OK.
3. This will reopen the Directory Permissions dialog box with the selected groups or individuals listed. Click OK.

NOTE See Chapter 15 for the steps to create your own local group—as in a special project workgroup—and to grant permissions for that group.

Customizing Permissions

Open the File Permissions dialog box to more carefully define the kinds of permissions that are granted. Highlight each name in turn, and the Type of Access field will show the level of access granted. You can change the access by opening the pull-down list and selecting a level.

By default, permissions you set for a folder apply only to the folder and its files. Clear the check box next to Replace Permissions on Existing Files to apply permissions to the folder only. If the Replace Permissions on Subdirectories box is checked, permissions are applied to all subdirectories as well.

NOTE
If you're setting directory permissions, the dialog box that pops-up is titled Directory Permissions. If you're setting file permissions the same dialog box is titled File Permissions.

Sharing Resources on a FAT Drive

Because a FAT drive is a low-security option, the method of sharing files, folders, and drives is reassuringly straightforward, though the degree of sharing is still configurable.

1. Locate the resource you'd like to share and right-click on it. Select Sharing from the resulting pop-up menu. This should bring up the resource's Properties sheet (Figure 8.12).

2. On the resource's Properties sheet, select the Sharing tab and click the Shared As button.

3. At this point, either you can accept the Share Name that NT Workstation suggests (it's usually the name of the file or folder in question), or you can type a new Share Name in the Share Name box. Add a comment in the Comment box if you wish.

WARNING
Don't change the default setting of Maximum Allowed in the User Limit box unless you're instructed otherwise.

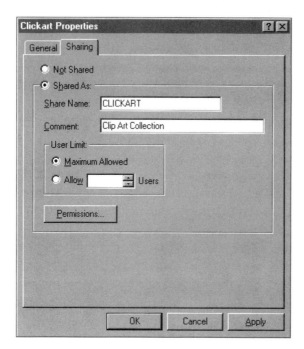

FIGURE 8.12:
The Sharing Properties sheet for a folder on a drive that was formatted as FAT

4. Click the Permissions button to set specific permissions. Make sure you read "Setting Permissions" *before* you change any of the permissions shown.
5. After you've set the resource's permissions as you want them, click OK; other users on your network will be able to start using your newly shared resource.

Using a Network Printer

When there's no printer directly plugged into your computer, you can easily find out what printers you can use.

1. Click the Start button and select Settings ➢ Printers.
2. In the window that opens, you'll see one or more printers plus the Add Printer icon.
3. If the printers all have totally cryptic names, right click on them in turn, selecting Properties each time. This should give you a little information (see Figure 8.13) about the type of printer and where it is.

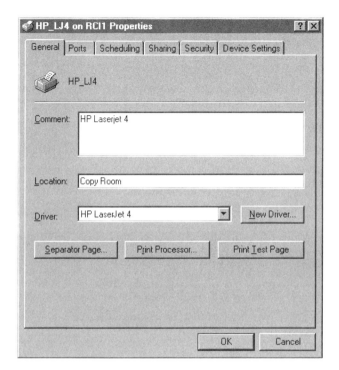

FIGURE 8.13:
Looking at a printer's properties

Picking an Everyday Printer

If you're lucky enough to have a whole bunch of printers you can use, you need to set one of them as the default printer. That means all your Windows print jobs will go to that printer unless you intervene.

Right-click on the printer you want to use most of the time and then click Set As Default (see Figure 8.14). A check mark in front of Set as Default means the printer has already been made the default printer.

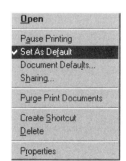

FIGURE 8.14:
The check mark means this printer is the one your Windows programs will use unless you change the default.

Only one printer at a time can be the default printer for your computer. To change which printer is the one used by default, right-click on the one you want and then click on Set as Default.

TIP

Want to use a different printer for just one print job? Look at the File menu in the program you're using. Select the Printer Setup item if there is one; otherwise just select Print. In the window that opens, look for a drop-down list of printers and choose the one you want.

Adding a Network Printer to Your Machine

When a new printer is placed on the network and shared with everyone, you'll be able to use it, but first you have to tell your computer about it. To add a printer to your Printers folder, follow these steps:

1. Click on Start ➤ Settings ➤ Printers.
2. In the Printers folder, double-click Add Printer. A helpful Wizard program opens (Figure 8.15). As you can see, it already knows this has to be a network printer. Click on next.

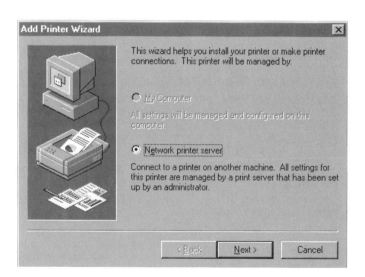

FIGURE 8.15:
The Add Printer Wizard does all the work for you.

3. On the Connect to Printer dialog box (Figure 8.16), you just have to select the printer you want to add, and then click the OK button.

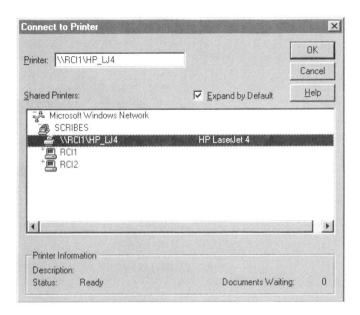

FIGURE 8.16:
Click the mouse button on the printer you want to add, then click OK.

TIP Even if a printer actually exists, you may not be able to see it on the network because you haven't been granted access to it. The administrator is the only one who can fix that for you. But if you can see it, you probably have the right to use it, so go ahead and try.

Next Step

In this chapter, you've seen how you can reap the benefits of networking by sharing resources with other users. In the next chapter, we'll move on to running programs on your workstation.

Chapter 9

RUNNING PROGRAMS

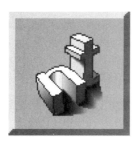

- **Using the Start menu**
- **Using the right mouse button**
- **Arranging menus**
- **Putting programs in the Startup group**
- **Finding and using Program Manager**

In this chapter, we'll cover the essentials of launching programs. There are lots of ways to get programs started, and where you'll start them from depends a lot on how often you use certain ones. The more frequently used programs can be placed in the most easily accessible spots, and the infrequently used can be easily accessible but still out of the way.

WARNING Once again, I need to caution you that networks being what they are, some of the functions in this chapter may not be available to you or may work slightly differently. This is because the administrator has the power to restrict all sorts of things, including what programs can be used and what you can do with the ones you have. But don't blame the administrator, it's sure to have been a decision made by the administrator's *boss*.

Starting a Program

As you might suspect by now, there are a lot of different ways to start a program. You may prefer having shortcuts to your favorite programs on your Desktop or on the Start button. Here's a refresher on how to do that.

Shortcut to a Program

To make a shortcut to a program on your Desktop, follow these steps:

1. Open Explorer (Start ➢ Programs ➢ Windows NT Explorer).
2. Using the scroll bars, find the folder for your program. Double-click on the folder.
3. In the right pane of the Explorer, click on the Type button at the top of the list until you see a file or a group of files labeled Application.
4. If there's a single file labeled Application, right-click on the file and drag it to your Desktop. When you release the mouse button, select Create Shortcut(s) Here from the pop-up menu.

NOTE If there's more than one file labeled Application, you may have to guess which one is the actual main program file—either by the name or the icon. If worse comes to worse, double-click on a file you think might be "it." If the program opens, you've hit the jackpot. If it doesn't, just close whatever did open and try again.

A shortcut to a program can be put wherever you find it handy—on the Desktop or inside a folder.

Putting a Program on the Start Menu

If you want a program to appear on the Start menu (as shown in Figure 9.1), the necessary steps are very similar to the ones above.

FIGURE 9.1:
The Start menu with some programs and a folder added

1. Open Explorer (Start ➤ Programs ➤ Windows NT Explorer).
2. Using the scroll bars, find the folder for your program. Double-click on the folder.
3. In the right pane of the Explorer, click on the Type button at the top of the list until you see a file or a group of files labeled Application.
4. Look for a file labeled Application, right-click on the file and drag it to the Start button. When the pointer is above the Start button, release the mouse.

TIP

Like the idea of having a shortcut to your very own Desktop on your Start menu? Open the Explorer and find your Desktop subfolder (open the WINNT folder, then the Profiles folder, then your personal User folder, which should be called by your username). Right-click on your Desktop folder, drag it to the Start button, and drop it.

Forcing the Order on the Start Menu

Programs on the Start menu are listed in alphabetical order, but what if this isn't what you want? To change the order, follow these steps:

1. Right-click on the Start button and select Explore.
2. In the window that opens, you'll see a Programs folder (it's another view of what you see when you click on the Start button and then click Programs) and the shortcuts you've placed on the Start button (see Figure 9.2).

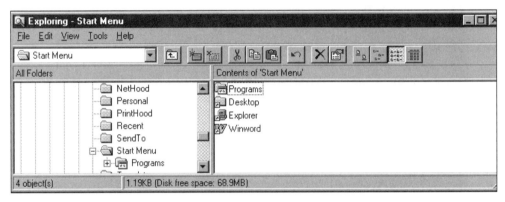

FIGURE 9.2: Programs and Folders on the Start menu are listed in alphabetical order.

3. Right-click on the program you want to move to the top of the list.
4. Rename it, making sure the first character is an underscore (_).
5. Click on the Start button and you'll see that the name that begins with an underscore has been moved to the top (Figure 9.3).

To force a program to be second on the list, no matter what its alphabetical ranking, just rename the shortcut, making a tilde (~) the first character.

TIP

Rename several files using the underscore as the first character, and they'll be listed together in alphabetical order at the top of the menu. Rename several with the tilde as the first character, and they'll also be listed together in alphabetical order but *after* the group with the underscore.

FIGURE 9.3:
The underscore character moves the program to the top of the list.

Using the Right Mouse Button

The right mouse button, not surprisingly, is useful for launching programs in addition to all its other talents. Right-click on a program in the Explorer or on the Desktop and select Open from the menu.

If the top item is Open With… and you haven't a clue as to what program might be able to handle the file, make a shortcut to the file viewers by following these steps:

1. Click on the Start button and select Find.
2. Search for QUIKVIEW.EXE (note the spelling!). Or you can open Explorer and look in the following folders: WINNT ➢ System32 ➢ Viewers. You'll find QUIKVIEW.EXE in the last folder.
3. Right-click on QUIKVIEW.EXE and drag it to the Desktop, selecting Create Shortcut(s) Here when you release the mouse button.
4. Next open the Explorer and locate your User folder (which should be called something resembling your username) by looking through the folders WINNT ➢ Profiles ➢ *Your username* ➢ SendTo. Drag the shortcut to QUIKVIEW.EXE to the SendTo folder and drop it inside.

Now when you right-click on an object, one of the options under SendTo will be Quikview. So when you see a file that you don't recognize, you can always send it to Quikview for a fast look.

Launching from Start ≻ Programs

Click once on the Start menu, slide the pointer up to Programs, and then select the program you want. This is an easy way to start up any program on your system However, you may dislike the multilevel menus—first there's a folder for each application and then another menu for all the stuff inside (see Figure 9.4). This is the default setup for NT Workstation, but you can change almost all aspects of it.

Many of the menus in NT Workstation contain a series of shortcuts easily accessible through Explorer. Find the window that represents the menu and you can add to it or subtract from it. To change the Programs menu, follow these steps:

1. Right-click on the Start button and select Explore.
2. Double-click on Programs and you'll see a listing of folders and shortcuts that correspond to the Start ≻ Programs menu.
3. Double-click on a folder to see the program inside. To move a program up a level, right-click on the shortcut and select Cut from the pop-up menu.

4. Click on the Up One Level icon on the toolbar.
5. Right-click in the right pane and select Paste from the menu. Remember that these are all shortcuts, so you can rename them or delete them without a thought. You can also drag new shortcuts to any level of the menu.

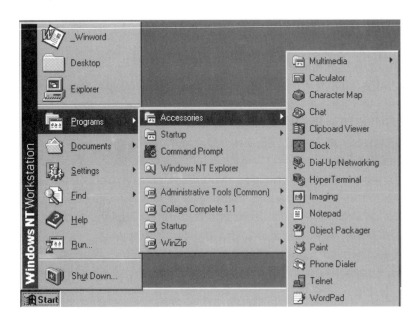

FIGURE 9.4: Maybe you'd rather *not* have your programs set up this way.

Adding a Program to the Start ➤ Programs Menu

You can add a program to the Start ➤ Programs menu quite easily. Just follow these steps:

1. Find the program (or a shortcut to the program) you want, either by searching the Explorer or by using Start ➤ Find.
2. Once you locate the program or shortcut, right-click on it and drag it to the Desktop, creating a new shortcut when you get there.
3. Right-click on the Start button and select Explore. Double-click on the Programs icon.
4. You can drag and drop your newly made shortcut to this window. That will put it on the first level of the Programs menu.

If you want, you can create a new folder in Programs (right-click on a blank spot inside the folder and select New ➤ Folder). Then you can put other shortcuts in the folder—these will then be on the second level of the Programs menu.

Removing a Program from the Start ➤ Programs Menu

Removing stuff from the Programs menu is equally easy:

1. Right-click on the Start button and select Explore.
2. Double-click on the Programs icon.
3. Right-click on anything you want to get rid of and select Delete from the pop-up menu. When you see the dialog box confirming that you want to send the item to the Recycle Bin, choose Yes.

WARNING   All the items in the Programs folder and any subfolders *should* be shortcuts, though the icons are too small in many cases to verify this at a glance. If you have any doubts, right-click on the object and select Properties. If there's not a Shortcut page within the Properties sheet, don't delete the file until you're sure it's not the *only* copy.

Starting Programs When You Start NT Workstation

Everyone has a program or two that they know they'll be using every single day. So you might as well have the program start when you start up your computer.

To add a program to the StartUp group, just right-click on the Start button and select Explore. Double-click on the Programs icon in the right pane. Then double-click on StartUp (this is a folder under Programs). This folder contains all the programs that will launch when you turn on the computer.

Next, open a second instance of Explorer and find the programs you want in StartUp. Right-click on your choice and drag it to StartUp. Release the mouse button and select Create Shortcut(s) Here from the menu. Or you can right-click on any shortcut on your Desktop and drag it to StartUp, also selecting Create Shortcut(s) Here when the menu appears.

Using Program Manager

If you really miss Program Manager from previous versions of NT Workstation, there's good news for you. It's included with NT Workstation 4. Look in your WINNT folder for a folder called System32, then look for a file called PROGMAN.EXE. Right-click on it and drag it to the Desktop and make a shortcut.

> **TIP**
>
> **When you know the name of the file, it's almost always fastest to use Find from the Start menu. Once Find locates the file, you can right-click on the file and make a shortcut or a copy, or even move it from its folder.**

Next Step

In the next chapter, we'll move on to one of the best tools in NT Workstation, the Recycle Bin. We'll cover how to use it to its best advantage, as well as some of the Recycle Bin's limitations and how to overcome them.

Chapter 10

THE RECYCLE BIN

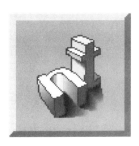

- **How the Recycle Bin works**
- **Deleting files safely**
- **Recovering deleted files**
- **Setup and configuration**

In the bad old days of computing, it was far too easy to accidentally delete a file from your system—and all you could do was wave bye-bye. Because there was no going back. You could buy a package of tools like Norton Utilities that included a utility to retrieve deleted files (providing you acted quickly enough). And DOS itself, starting with version 5, included a program to undelete files. The weakness of both approaches was that if you didn't undelete right away, your file could easily be overwritten by another file, and then there was *no way* to recover.

The Recycle Bin will retain all your deleted files for as long as you want, and you can adjust the amount of security from "just a little" to "all I can get" to match your own personal comfort level.

What It Is

The Recycle Bin is a reserved space on your hard drive. When you delete a file or drag it to the Recycle Bin icon, the file is actually moved to that reserved space. If you have more than one hard drive, each drive has its own reserved space. There's an icon that represents the Recycle Bin on each drive (but only one Recycle Bin icon is ever displayed on the Desktop)—though the contents displayed when you double-click on any icon will be the same as the Recycle Bin on any other drive. If you want a deleted file back, you can double-click on the Recycle Bin icon to open it and retrieve any file.

The Recycle Bin functions as a first-in, first-out system. That is, when the bin is full, the oldest files are deleted to make room for the newest ones.

As configurable as the rest of NT Workstation is, this is one place where Microsoft draws the line. The Recycle Bin cannot be

- Deleted
- Renamed
- Removed from the Desktop

though there are a number of settings you can change to make the Recycle Bin suitable for your use.

NOTE   See "Settings" later in this chapter for information on how to determine the amount of disk space used by the Recycle Bin as well as other settings.

Sending Files to the Recycle Bin

By default, NT Workstation is set up to deposit all deleted files in the Recycle Bin. When you right-click on a file and select delete or highlight a file and press the Del key, you'll be asked to confirm if you want to send the file to the Recycle Bin. After you click on Yes, that's where the file is moved to. Deleted shortcuts are also sent to the Recycle Bin.

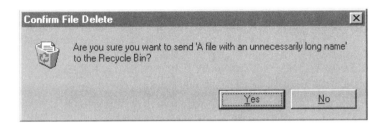

Sending a Floppy Disk's Files to the Recycle Bin

Normally, files that you delete from a floppy drive are *not* sent to the Recycle Bin. They're just deleted. However, if that strikes you as just a little too impetuous, there's an easy way to make sure the files on your floppy do go to the Recycle Bin.

1. Open Explorer. Use the scroll bar for the left pane to move up so you can see the entry for your floppy drive.
2. Click with the left mouse button on the Floppy Drive icon. In the right pane, select the file(s) you want to delete but still want in the Recycle Bin.
3. Right-click on the file(s) and select Cut. Right-click on the Desktop and select Paste.
4. Highlight the file on the Desktop. (If there's more than one, hold down the Ctrl key while you click on each one in turn.) Right-click on a highlighted file and select Delete. You'll be prompted to confirm that you want to send the file(s) to the Recycle Bin.

There's no more direct way to do this function because the Recycle Bin stubbornly refuses to see any files that are sent directly from a floppy.

Bypassing the Recycle Bin

If you've got a file you know for sure you want to delete and you therefore don't want it taking up space in the Recycle Bin, just hold down the Shift key when you select Delete. But be sure that's what you want to do because there's no way in NT Workstation to recover a deleted file that's bypassed the Recycle Bin.

Throwing Unwilling Files into the Recycle Bin

Some older programs (not written specifically for NT Workstation) allow you to delete files from within the program. Files deleted this way will not be sent to the Recycle Bin. Similarly, files you delete at the DOS prompt will also disappear into never-never land rather than into the Recycle Bin.

Therefore, you should make all your deletions through the Explorer or My Computer or on the Desktop. If NT Workstation knows about the deletion, the file will automatically go to the Recycle Bin.

NOTE   Using the command prompt is covered in Chapter 11.

Recovering a Deleted File

Retrieving a file from the Recycle Bin is remarkably easy. Just double-click on the Recycle Bin icon. The Recycle Bin window can be set up with any of the usual choices on the View menu. The most useful are probably Large Icons (as shown in Figure 10.1) and Details.

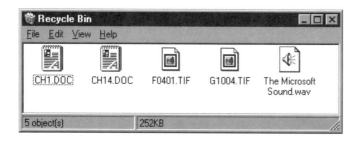

FIGURE 10.1:
In the Large icons view, you can quickly identify files that were made by a particular program.

The Details view (Figure 10.2) is the best view if you're looking for a file that was recently deleted. Just click on the Date Deleted bar to arrange the files in date order. A second click will reverse the order. Similarly, if you know the file name, a click on the Name bar will list the files in alphabetical order.

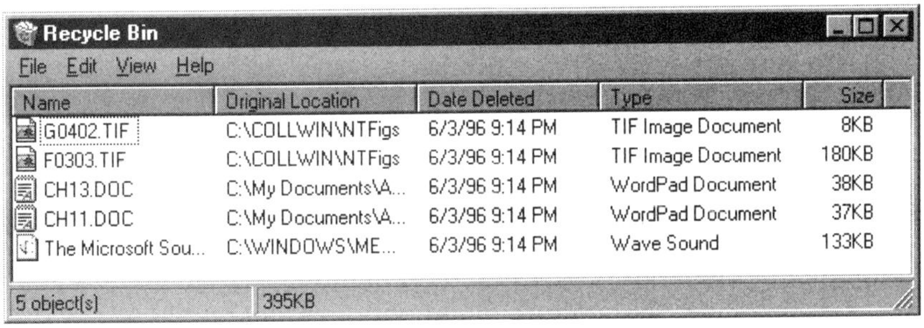

FIGURE 10.2: The Details view is useful if you're searching by date or name.

To retrieve a single file, click on it with either the left or right mouse button and drag it to a folder or to the Desktop. If you just want to send it back to its original location, right-click on the file name and select Restore from the pop-up menu.

Recovering More Than One File

To recover more than one file at a time, hold down the Ctrl key while selecting the file names. Then right-click on one of the highlighted names and select Restore. Or use cut and paste to send the whole bunch to a different location. Using either the right or left button, you can click and drag the files to your Desktop or another open folder.

To retrieve a number of files all in a series, click on the first one and then hold down the Shift key while selecting the last one in the series.

Let's say you deleted all the contents of a folder, and the only thing all the parts of the folder have in common is that all were deleted at the same time. Here's how to recover them:

1. Open the Recycle Bin with a double-click on the icon.
2. Select Details from the View menu.
3. Click on the Date Deleted button. Use the scroll bar to move through the list until you find the group of files you want to retrieve.
4. Click on the first one's name. Then, while holding down the Shift key, click on the name of the last one you want. All the files between the first and last click will be highlighted.
5. Right-click on one of the highlighted files and select Restore from the pop-up menu.

All the files will be returned to their original home, and even though the original folder is not listed in the Recycle Bin, the files will be in the original folder.

Settings

You can adjust the amount of space the Recycle Bin claims and change other settings that affect how the Recycle Bin works. Mostly, you have to decide just how much safety you want and are comfortable with.

How Much Space?

Right-click on the Recycle Bin icon and select Properties. The Recycle Bin's Properties sheets will open, as shown in Figure 10.3.

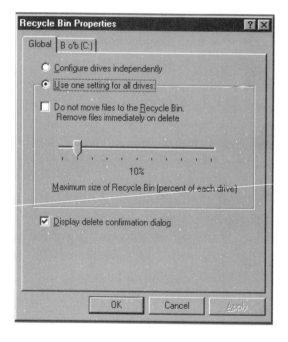

FIGURE 10.3:
The Recycle Bin's Properties sheets

As you can see, you can set the amount of space reserved for the Recycle Bin for each hard disk drive individually or globally. By default, 10 percent of each drive is set aside for the Recycle Bin. On a large drive, that's a lot of megabytes, so you may want to reduce the size a bit.

Click on Configure Drives Independently and then click on each drive tab in turn. Click on the sliding arrow and move it up or down until the Space Reserved is to your liking.

NOTE There's also a field below the slider, showing the percentage of the drive that is reserved. If your drives are different sizes, you might want to make things easier for yourself by just reserving the same percentage on each drive.

Remember that the Recycle Bin is first-in, first-out, so if you make the reserved space very small, deleted files may pass into oblivion faster than you might wish.

Getting Rid of Confirmations

On the Global page of the Recycle Bin Properties sheet, there's a box to clear if you don't want to be questioned every time you delete a file.

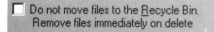

If there's no check in this box, you won't see any messages when you select Delete. If, however, you like the comfort of being consulted about every deletion, make sure this box is checked.

Doing Away with the Recycle Bin

Well, you can't exactly do away with the Recycle Bin completely. As mentioned before, you can't delete it or remove it from the Desktop. However, you can check this box on the Recycle Bin Properties sheet.

☐ Do not move files to the Recycle Bin.
Remove files immediately on delete

If you have selected Configure Drives Independently, you can pick which drives you want this to apply to.

WARNING Doing away with the Recycle Bin is a *very bad* idea unless you have another program for undeleting files. Files that are deleted and not sent to the Recycle Bin are gone forever.

Even if you do have a program that will rescue files deleted in error, it's still not a good idea to bypass the Recycle Bin completely because most of the undelete programs are dependent on you getting to the deleted file before it is overwritten by something else. And that can easily happen in NT Workstation where there's almost always something going on behind the scenes.

WARNING If you begrudge large portions of your hard drive, make the reserved space on the hard drive very small—maybe 5 or 10 MB. Check the box on the Properties sheet to disable the confirmation requests. Then the Recycle Bin will be quite unobtrusive, but you'll still have some margin of safety.

Emptying the Recycle Bin

To get rid of everything in the Recycle Bin, right-click on the Recycle Bin icon and select Empty Recycle Bin. There's also an option to Empty Recycle Bin on the Recycle Bin's File menu.

To remove just *some* of the items in the Recycle Bin, highlight the file names, right-click on one of them and select Delete from the pop-up menu. You'll be asked to confirm the deletion, and when you say Yes, the files will be deleted permanently.

Next Step

Up until now we've talked about NT Workstation as a graphical environment—and an excellent one it is. In the next chapter, we'll see how NT Workstation runs from the command line.

Chapter

11

USING THE COMMAND PROMPT

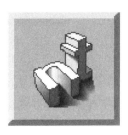

- **What is the Command prompt?**
- **Running DOS programs under the Command prompt**
- **DOS Property sheets in NT Workstation 4**
- **DOS commands in NT Workstation 4**
- **Changing Console window options**
- **Selecting Console window font, layout, and colors**

Although it's not immediately apparent when you open the box, NT Workstation 4 will allow you to run most DOS programs without muss and fuss. But what happened to the old DOS prompt? Well, the DOS prompt still exists, but it's been renamed and dressed up a bit. In NT Workstation 4, what was the *DOS prompt* is now called the *Command prompt*. Fortunately for those of you who use the Command prompt a lot, NT Workstation comes complete with a handy Console element in the Control Panel that lets you change the properties of the Console window, which is where your DOS programs will run. In this chapter, you'll learn how to run DOS programs from the Command prompt and how to customize the Console window to suit your individual taste.

Running DOS Programs from the Command Prompt

Running a DOS program from the Command prompt really couldn't be simpler. To access the Command prompt, click on the Start button in the Taskbar, then select Programs ➢ Command Prompt to display the window shown in Figure 11.1. Once you've done that, do whatever you'd normally do to start the DOS program in question.

FIGURE 11.1: The basic Console window is useful even if it isn't much to look at.

DOS the Easy Way

If you're planning to run one or more DOS programs on a regular basis, it's helpful to know that DOS programs aren't automatically placed on your Programs menu the way Windows programs are when you first install them. But you can create a shortcut to a DOS program and put the shortcut either on your Desktop or in one of the folders that make up the Programs menu (as discussed in Chapter 8).

Open the Explorer and find the folder with your program in it. Right-click on the program name and drag it to the Desktop to make a shortcut. Then you can put it on your Start menu or in a folder. In other words, you can handle DOS programs like Windows programs. Almost every DOS program will open with a simple double-click on the icon. But what if it won't? Or what if it opens in a window and you'd like it to run full screen? Fortunately, every DOS program has an extensive collection of Properties sheets you can use to tweak your DOS performance.

DOS Properties Sheets

When you run a DOS program, whether from the Desktop or off the Start menu, you can set a wide variety of properties for the program. As elsewhere in NT Workstation, you get to those properties by right-clicking on the icon for the program or on its shortcut in either of two different places:

- Highlight the program's executable file in the Explorer or My Computer, and right-click on it.
- Right-click on a shortcut to the program.

In either case, you'll select Properties from the menu that opens. This will open up a Properties sheet for the DOS program like the one in Figure 11.2.

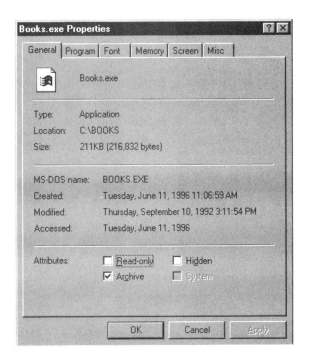

FIGURE 11.2:
The first page of a DOS program's many Properties sheets

There are six pages on the Properties sheet:
- General shows information about the file and file attributes.
- Program sets command line options and sets the program's icon.
- Font sets the font to be used when the program is run in a window.
- Memory sets how much and what kind of memory is made available to the DOS program.
- Screen changes whether the program runs full screen or in a window and the characteristics of the window.
- Misc, like miscellaneous files everywhere, sets stuff that doesn't fit in any other category.

The default settings are usually adequate for most programs, but if you need to fuss with one or more of these pages, the following sections will give you some guidance.

General Properties

The General tab shows information about the program and allows you to set the attributes of the underlying file. As you can see in Figure 11.2, this tab shows you the type of program or file, its location and size, the DOS file name associated with it, and when the file was created, modified, and last accessed.

If you're looking at a shortcut, the information about the file size, location, and type will refer to the shortcut and not to the original object (the file itself).

On this tab, you can change the MS-DOS attributes of the program, including whether the archive bit is set, whether the file can be modified or not (read-only bit), and whether the file is a hidden file. Generally, you won't want to change these bits except in very special circumstances. And then only if you're sure you know why you're making the change.

Program Properties

The Program tab of the Properties sheet (see Figure 11.3) lets you change the running parameters of the program as well as the name and icon associated with it.

Some Basic Settings

Here's what those settings mean:

Cmd Line This box shows the actual command line executed. Here you can add any command line parameters that you need. (If you want to be able to add parameters each time you run the program, add a question mark as the only command line option, and NT Workstation will prompt you for parameters.)

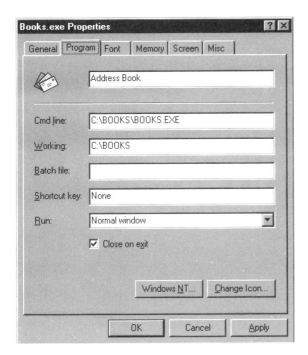

FIGURE 11.3:
The Program tab lets you control the command options of a DOS program.

Working If your program has a favorite working directory, set that here. This isn't common anymore, but some older programs need to be told this information. If there's already an entry in this box, NT Workstation and the program have figured out that it's necessary. Don't change this setting unless you're sure you know why.

Shortcut Key This box lets you add a shortcut key. (Some DOS programs may not work well with this option, but there's no harm in trying.)

Run You can decide whether the program will run in a normal window, maximized, or minimized. Some DOS programs may pay no attention to this setting.

Close on Exit When this box is checked, the DOS window will close when you exit the program.

Windows NT PIF Settings

If you click on the Windows NT button on the Program tab of a DOS program's Properties sheet, you'll see the Windows NT PIF Settings dialog box, shown in Figure 11.4.

FIGURE 11.4:
The Windows NT PIF Settings dialog box lets you specify which AUTOEXEC.BAT and CONFIG.SYS files this program will use.

Here, you can specify which AUTOEXEC.BAT and CONFIG.SYS files this DOS program will use. Don't change these settings unless you have a really good reason to do so; most DOS programs will be perfectly happy using the default files supplied with NT Workstation, so why ask for trouble?

Change the Icon

Click on the Change Icon button on the Program page to change the way the program displays in icon form. You can accept one of the icons offered or use the Browse button to look elsewhere.

Font Properties

The Font tab of the Properties sheet (see Figure 11.5) lets you set which fonts will be available when the program is running in a window on the Desktop. You can select from either bitmapped or TrueType fonts or have both available.

In general, bitmap fonts look better on high resolution displays and are easier to read. If you want to be able to scale the window when it's open on your Desktop, set the Font Size to Auto, and the fonts will change as you resize the open window.

Resizing the Console Window

To change the size of a DOS window, go to the program's Properties sheet; try setting the font size to Auto and then clicking on and dragging the edge of the DOS window. Sometimes setting the Font to a fixed size and then dragging the edge of the window will also work. Different programs have different abilities to shrink and expand.

Memory Properties

The Memory tab of the Properties sheet (see Figure 11.6) lets you control how much and what kind of memory DOS programs have available when they run.

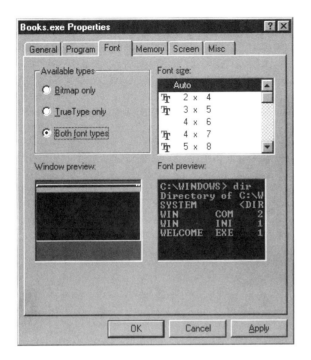

FIGURE 11.5:
The Font tab of the Properties sheet lets you control which fonts are available and used for the DOS program when it's running in a window.

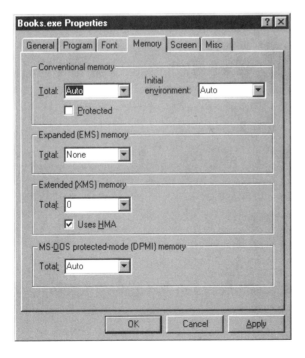

FIGURE 11.6:
The Memory tab lets you fine-tune the memory available for your DOS programs.

On this tab you can make sure your program has a specific amount of conventional, expanded, and extended memory. You can also let NT Workstation automatically determine how much to make available. Generally, you'll want to leave the settings here on Auto, but if you know you have a program that requires a specific amount of expanded memory to run well, you can set that here.

And Memory Problems

If you have a program that has a habit of crashing occasionally and you want to be sure it doesn't cause problems for the rest of the system, check the Protected box in the Conventional Memory section. This may slow down the program a little, but it will provide an additional layer of protection.

> **TIP** Windows NT is well protected against badly behaved DOS programs. Your program may crash, but Windows NT will survive unscathed. You adjust the program's properties to keep the program alive, well, and running enthusiastically.

Screen Properties

The Screen tab of the Properties sheet (see Figure 11.7) lets you set your program's display. If you're running a graphical program, set it for full screen. Most text-based programs run better in a window.

Except for the full-screen versus window option, the options on this page are best left alone unless you know why you're changing them.

> **NOTE** If you're determined to do something, right-click on an item and select What's This? If you understand what's in the box, you are hereby authorized to make the change.

Switching from a Window to Full Screen (and Back Again)

To switch a DOS program window to full screen, just press Alt+↵. Press Alt+↵ a second time to return to the window.

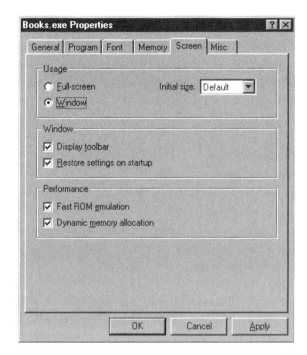

FIGURE 11.7:
The Screen tab lets you decide how your DOS programs are displayed.

To switch from a DOS Program running full screen to the NT Workstation Desktop, press Alt+Tab.

Miscellaneous Properties

The Misc tab of the Properties sheet, shown in Figure 11.8, lets you tweak several characteristics that don't fit in any of the other categories.

The properties you can set here include the following:

Allow Screen Saver   When this box is checked, the Windows screen saver is allowed to come on when the DOS program is in the foreground. If this box isn't checked, an active DOS program will keep your screen saver from kicking in.

Exclusive Mode   Lets the mouse work exclusively with this program. This means that when this program is open, the mouse won't be available outside this program's window.

Always Suspend   When this box is checked, no system resources are allocated to this program while it's in the background (open, but not the active window). If this is a communications or other type of program that you want churning away in the background while you do something else, don't check this box.

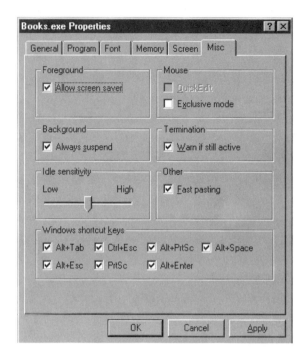

FIGURE 11.8:
The Misc tab lets you set other characteristics of your DOS program's behavior.

Warn If Still Active   Some DOS programs are very fussy about being closed properly (like WordPerfect for DOS). When this box is checked, you'll get a warning message if you try to close the window without closing the program first.

Idle Sensitivity   When this slider is set to high, the DOS program will release resources and processing time more quickly to other foreground tasks. For communications programs, however, you will probably want to set this on the low side.

Fast Pasting   This allows a faster method of pasting, but if you have troubles with pasting correctly in this application, clear the box.

Windows Shortcut Keys   Generally you will want to leave these alone unless your DOS program absolutely needs to use one of these keystrokes. Clear the appropriate box or boxes if there are special keystrokes normally used by NT Workstation that you want passed on to your DOS program instead.

DOS Commands

The NT Workstation Help files proudly advertise that Windows NT retains and enhances almost all the functionality of MS-DOS. How you feel about this claim will be determined by how often you actually use DOS; most of us have long since stopped using DOS programs, and we've consequently forgotten most of the DOS commands we ever knew. Just in case you're feeling nostalgic for the command line, here's a table of some of the more useful DOS commands available in NT Workstation and a brief description of what each one does.

Command Name	Description
attrib.exe	Displays or changes file attributes. But this task is better accomplished by checking the appropriate boxes on a file's Properties sheet.
choice.com	Allows for user input in a batch file.
diskcopy.com	Makes a full copy of a diskette. Same function also available in Explorer.
doskey.com	Beloved of all DOS-geeks, edits command lines and makes macros.
fc.exe	Compares file compare.
find.exe	Locates text in a file. But why anyone would prefer find.exe to using Find is beyond me.
format.com	Formats disks.
label.exe	Adds, removes, or changes a disk label.
more.com	Displays output one screen at a time.
move.exe	Moves one or more files.
sort.exe	Sorts input.
start.exe	Runs a program.
subst.exe	Associates a drive letter with a particular path.
xcopy.exe	Copies whole directories including subdirectories.

There's not a whole lot of help available for DOS commands in NT Workstation, but you can get basic information if you go to a DOS prompt, type in the name of the command followed by / ?, and then press ↵. Another way to get help is to use the Find tab on the Help Topics dialog box to search for Command Index. The Command Index is a list of all the commands available in NT Workstation, including old familiar

DOS commands. Click on one of the command names to open a window with a complete description and all the parameters for that command.

Customizing the Console Window

Customizing the Console window is easy thanks to the existence of the Console element in the NT Workstation Control Panel. To have a look at what the Console element can do for you, double-click on its icon, and you should see a dialog box that resembles Figure 11.9.

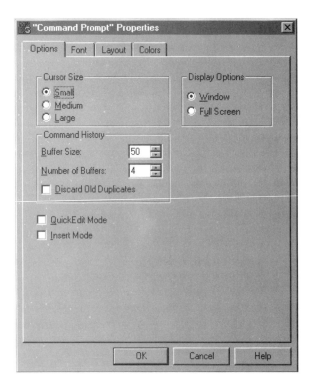

FIGURE 11.9:
The Console element in the Control Panel lets you make your Console window look the way you'd like it to.

Before you get carried away customizing your Console window, it's useful to know that the tabs on the Console Windows Properties sheet overlap with the DOS Properties sheet for a given program. Most of the time, it's easier to customize the Console window for a particular program (which you do on the DOS Properties sheet, as described in the previous section). Doing this will allow you to set things up so that particular program will run as happily as it can under NT Workstation.

Options Properties

The Options tab, shown in Figure 11.9, gives you control over a number of things you may want to know about. Here's an overview of what these settings mean:

Cursor Size   You can set the cursor size to small (the default), medium, or large, depending on how much you plan to use the Command prompt and how good your eyes are.

Display Options   See the advice under "Screen Properties" in "DOS Properties Sheets" for information about how to use this setting.

Command History   By default, you're given a space in memory (called a *buffer*) large enough to "remember" the last 50 commands you've executed, which should be enough for even the nerdiest among us. My advice: don't touch that dial. If you're really into having squeaky-clean buffers, check the Discard Old Duplicates box, and any duplicate commands will magically disappear.

Quick Edit Mode   Allows you to use your mouse to select text for cut-and-copy operations. If this box is cleared, you must use Mark on the Edit menu of the program to mark text.

Insert Mode   Select this check box if you want text to be inserted at the cursor. If Insert Mode is not enabled, text typed at the cursor replaces (*overtypes*) existing text.

Font Properties

The Font Properties tab (see Figure 11.10) lets you choose a font style and size for your Console window. There's even a Window Preview feature here, so you can see how your selection will look.

To choose a font size, scroll up and down the list in the Size box until you see a size you like and highlight it. That's all there is to it. To choose a typeface, highlight one in the Font box. Before you OK your way out, check the Window Preview box to make sure you're pleased with the results of your efforts.

Layout Properties

The Layout Properties tab, shown in Figure 11.11, lets you select a screen buffer size, a window size, and a window position. Frankly, you'll probably never need to change these settings, but in case you're curious, here's what they mean:

Screen Buffer Size   This setting determines the width and height of the Console window screen buffer. The width setting determines the number of characters in

FIGURE 11.10:
The Font Properties tab lets you make the text on your Console window look just the way you'd like it to.

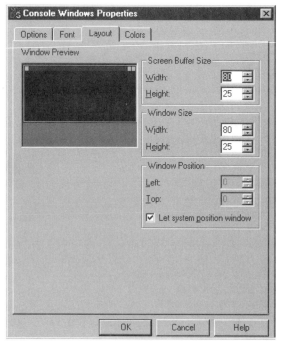

FIGURE 11.11:
On the Layout Properties tab, you can make the Console window bigger or smaller, as you wish.

each line, while the height setting determines how many lines are stored in memory. If the current window size is smaller than the screen buffer size settings, scroll bars are displayed, so you can scroll back through the information.

Window Size   Here you can specify the visible width and height, in characters, of the Console window.

Window Position   This setting specifies the left and top position of the Console window. If you'd like the system to position the window (this is usually the best thing to do), select the Let System Position Window check box.

Color Properties

The Color Properties tab (see Figure 11.12) is where you can really display your individualistic (and perhaps artistic) tendencies. Some people prefer the plain-old black background with grayish text, while others prefer to perform Command prompt functions in living color. Suit yourself. Here's what you need to know about the settings the Colors tab offers you:

Screen Text   Select this option to change the color of the screen text in a Console window.

Screen Background   This setting lets you change the color of the screen background in a Console window.

Popup Text   Select this option to change the color of the text in a pop-up window.

Popup Background   This setting lets you change the color of the background in a pop-up window.

Selected Color Values   If you'd like, you can use these boxes to increase or decrease the amount of primary color used in a particular color. The valid range is from 0 to 255 in the red, green, and/or blue boxes. Play around with them until you have everything *all* messed up. Click Cancel to avoid making any messed-up colors permanent. (Then you can start over!)

Selected Screen Colors   This little window gives you a preview of your selected screen colors. Be sure you like your selections before you OK your way out of here.

Selected Popup Colors   This window, like the Selected Screen Colors window, is for preview purposes. If you've monkeyed with the pop-up text and/or background settings, it's probably a good idea to make sure your new settings will be legible.

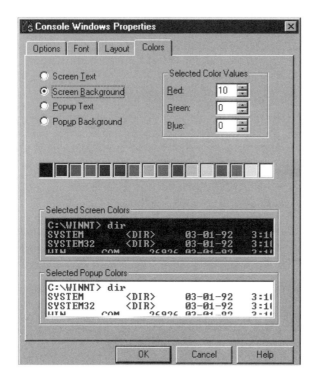

FIGURE 11.12:
You can show your true colors on the Color Properties tab.

Next Step

You now know all you need to know about how to use the Command prompt to your best advantage and how to customize the Console window to suit your tastes. The next chapter will cover how to install and uninstall hardware on your NT Workstation, so hold onto your hat.

Chapter 12

HARDWARE MADE EASY

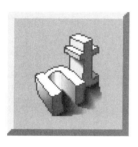

FEATURING

- **Making a modem work**
- **Installing a sound card**
- **Adding or removing a printer**
- **Troubleshooting the troublesome**

Changing hardware on a PC has always been a challenge, to say the least, because most PCs are made up of a hard drive from one manufacturer, a video card from another, a sound card built somewhere in Asia, and a modem manufactured by someone you never heard of. Before NT Workstation, getting all these disparate parts to work together was a real chore. And once everything was functioning, changing your system by installing a new hard drive or a different modem was more grief than most could bear.

While NT still can't quite equal the ease of Windows 95 with its *Plug-and-Play* standard, under NT Workstation 4 hardware installation is far less painful than it used to be. In this chapter, you'll see how to get NT Workstation to recognize your new hardware as well as how to troubleshoot any hardware that gets flaky.

> **WARNING** Be aware that some things described in this chapter may not work for you because what you can and can't do depends on how your system administrator has set network privileges for your account. So if you encounter difficulties, try consulting he or she who knows all.

Modems

Modems

In these days of the ubiquitous Information Superhighway, a modem has become a must in any computer that's not connected directly to the Internet. Because at least some of you will realize this only *after* you've installed NT Workstation, it's probably a good idea to know how to add a modem after the fact. Or, if your modem isn't working and you'd like to remove it, you need to know how to do that too. In this section, you'll learn how to add and remove modems, how to change modem settings and dialing properties, and, last but certainly not least, how to troubleshoot a modem that's acting up. Note that in order to perform some of these actions, you must be logged on using an account with administrative privileges; if you find that many options are grayed out, you'll need to ask your system administrator for assistance.

Adding a Modem

If you have no modem in your computer and want to install one, follow these steps:

1. Shut down NT Workstation by clicking on the Start button and selecting Shut Down. After turning off the computer, connect the modem.
    *   If it's an external modem, you need to plug it into a serial port on the back of the computer box. You'll also need to plug the modem's electrical cord into an outlet, then make sure to turn the modem *on* before proceeding.
    *   For an internal modem, you'll need to open the computer box. The instructions that came with the modem should help.
    *   For a PC Card (the new name for PCMCIA cards), plug it into the PC Card slot on the laptop and connect it to the phone line.

2. Turn your computer back on, and let NT Workstation start. Double-click on the Modems icon in the Control Panel.

3. NT Workstation's Install New Modem Wizard will volunteer to find the modem for you and install it. Take advantage of this offer and click on Next.

4. The system will search the communications ports and report its findings. Figure 12.1 shows what was found on my computer.

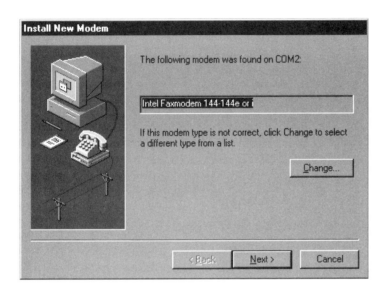

FIGURE 12.1:
NT Workstation reports on the kind of modem it found.

5. If the finding is correct, click on the Next button. If NT Workstation came up with wrong information, click on the Change button, select the right manufacturer and type from the list provided, and *then* click on Next.

The process will continue, and you'll be notified of a successful installation.

Removing a Modem

If you change modems (or install the wrong one), it's easy to correct the situation.

1. Open the Modems icon in the Control Panel.

2. On the General page, highlight the modem name.

3. Click on the Remove button, confirm, and it's gone!

TIP | **Some modem problems in NT Workstation arise when older communications software intervenes and changes a modem setting without your knowledge. If you repeatedly get a `modem will not initialize` message, try removing the modem from NT Workstation and then installing it again. Sometimes, just shutting down the computer and starting it up again will do the trick. You may even need to switch software or upgrade your existing software.**

Modem Settings

To find the hardware-type settings for your modem, double-click on the Modems icon in the Control Panel. Highlight your modem (if it isn't already) and select Properties. What opens is the Properties sheet for this particular modem (see Figure 12.2).

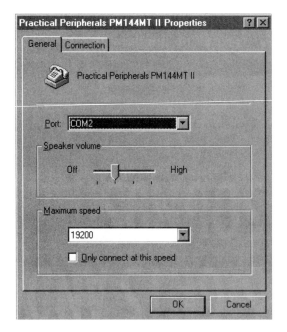

FIGURE 12.2:
This is the place to check up on the settings for your modem.

On the General page you'll find
- The full name of the modem
- The port it's connected to
- A slider for setting the volume of the modem speaker
- A drop-down box for setting the maximum speed

These settings (except for volume, which is strictly a matter of preference) rarely need to be fooled with. That's because they come from what NT Workstation knows about your specific modem. Only change the settings when you've had some difficulty with your modem being recognized or you're sure a particular setting is wrong.

On the Connection page are more of the hardware settings. Again, unless you have a good reason for changing the Connection preferences, leave them alone. The Call preferences can be changed if you find the default ones unsuitable.

If you click on the Advanced button, you'll see the dialog box shown in Figure 12.3. These settings are rarely anything to be concerned about. They're just here for those odd and infrequent times when it might be necessary to force error correction or use software for flow control. The one thing on this page that might be used more often is the Log File. If you're troubleshooting a bad connection, check Record a Log File before you try to connect, and NT Workstation will produce a text file that will tell you exactly what happened. The file will be called MODEMLOG.TXT and will be placed in the WINNT folder. Some communications software will not produce a MODEMLOG.TXT.

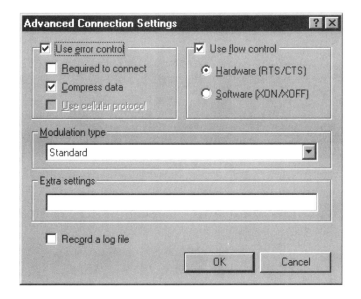

FIGURE 12.3:
The Advanced settings can sometimes help with a difficult connection.

Dialing Properties

In addition to the modem's hardware and software settings, you'll also want to enter information about how you're dialing and where you're dialing from. NT Workstation allows for the configuring of multiple dialing locations, so if you travel with your computer, you can make calls from your branch office (or someplace you visit often, like Michael Jordan's house in Saint Croix) without having to make a lot of changes. Double-click the Modems icon in the Control Panel, and then click the Dialing Properties button. This will open the My Locations page shown in Figure 12.4.

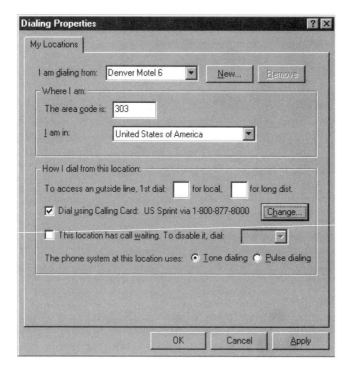

FIGURE 12.4:
When you travel with your computer, you don't have to redo your communications settings when you change locations.

My Locations

You can also reach the My Locations page by double-clicking on the Telephony icon in the Control Panel. As you can see in Figure 12.5, the settings here are identical to the ones in Figure 12.4, so it doesn't really matter which way you get to them.

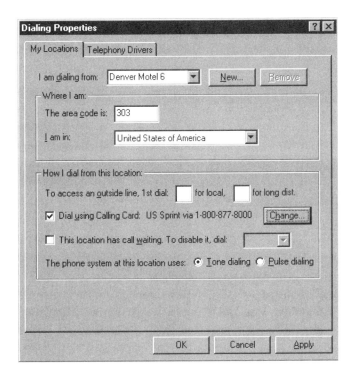

FIGURE 12.5:
You can also access the My Locations page by double-clicking on the Telephony icon in the Control Panel.

Telephony Drivers

The Telephony Drivers page (see Figure 12.6) is an element of NT Workstation that's definitely not for the novice. If you'd like to look at it just to see what's there, double-click on the Telephony icon in the Control Panel, and then select the Telephony Drivers tab. Here, you can install and configure telephony drivers, which are the software your modem uses to "talk" to other computers. In most situations, the NT Workstation default, TAPI Kernel-Mode Service Provider, will work just fine. If it doesn't, consult your system administrator to find out which driver might work better for you, and while you're at it, ask him or her for advice on how to configure the driver in question.

Modem Solutions

As a general rule, when your modem is uncooperative, it's for obvious reasons:

- It's not plugged into a phone line.
- The modem's turned off, or it's not plugged into an active electrical socket (external modems).
- One or more programs have confused the settings.

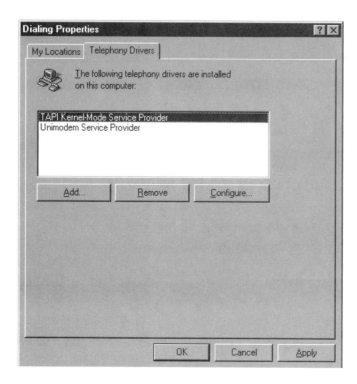

FIGURE 12.6:
The Telephony Drivers page lets you view or change the drivers your modem uses to "talk" to other computers.

This last item happens more often in NT Workstation because of the new TAPI (short for *Telephony Applications Programming Interface*) standard. Like most technology designed to make things better in the future, it has a way of making life somewhat worse here in the present.

> **NOTE** For more on TAPI and what it means, see Chapter 17.

Suffice it to say here that communications programs written for previous versions of Windows or Windows NT Workstation and not yet updated can change your modem's settings. Not all older programs—just some. If this happens, when you try to use another communications program, you'll get an error message that says something like **"the port is already in use," "initialization failure," or "modem not recognized."**

The problem can usually be fixed by removing your modem (as described earlier in this chapter) and then reinstalling it. This isn't really difficult, but it is a pain and a delay. More permanent solutions are

- Upgrade to the NT Workstation 4 or Windows 95 version of the software;
- Change to a communications program that doesn't cause other programs to fail.

Another problem in NT Workstation is that most programs can't share a communications port. You become aware of this when you have fax software loaded, you're ready to receive a fax, and then you try to connect to America Online or CompuServe or your Internet provider. In this case, you'll get a message like **"the modem can't be found" or "the modem is not responding."** The immediate solution is to close the fax software before starting another communications program. The long-term fixes are

- Upgrade all your communications programs to ones that are TAPI-aware;
- Use programs that combine fax and communications in one package.

Printers

Printing is generally a lot easier in NT Workstation than in any previous system. As in NT Workstation 3.51, printers are set up to use a common set of drivers, so you don't have to configure each program independently for printing. Adding or removing a printer is as easy as pointing and clicking, and sharing printers over a network is painless.

Printers are accessible through the Printers folder inside My Computer, off the Start menu under Settings, or in the Printers folder in the Control Panel. And, of course, you can drag a shortcut to the Printers folder (or any of the printers in it) to your Desktop. Open the Printers folder to see what printers are installed for your system.

Adding a Local Printer

Setting up a printer is part of the installation routine. But if your printer isn't installed or you want to add another printer or a network printer, it's very easy to do.

For a printer that's connected directly to your computer, double-click on the Printers folder and follow these steps:

1. Double-click on Add Printer.
2. When the Add Printer Wizard starts, check the My Computer entry.
3. Click the check box next to the port(s) you want to use. Unless you know of some special circumstances, choose LPT.

4. Highlight the name of the printer's manufacturer and the model name, and click Next.

5. Type in the name you want the printer to be known by. If this is not the first printer you're installing onto your computer, specify whether this should be the default printer for Windows applications.

6. Indicate whether or not you'd like this printer to be shared by clicking next to Shared or Not Shared. If you've selected Shared, you'll need to type a name for this printer in the Share Name box and select the operating systems that will be printing to your printer.

7. Opt to print a test page to verify all is well. Then click on Finish.

Adding a Network Printer

SHHPLJII on
SPEEDYG

A network printer (indicated by this icon) is plugged into someone else's computer—a computer you have access to via a network. Once again, be aware that you may not have the network permissions necessary to perform this operation; if you experience technical difficulties, do what you must—consult your system administrator.

To install a network printer so you can use it, double-click on the Printers folder, and follow these steps:

1. Double-click on Add Printer. When the Add Printer Wizard starts, select Network Printer Server, and then click Next.

2. You'll need to show the system where the printer in question is, so double-click on the appropriate domain or workgroup, then double-click on the icon of the computer to which the printer is attached (unless the printer is attached directly to the network), then on the icon for the printer you'd like to use, and click OK. Depending on how your system administrator has set this printer up, you may see a message telling you that you need to install an appropriate printer driver. If this happens, just follow the Wizard's instructions; if it doesn't, follow the Wizard's instructions anyway.

3. If this is not the first printer you're installing onto your computer, specify whether this should be the default printer for Windows applications to print to.

4. Click on Finish.

To be able to use a printer set up this way, both the printer and the computer it's connected to must be switched on.

NOTE Many times printers on the network are not connected to anyone's computer. They're connected to a dedicated machine called a printer server, or they're just "on the network" and take their orders from a controller. You won't be able to add or remove these printers unless you have permission.

Removing a Printer

Sometimes you may need to uninstall a printer, which is quite easily done. Just right-click on the printer's icon in the Printers folder and select Delete. You'll be asked to confirm the deletion. You may also be asked if you want to delete files that are associated with this printer and that won't be necessary if the printer is gone. If you're getting rid of the printer permanently, select Yes. If you're planning on reinstalling the same printer soon, select No.

Printer Settings

To get at the settings for a printer, you need to right-click on the printer's icon and select Properties. On the Properties sheet that opens, you can set details as to fonts, paper, graphics, and so on.

Most of these settings are made by the printer driver that NT Workstation installed to run the printer. Change ones that you need to change, but avoid changing settings if you're not clear what the setting does. You can inadvertently disable your printer. If this happens, you can usually cure it by removing the printer (see the previous section) and then installing it again.

Printer Solutions

Besides the usual paper jam problems we all hate, you can easily run into subtle conflicts between your application program and the printer drivers, as well as downright bugs in either. Here are some things to try, in roughly the order to try them.

Printer Online This happens all the time, especially if the printer's not right next to you where you can see it. Make sure the Online light is on. A network printer shared by others can easily be taken offline by someone who then forgets to press that Online button again.

Power Turn the power off and back on. This does two things. It forces you to check that the power is actually on, and, more to the point, it causes the printer to do a complete reset, getting back to the known starting point that NT Workstation expects to find it in.

Network Print Servers Try connecting directly to the printer without the intervening network connection. Now try printing. If you can print now, you know the problem isn't the printer itself. It's the device between your computer and the printer.

Test File Print a simple test file from Notepad—a few words are enough to know if the printer is being recognized by NT Workstation. If the test file prints, but you have a problem with more complicated printing from your application, chances are you have a problem with the application or possibly the printer driver. Check with the company that makes the application for a newer version, or check with the manufacturer of your printer to see if there's a newer driver.

If none of these help, you can either put out an APB for the system administrator or try the Print Troubleshooter that comes with NT Workstation. To use the Troubleshooter, select Help from the Start menu. On the Contents page, double-click on Troubleshooting and select If You Have Trouble Printing. The guide is interactive in that you select the problem you're having, and then you're guided through the process of finding a solution.

No matter how much NT Workstation does to help you install your hardware quickly and easily, sooner or later you're going to have problems with either a new piece of hardware or an existing one. Sometimes the source of the problem is a subtle conflict between two (or more) pieces of hardware, but much more often the root cause is something fairly simple and straightforward. The best advice has already become like the refrain in a familiar song—consult your system administrator. Hopefully he or she will be able to rescue you yet again.

If you're feeling brave or your system administrator's vacationing in Bora Bora and your problem is a sort of general "it doesn't work"—where "it" is a printer or some other device—start the NT Workstation Help system, and see if there's a Troubleshooter for it in the Troubleshooting section, as shown in Figure 12.7.

FIGURE 12.7:
The NT Workstation Help system has excellent Troubleshooting Wizards to help you locate and resolve problems.

Adding a Sound Card

Windows NT Workstation may have already recognized your sound card, but if it hasn't—or you didn't have a sound card when Workstation was installed but want to add one now, here's how to do it.

First, install the sound card following the instructions that came with it. Make note of the settings used by the sound card. This includes nasty stuff like the IRQ number, I/O address range, and the DMA address.

NOTE If the sound card is already installed, check the documentation to find out how to locate these settings.

You don't have to know what any of this silliness means—just write it down, and don't lose it. Then follow these steps:

1. Open the Control Panel and double-click on the Multimedia icon.
2. Click the Devices tab to open a dialog box that looks like Figure 12.8.

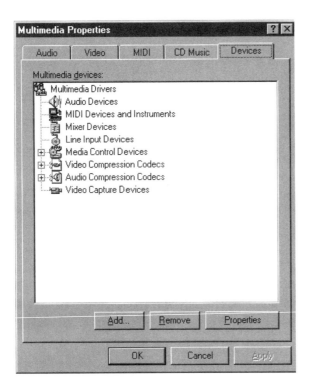

FIGURE 12.8:
All sorts of audio and video multimedia devices are installed from this dialog box.

3. Highlight Audio Devices and click the Add button. This will open a dialog box with a list of possible multimedia gadgets.
4. Select the one on your computer and click OK.
5. You'll be asked to supply a source for the driver NT Workstation needs. This will probably be on the NT Workstation CD, or it may be on the disk that came with the sound card. (Use the one on the NT Workstation disk if you have a choice.)
6. After the driver is installed, you'll be shown the settings for the sound card. Lo and behold, they're the same things you wrote down. Make the settings on the computer match the ones in your notes, not the other way around.

Now all you have to do is reboot, and your sound card will be working. If it's not, you may need to contact the manufacturer about newer drivers.

Next Step

In this chapter, we've covered some of the most common hardware questions and answers. Next we'll move on to the features and programs that come with NT Workstation, starting with some treats for your eyes and ears.

Chapter 13

SIGHTS AND SOUNDS

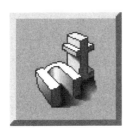

FEATURING

- **Setting up multimedia**
- **Playing and programming CDs**
- **Playing video**
- **Recording and playing sound**
- **Turning the volume up (and down)**

The multimedia capabilities built into many computers and now implemented by NT Workstation may strike you as more of a toy than anything useful. People who use computers as intensely as writers, accountants, and computer consultants do are not looking for more ways to get distracted but for ways to remove distractions. Who needs moving pictures or music to get a book written?

Turns out that's the wrong question. The fact is publishing is different in the age of the computer as are accounting and data crunching. Books can be published online with animation, pictures, or music. Spreadsheets can include pictures of products or factories to make data more concrete. Databases can include pictures of clients and employees to make information more personal.

This chapter examines the CD Player, Media Player, and Sound Recorder built into NT Workstation. The first can be used for your private enjoyment or to accompany a presentation with a soundtrack. The second and third can be used to display and enhance multimedia presentations.

You'll find all the Multimedia applications by clicking on the Start button and proceeding through Programs ➤ Accessories ➤ Multimedia.

Can't Find Multimedia?

You won't have a Multimedia menu on your Accessories menu if the Multimedia applications weren't installed at the time NT Workstation was installed. If this is the case, it's easily remedied:

1. Go to the Control Panel, and click on Add/Remove Programs.
2. Click on the Windows NT Setup tab at the top of the Add/Remove Programs Properties dialog box.
3. Scroll through the list of options in the dialog box until you locate Multimedia.
4. Double-click on Multimedia to see a list of multimedia programs available.
5. Click on the check boxes next to as many programs as you want to install. (For the purposes of this chapter, make sure CD Player, Media Player, Sound Recorder, and Volume Control are selected.)
6. OK your way out, and insert your NT Workstation disk as requested to complete the installation.

NOTE You can associate sounds with different events—for example, a program opens and a particular sound plays. Chapter 14 covers how to do this.

The CD Player

The CD Player lets you play audio CDs using your CD-ROM drive, sound card, and speakers. You can plug speakers or headphones into the sound card or into the jack on the front of the CD-ROM drive.

To open the CD Player, follow these steps:

1. Click on the Start button on the Taskbar.
2. Select Programs.
3. Select Accessories in the Program menu.
4. Select Multimedia in the Accessories menu to open the Multimedia menu.

Depending on the programs you selected when you installed NT Workstation, you'll probably have several applications on this menu.

Starting It Up

To start the CD Player, follow these steps:

1. Locate CD Player among the programs in the Multimedia menu.
2. Click on the CD Player option to start the program. You will see the window shown in Figure 13.1.

FIGURE 13.1:
To change the look of the CD player, check out the View menu.

All you have to do is supply a music CD. The Player will play it through your sound card and speakers (plugged into the audio jacks on the back of the CD-ROM controller) or through the headphone jack in the front of your CD-ROM drive.

> **TIP**
>
> Windows NT Workstation 4 has an automatic play feature for the CD-ROM drive. Put a music CD in the drive and close it. The CD player will start up. Similarly, put a data CD in the drive, and Windows NT shows the opening screen.

How It Works

Just as a demonstration, I popped a music CD in the drive and clicked on the large triangle next to the digital read-out (the Play button). The CD Player (with Disc/Track info enabled from the View menu) can be seen in Figure 13.2.

FIGURE 13.2:
Here's what the CD Player at work looks like.

Notice that several of the buttons that were gray and unavailable in Figure 13.1, when there wasn't a CD in the drive, are now black and available in Figure 13.2.

Play   At the top, the large triangle is gray because the CD is playing. (There's no reason to click on the Play button when the CD is playing, but if you do, no harm is done.)

Pause   Next to the Play button is a button with two vertical bars. This is the Pause button. Click on it to hold your playback while you run to answer the door or the phone.

Stop   The last button at the right end of the top tier is the Stop button. Click on it when you're tired of listening to the music or when the boss walks into your office. It will stop playback dead.

Previous Track   The first button at the left end of the second tier of buttons looks like a double arrowhead pointing left toward a vertical line. Click once to move to the beginning of the current piece; click twice to move to the previous track on the CD.

Skip Backwards   The second button on the second tier looks like a double arrowhead pointing left. This is the Skip Backwards button. Each time you click on it, you will move back one second in the music.

Skip Forwards   The third button on the second tier is the Skip Forwards button. It looks like a double arrowhead pointing to the right. Each time you click on it, you will move one second forward in the music.

Next Track   The fourth button on the second tier is the Next Track button. It looks like a double arrowhead pointing right toward a vertical bar. It will instantly take you to the next song.

Eject   The final button at the right end of the second tier of buttons looks like an arrow pointing upward. Click on it and the CD-ROM drive pops open.

Setting Time and Play Options

Is that all there is? Certainly not. If you're an information freak, click on the digital readout. Before you click, the readout will tell you the current track number and the elapsed time for that track. The first time you click, you'll see the track number and the time remaining on the track. The second click will display the time remaining for the whole CD (shown in Figure 13.3).

FIGURE 13.3:
Getting instant information about the play time remaining on the whole CD

If you want to set these without clicking on the digital display, pull down the View menu and select from

- Track Time Elapsed
- Track Time Remaining
- Disc Time Remaining

The Options menu lets you opt for Continuous Play, Random Play, or Intro Play. Select the Preferences option. It allows you to set the font size for the digital readout as well as the length of intro play (ten seconds is the default).

> **TIP**
>
> **Want a shortcut to CD Player or Media Player on your Desktop? Open the WINNT folder, then open the System32 folder and look for the file CDPLAYER.EXE or MPLAY32.EXE. Right-click and drag the file to the Desktop. Release the right mouse button, and select Create Shortcut(s) here.**

Editing the Play List

And if that's not enough, there's an entire layer of the CD Player we haven't even touched yet. Here's how to access it:

1. Pull down the Disc menu.
2. Select Edit Play List. You will see the dialog box shown in Figure 13.4.

Using this dialog box, you can do something owners of CD players often never get the hang of—programming your player to play specific songs in a specific order.

By Track Number

As an example, let's set up the CD Player to play Tracks 5, 12, and 3 on this particular disc. Here's how:

1. Click on the Clear All button to clear all the entries on the Play List.
2. Double-click on Track 5 in the Available Tracks list box. It will appear in the Play List.
3. Double-click on Track 12, and then double-click on Track 3 in the Available Tracks list box.

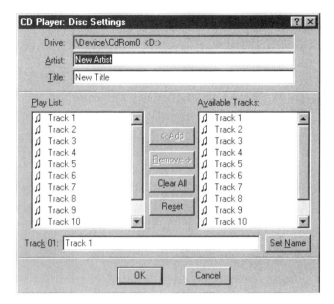

FIGURE 13.4:
The Disc Settings dialog box lets you program a play list.

By Track Name

If you'd rather deal with track names than track numbers, you can insert names for each of the tracks (or just the ones you care about) as follows:

1. Click on a track—for this example, we'll click on Track 3 in the Available Tracks list.
2. Click in the text box next to the Set Name button.
3. Refer to your CD packaging to get the name of the third song on the CD.
4. Type the name in the text box. (You can type it next to Track 3 or delete the track and type the name instead.)
5. Click on the Set Name button. In the Available Tracks list and in the Play List, Track 3 will be replaced with the name you just typed.
6. Just for the sake of completeness, click on the text box marked Artist, and type the performer(s) name.
7. Highlight the text box marked Title, and type the CD's title.
8. Click on the OK button.

Once you've supplied your CD Player with this information, the program will remember it, recognize the CD, and follow your programmed instructions every time you play it.

TIP   If you have a CD-ROM player capable of playing multiple discs, Multidisc Play will be an option on the Options menu. Select it, and when you click on the downward-pointing arrow at the right end of the Artist box, you will see each of the CDs available to you. Select the CD you want to play.

The Media Player

These days the word *media* conjures up more talk show blather about how everything's the fault of the media—whoever they are.

Not this media. The media in this section are fun—never trouble.

Let's begin, as always, by first opening the program:

1. Click on the Start button on the Taskbar.
2. Select Programs.
3. Select Accessories from the Programs menu.
4. Select Multimedia from the Accessories menu.
5. Select Media Player from the Multimedia menu.

You should see something similar to the window shown in Figure 13.5.

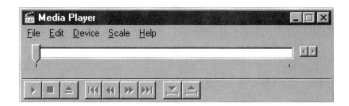

FIGURE3.5:
The Media Player looks like this.

The Media Player will play Video for Windows animated files (.AVI), sound files (.WAV), MIDI files (.MID and .RMI), or your audio CD. Yes, that's right. You can use Media Player to play your music CDs. It's just like the CD Player; except, Media Player offers fewer customization options.

Playing Files

NT Workstation comes with a variety of multimedia files—especially on the CD-ROM version. To play a file, follow these steps:

1.   Pull down the Media Player Device menu, and select the type of file you want to play.
2.   Locate the file you want to play, double-click or highlight it, and select Open.
3.   Click on the single right-pointing arrow (the Play button).

You can select sections of animation or movies just like you select recorded music tracks (see the CD Player section earlier in this chapter). Although the buttons are in different places than the ones on the CD Player, you should be able to identify them by their icons (see "How It Works").

Copying and Pasting Files

You can copy and paste sound, animation, or movie files using the Select buttons, which look like tiny arrows above a horizontal bar pointing down (start selection) and up (end selection).

Selecting a Piece of the File

To select a section of either an audio or video file:

1.   Listen (or watch) until you reach the point where the section begins.
2.   Click on the Begin Selection button.
3.   Continue listening or watching until you reach the end of the section.
4.   Click on the End Selection button.
5.   Pull down the Edit menu and select Copy Object. (The piece you have selected will be placed on the Clipboard for pasting into any document that supports sound or video files.)

Getting Looped

If you want a piece of music, film, or animation to repeat continuously, pull down the Edit menu and select Options. Click on the option marked Auto Repeat. Your media file will play over and over until

1.   The end of time;
2.   You turn off the media player;
3.   Or you lose your mind and destroy your computer with a fire ax.

The Sound Recorder

If you have an audio input device on your computer (either a microphone or a CD-ROM player), you can use the Sound Recorder to make a .WAV file that you can associate with a Windows event or send in a message.

Making .WAV Files

Here's how to make a .WAV file with the Sound Recorder:

1. Open Sound Recorder in the Multimedia menu under Accessories.
2. To begin recording, click on the button with the dark red dot.
3. Start the CD, or start speaking into the microphone.
4. Click on the button with the black square to stop recording.
5. Select Save from the File menu to save the sound clip, and enter a name for the file in the Save dialog box that appears.

Figure 13.6 shows the Sound Recorder recording from a CD being played in the Media Player.

FIGURE 13.6:
Make your own .WAV files from a CD-ROM with the Sound Recorder.

The Sound Recorder also lets you play other types of sound clips in the Media Player and record them as .WAV files. The .WAV files you make can be played back with the Sound Recorder or the Media Player.

Special Effects and Editing

Use the Effects menu to change some of the sound's qualities—to add an echo or decrease the speed, for example. The sound can also be edited using the menu controls.

Volume Control

The Volume Control panel lets you not only adjust the sound level but also individually tune levels for different types of files. The best way to reach the Volume Control panel is to open it from the Multimedia menu under Accessories (Figure 13.7).

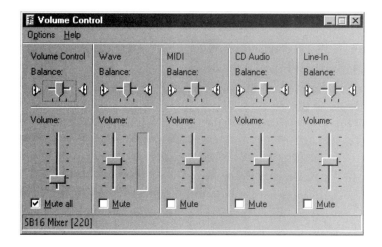

FIGURE 13.7:
The Volume Control panel lets you make adjustments in your sound files.

Tone Controls

For tone controls (bass and treble), select Advanced Controls from the Options menu. This will put an Advanced button at the bottom of the Volume Control window. Click on this button to open the dialog box shown in Figure 13.8.

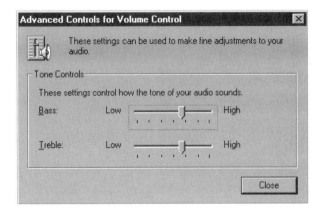

FIGURE 13.8:
Use the slider controls
to adjust tone.

Use the slider controls to increase or decrease the treble and bass tones. These settings will affect all the sound files you play.

NOTE If Advanced Controls is dimmed on your screen, it just means your hardware doesn't support these functions.

Setting Volume Control Display

Figure 13.7 shows the default settings for volume control, but you can decide which devices you want to show on the Volume Control panel. Open Volume Control and select Properties from the Options menu. This will open the Volumn Control dialog box.

Select Playback and check the devices you want shown on Volume Control. Likewise you can display recording levels. The choices will probably differ based on your specific computer hardware.

More Multimedia Settings

There's also a Multimedia icon in the Control Panel that contains mostly advanced settings, but some basic ones too.

Multimedia   Double-click on this icon, and poke around, right-clicking on anything you don't understand to get an explanation box. There are a lot of terms here that will be unfamiliar to anyone who's a novice at computer-based sound and video. Experiment but also take care not to remove a device unintentionally.

> **TIP**
>
> **The Multimedia icon is the place you go to install a sound card or other audio/video devices. The steps for installing a sound card— or making Windows NT recognize a sound card already installed— are in Chapter 12.**

Next Step

This chapter hasn't exhausted all the features for the eyes and ears. In the next chapter, we'll go on to some neat functions in the Control Panel that also affect how your computer looks and sounds, and you'll learn how to customize settings to make your computer truly your own.

Chapter 14

IN THE CONTROL PANEL

- **Adding and removing programs and hardware**
- **Configuring your mouse, keyboard, and printer**
- **Using all the Control Panel icons**

If you've fiddled around with the Control Panel at all, you can see that it acts as a sort of "mission central" for NT Workstation. Some of the settings behind the icons can be reached from other directions, but others can be reached only by way of the Control Panel. Most of the items in the Control Panel help you customize your NT Workstation even further.

You'll find a heading in this chapter for all the usual icons in the Control Panel (listed alphabetically). If the settings behind an icon are detailed elsewhere, you'll be pointed to the correct location.

Accessibility Options

The Accessibility Options are installed automatically when NT Workstation is installed. If you want them and they're not on your system, use Add/Remove Programs to add them. Double-click on this icon, and you'll find options for adding sound to the usual visual cues, adding visual cues to the sound cues, and making the keyboard and mouse easier to use for those of us with dexterity problems (see Figure 14.1).

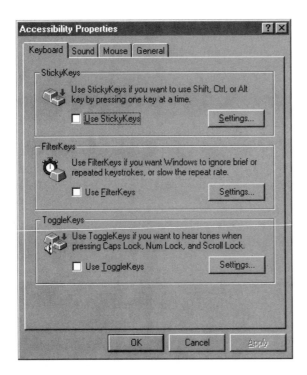

FIGURE 14.1:
Here's where you can add sounds to visual cues and visual cues to sound.

Not all the settings are obvious, so when you come across one that's unclear, right-click on the text and then click on the What's This? button for more information.

After you've made your settings, don't leave until you click on the General tab to check the Automatic Reset section. Put a check mark next to Turn Off Accessibility Features after Idle to turn off the options if the computer isn't used for the period specified in the Minutes box. Clear the check box if you want to make the selected options permanent.

> **TIP**
>
> The Toggle Keys option on the Keyboard page is of great help if you often hit the Caps Lock key inadvertently and lookup to find your text looking like: "cALL mR. jAMES IN cAPE vERDE." With Toggle Keys on, you'll hear a quiet but distinct warning beep when Caps Lock is switched on.

Add/Remove Programs

Add/Remove Programs

NT Workstation provides a good deal of aid and comfort when it comes to adding or removing programs from your system, especially adding and removing parts of NT Workstation itself. Double-click on this icon in the Control Panel.

The Add/Remove function has two parts, one on each tab:

- Installing or uninstalling software applications
- Installing or removing portions of NT Workstation

Install/Uninstall

A software producer who wants the right to put a Windows 95 or Windows NT logo on a product is supposed to make sure the program can uninstall itself. The idea is to correct a problem that made it difficult to completely remove a program and all of its associated files in previous versions of NT Workstation.

Programs written for previous versions of Windows (and that's the software we're mostly using) don't have this uninstall capability. And some programs actually written for Windows NT and Windows 95 can be uninstalled and still leave bits of themselves cluttering your hard disk. This will probably improve over time. How the major programs written for NT Workstation 4 handle Add/Remove varies widely. Some will just uninstall themselves without a fuss; others will give you the option of removing all or just parts of the program. You'll have to click on the program and select Remove to see what happens. *Nothing* will be uninstalled without your OK.

For now, this is an easy-to-use tool for installing new programs. Just put the program's first floppy disk in the drive (or if the program came on a compact disc, insert the CD in the proper drive), click on the Install/Uninstall tab, and then click on the Install button.

The program searches for an install routine first in drive A:, then in drive B: (if you have one), and finally in the CD drive. Figure 14.2 shows the result of one search. Click on Finish to continue. After this, the program's install routine takes over.

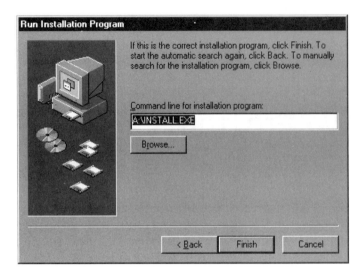

FIGURE 14.2:
The Installation program finds the INSTALL or SETUP file and proceeds to install the program.

Windows NT Setup

Click on the Windows NT Setup tab to add or remove a component of NT Workstation. The various parts are organized by groups (see Figure 14.3). For certain groups, you can highlight the group and click on Details to see the individual components.

As you click on each item in a group, a description of the item's function is displayed at the bottom of the page. The rules are simple:

- If an item is checked, it's installed. Remove the check mark, and it'll be removed.
- If an item is not checked, it's not currently installed on your system. Put a check mark next to it, and it'll be installed.
- If the check box is gray, a part of the component is selected for installation. Click on the Details button to specify which parts you want.

Click on OK once or twice until the window closes. You'll be prompted to put the NT Workstation compact disc in the CD drive.

FIGURE 14.3:
Here's where you can install or uninstall various parts of NT Workstation.

Console

Console

There's a whole chapter devoted to using the command prompt in this book; see Chapter 11 for the details of how the Console icon works.

CSNW

CSNW

If you have this icon, it means that Client Services for NetWare is installed on your computer. This service allows you to use the printers and drives of a NetWare server on your NT Workstation. If you need to change something here, call your system administrator.

Date and Time

Date/Time

Unless you're logged in using an account with administrative privileges, this Control Panel option is unavailable to you, which makes sense since you don't have permission to change the system date and time.

Devices

Devices

If you double-click on the Devices icon in the Control Panel, you'll see a mysterious-looking list of items. What you've got in front of you is actually an inventory of devices on your system, which includes basic things, such as your keyboards, ports, and mouse, but also more complicated things, such as hardware and software drivers. My advice on this one is *don't touch!* You'll probably never need to change any of the settings behind the Devices icon, and if you do, it's probably best to call your trusty system administrator, whose job it is to know more about such arcane matters than you do.

Dial-Up Monitor

Dial-Up
Monitor

If you have Dial-Up Networking or Remote Access Service installed, you may have an icon for the Dial-Up Networking Monitor, which lets you keep tabs on your modem network connection. Remote Access Service is covered in Chapter 17, where you'll find out all the details of connecting to the outside world.

Display

Display

Behind the Display icon in the Control Panel are all the settings that affect your screen display, including colors, screen savers, type faces in windows and dialog boxes, and resolutions. See "Desktop Settings" in Chapter 3 for details on these settings.

Fonts

Fonts

TrueType fonts are managed in NT Workstation in a clear and understandable way. To see the list of fonts on your computer, double-click on this icon in the Control Panel.

Selecting and Viewing Fonts

The Fonts folder is a little different from the usual run of folders in that the menus show some new items. In the View menu shown in Figure 14.4, you'll find, in addition to the choices for viewing icons and lists, an option called List Fonts by Similarity.

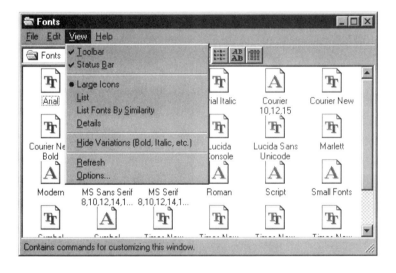

FIGURE 14.4: The View menu is a little different in the Fonts folder.

> **NOTE** If your font list is very long and unwieldy, select View ➤ Hide Variations. That will conceal font variations, such as bold and italic, and make the list easier to look through.

Select List Fonts by Similarity from the View menu and then select a font in the drop-down box at the top of the Fonts folder, and the other fonts will line up in terms of their degree of similarity (see Figure 14.5). Before you make a commitment, you can right-click on any of the font names and select Open (or just double-click). A window will open with a complete view of the font in question.

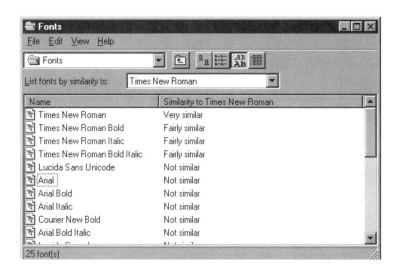

FIGURE 14.5:
Fonts can be viewed in terms of their resemblance to one another.

TrueType fonts that you may have located elsewhere can be moved into this folder. Figure 14.6 shows a newly acquired font being dragged into the folder.

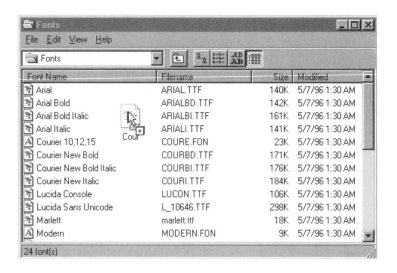

FIGURE 14.6:
Move fonts into the Fonts folder just as you'd move any object—drag and drop or cut and paste.

Fonts don't have to be physically located in the WINNT/Fonts folder to be recognized by NT Workstation. You can make a shortcut to a font in another folder and put the shortcut in the Fonts folder. The shortcut is all you need for the font to be installed.

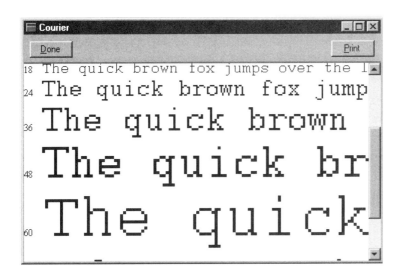 Fonts that are identified with an icon like this are not TrueType fonts. They're not *scaleable,* which means they tend to look quite crummy at large point sizes (see Figure 14.7). Many of these fonts can be used only in certain limited point sizes.

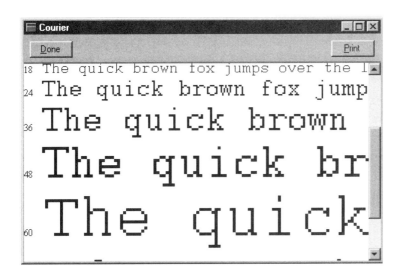

FIGURE 14.7:
The non-True Type fonts are not much to look at in the larger sizes.

Installing New Fonts

Installing new fonts is a pretty easy project. Just open the Fonts icon in the Control Panel and select Install New Font from the File menu. In the Add Fonts dialog box (Figure 14.8), you can tell the system the drive and directory where the font(s) resides. If there's one or more TrueType or Postscript fonts at the location you specify, they'll show up in the List of Fonts box.

Highlight the font or fonts you want installed, and click on the OK button. Packages like Microsoft's TrueType Fonts for Windows may need to be installed like other programs. Use Add/Remove Programs, described earlier in this chapter.

NOTE Postscript fonts can't be used for display in NT Workstation, but they can be used for printing to a Postscript compatible printer, or they can be converted to TrueType fonts. NT Workstation includes a license to convert existing Postscript fonts to TrueType from many of the major font houses, including Adobe, Bitstream, and others.

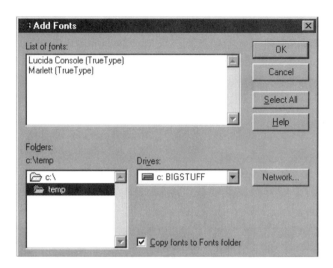

FIGURE 14.8:
Here's where you add fonts to the Fonts folder.

Internet

Internet

If your favorite NT Workstation is connected to the Internet, you can use this icon in the Control Panel to specify a *proxy server*. If you're not sure what a proxy server is and you've never needed one before, chances are you won't have to bother changing these settings. Should the need for a proxy server ever arise, consult your system administrator, who should be able to tell you what the correct settings are.

Keyboard

Keyboard

The installation routine of NT Workstation finds the keyboard plugged into your computer and recognizes it, so you normally don't have to fuss with these settings. But if you need to change keyboards, adjust the keyboard's speed, or install a keyboard designed for another language, double-click on this icon in the Control Panel.

The three tabs on the Keyboard Properties sheet cover these different types of settings and are explained in the following sections.

Changing Your Keyboard

If you're changing keyboards or NT Workstation recognizes one type of keyboard when in fact you have a different kind, go directly to the General tab. The Keyboard Type box shows what NT Workstation thinks is your keyboard. If it's wrong, click on the Change button and follow these steps:

1. On the Select Device page, click on Show All Devices.
2. Select the correct keyboard from the list shown. If you have some special installation software, click on Have Disk.
3. Click on OK and NT Workstation will install the correct keyboard either from your disk or from its own set.

You *may* have to shut down and restart your computer for the keyboard to be completely recognized.

Adjusting Your Keyboard's Speed

Click on the Speed tab to adjust keyboard rates. Here are the available settings:

Repeat Delay   Determines how long a key has to be held down before it starts repeating. The difference between the Long and Short setting is only about a second.

Repeat Rate   Determines how fast a key repeats. Fast means if you hold down a key you almost instantly get vvvvvvvvvvery long streams of letters. (Click in the Practice area to test this setting.)

Cursor Blink Rate   Makes the cursor blink faster or slower. The blinking cursor on the left demonstrates the setting.

Keyboard Languages

If you need multiple language support for your keyboard, choose the Input Locales tab. Click on the Add button to select languages from Afrikaans to Ukrainian—including 15 varieties of Spanish.

If you have more than one language selected, the settings on the Input Locales tab let you choose a keyboard combination to switch between languages (see Figure 14.9).

Highlight the language you want to be the default (the one that's enabled when your start you computer), and click on the Set as Default button.

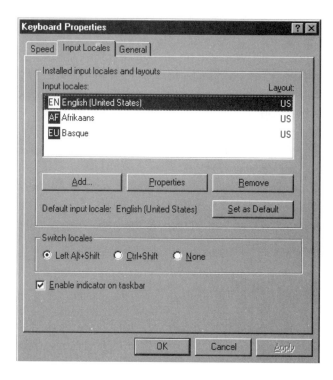

FIGURE 14.9:
Set up your keyboard for more than one language.

Check Enable Indicator on Taskbar, and an icon will appear on your Taskbar. Click on the taskbar and you can instantly switch between languages.

Mail

Mail

The Mail icon will appear in the Control Panel if you opted to install mail services when you installed NT Workstation.

Mail services have most of a chapter devoted to them. See Chapter 17 for mail and other communications information.

Microsoft Mail Postoffice

Microsoft Mail Postoffice

The Microsoft Mail Postoffice icon will appear in the Control Panel if you opted to include Microsoft Mail when you installed mail services. If you have this icon, you can use it to administer or create a Microsoft Mail Workgroup postoffice. Don't. Save this job for your System Administrator who gets paid the big bucks. See Chapter 17 for mail and other communications information.

Modems

Modems

The settings behind this icon are covered in the "Modems" section of Chapter 12.

Mouse

Mouse

Everything you ever wanted to know (and more) about mouse settings—including the settings connected to this icon—can be found in Chapter 5, which is devoted entirely to mouses and their uses.

Multimedia

Multimedia

Read Chapter 13 for information on the multimedia applications that come with NT Workstation and how to set them up. The settings behind this icon are covered there as well.

Network

Network

Fortunately or unfortunately, the majority of options that the Network icon offers are unavailable to you unless you're logged on to an account with administrative privileges. These things really *are* the business of the system administrator, whose job it is to keep the network up and running. If other users were allowed to muck around with network settings, the poor system administrator's job would be that much harder, so it's really a good thing that we plain-old users can't put our grubby paws where they don't belong.

If you double-click the Network icon just because you're curious, you'll see the Network pages in *viewing* mode, which means all the buttons that do anything are grayed out. On the Identification page, you'll see the name of your computer and the domain to which it belongs. On the Services, Protocols, and Adapters pages, you'll see a whole lot of arcane settings, so be glad you're not the person who's supposed to know what they all mean.

ODBC

ODBC

The ODBC icon will appear in the Control Panel if you have any database applications installed which provide ODBC (Open Database Connectivity) drivers. If you do, follow the instructions provided with the application or contact your system administrator for more information.

PC Card

PC Card
(PCMCIA)

The PC Card icon in the Control Panel enables PCMCIA sockets and allows you to change PC Card settings. This option is relevant only if you've got a laptop with a PC Card installed, and chances are if the card was already in the machine when you installed NT Workstation, you'll never have to bother with these settings anyhow.

Ports

Ports

The Ports box (see Figure 14.10) displays which ports are currently installed on your NT Workstation, and it lets you view and/or change the settings for a given port. Here, you can also add or delete a port, but consult your system administrator before doing this, since he or she usually knows best about this kind of hardware issue.

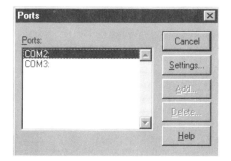

FIGURE 14.10:
Here's where you can
add or delete a port.

Printers

Printers

This icon in the Control Panel is a shortcut to your Printers folder (also seen in My Computer and the Explorer).

Details on how to install, remove, or change the settings of printers are all in Chapter 12, "Hardware Made Easy."

Regional Settings

Regional
Settings

The Regional Settings icon in the Control Panel is where you set the variations in how numbers and the time and date are formatted in different parts of the world. For example, if you're using a program that supports international symbols, changing the Regional Settings can affect how the program displays currency, time, and numbers.

First select the geographic area you want to use on the Regional Settings tab, then confirm or change the individual settings on the other tabs. Your system will have to be rebooted for the settings to take effect system-wide.

SCSI Adapters

SCSI Adapters

This icon in the Control Panel lets you add or remove an SCSI adapter and view the properties of any and all SCSI adapters installed in your system. If you double-click on the SCSI Adapters icon, highlight the adapter whose properties you'd like to view and then click the Properties button. You should see something that looks like Figure 14.11. The settings on these tabs won't mean much to most of us; what's important is that you make sure there's a message on the CardInfo tab that says, "The device is working properly."

FIGURE 14.11:
Viewing the properties of your SCSI adapter

If the device *isn't* working properly, it's time to yell for your system administrator, whose job it is to help you with just this sort of problem. If you notice the buttons on the Driver tab are grayed out, don't panic—this is so you can't accidentally modify the device driver for your SCSI adapter. If you ever need to fiddle with the device driver, contact your system administrator (or anyone else who has the proper administrative privileges).

Server

Server

Unless you're logged in using an account with administrative privileges, this Control Panel option is unavailable to you, which makes sense since you don't have permission to view Server properties.

Services

Services

The Services icon on the Control Panel, like the Server icon, shouldn't really concern mere mortals who just happen to be using a networked NT

Workstation. These settings are the exclusive purview of the system administrator, who should know better than anyone else how to change them when necessary.

Sounds

Sounds

What with NT Workstation's emphasis on multimedia, it's no surprise that using sound with your computer is easier than ever. Double-click on the Sounds icon in the Control Panel to set and change sound schemes. (See Chapter 13 for more on sounds.)

NOTE To play the sounds that come with NT Workstation, you'll need a sound card and speakers (or you'll have to wear headphones all the time).

A Sheet Full of Sounds

The Sounds Properties sheet is shown in Figure 14.12. The Events box lists everything on your system associated with a sound. Most are NT Workstation events. For example, opening a program can cause a sound, as can maximizing or minimizing a window along with many other actions.

Many of the new programs coming out now also include sound capabilities. Their sounds may not end up in the list shown on this sheet because they're configured in the program.

If there's a Speaker icon next to the event, a sound is associated with it. Highlight the event—the name of the sound file will appear in the Name text box—and click on the button next to the Preview box to hear its sound.

Sound schemes are included with NT Workstation, and you can choose one of them from the drop-down list.

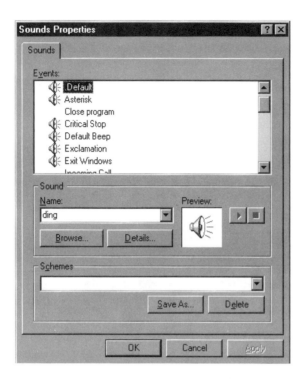

FIGURE 14.12:
Use the Sounds Properties sheet to associate a sound with an event.

> **TIP**   If sound schemes don't appear in the Schemes drop-down list, you'll need to install them. Go to the Add/Remove Programs icon in the Control Panel. Under the Windows NT Setup, double-click on Multimedia and select the sound schemes you want. Select OK twice, and then follow the instructions.

Customizing a Sound Scheme

All the sound schemes that come with NT Workstation are nice enough, but none of them is perfect. There are either too many sounds, not enough, the wrong sounds are attached to the wrong events, or whatever. Fortunately, there's a way to make as many customized sound schemes as you like. Here's how:

1. Double-click on the Sounds icon in the Control Panel.
2. If there's a sound scheme that's close to the one you want, select it from the Schemes drop-down list. Otherwise, select Windows default.

3. In the Events list, select an item that you want a sound associated with.
4. Select a file from the Name drop-down list. To make sure it's the one you want, click on the Preview button to hear it.
5. Select (none) from the Name drop-down list for events you want to keep silent.
6. Repeat steps 3–5 until you've completed the list.
7. Select Save As to save this particular assortment of sounds under a specific name. (The new scheme will appear in the Schemes drop-down list.)

> **TIP**
>
> NT Workstation stores all its sound files in the WINNT\Media folder. You'll probably want to move any additional sound files you acquire to that folder because using a single location makes setting up and changing sound schemes much easier.

System

System

The Properties sheet that opens when you double-click on the System icon in the Control Panel can also be accessed by right-clicking on My Computer and choosing Properties.

You won't use most of the settings if your computer is working properly. It's only when things go awry that you need to be changing anything here.

> **NOTE**
>
> There's much more on hardware troubleshooting in Chapter 12.

Environment

The Environment page displays information about system and user variables on your NT Workstation. Unless you really know what you're doing, you should never attempt to change any of the settings here; who knows what might happen if you do!

General

The General page only tells you which version of NT Workstation you're using, the registered owner, and a little bit about the type of computer. You'll find the main computer information on this page of the Properties sheet.

Hardware Profiles

Hardware profiles are something you may need if you're using a portable computer with a docking station. In a limited number of circumstances, you may need to configure alternate setups when the hardware on your system changes.

If you think this might be your situation, consult the NT Workstation Help files and/or your system administrator for instructions.

Performance

On this page, you'll see two entries (see Figure 14.13). The first is for Application Performance. By default, the slider is set to Maximum, which means the active application (the foreground application) will get the most attention from the processor. You can move the slider to the left to get more processor power for any background applications, but be aware that it may slow down the program you're actually working in.

The second setting is for Virtual Memory. Don't mess with this unless you're sure you know what you're doing, or the operating system tells you to change the setting. Windows NT Workstation is very good at determining how much virtual memory it needs. It's a losing game to try to outsmart the system.

Startup/Shutdown

The Startup/Shutdown page allows you to specify startup and shutdown options, such as which operating system should be the default when you boot up your computer and what should happen in case you experience a dreaded STOP error (most of us just call our friendly neighborhood system administrator; that's what he or she is there for!).

NOTE This Startup/Shutdown page won't be present in your Control Panel unless you're running multiple operating systems on one computer.

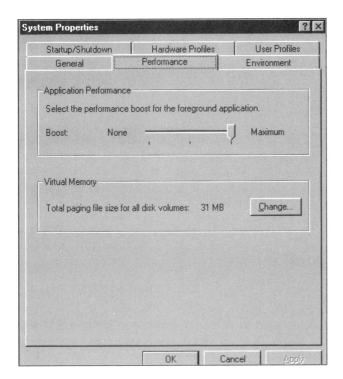

FIGURE 14.13:
The Performance tab lets you adjust the amount of time your active application gets from the processor.

User Profiles

The User Profiles tab on the System Properties page lets you switch between two different types of user profiles, which are files that contain Desktop settings and other information related to your NT Workstation logon. Just in case you're wondering, a user profile is created for you when you log on to your favorite NT Workstation computer for the first time. If you often use different computers, a different (local) user profile can be created on each computer you use, or you can set up what's called a *roaming user profile* that is the same on every computer you use. By default, a *user profile* is a local profile. If you'd like to try using a roaming profile, ask your system administrator to arrange this for you.

Tape Devices

Tape Devices

The Tape Devices icon on the Control Panel displays information about any tape device(s) installed on your system and the drivers that run them.

Since your system administrator is presumably the one who is responsible for hardware and any problems therewith, it's a good idea here (as elsewhere) to look but not touch.

Telephony

Telephony

Double-clicking the Telephony icon on the Control Panel leads you to two pages whose contents relate to your modem's dialing properties and the drivers it uses to communicate with other computers. Complete details on NT Workstation's Telephony features can be found in Chapter 12.

UPS

UPS

Unless you're logged in using an account with administrative privileges, this Control Panel option is unavailable to you, which makes sense since you don't have permission to configure a UPS (an *uninterruptible power supply,* in case you were wondering what the initials stand for!).

> **NOTE** How to install one of these devices is covered in Chapter 19.

Next Step

In the next chapter, we move on to administrative tools for non-administrators. We'll tell you how to view events on the network, monitor your computer's performance, manage your user profile, and (if you're feeling brave) diagnose any problems on your computer before you call the system administrator.

Chapter 15

ADMINISTRATIVE TOOLS FOR NON-ADMINISTRATORS

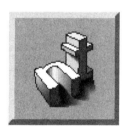

FEATURING

- **Viewing the Event Log**
- **Checking out Performance Monitor**
- **Making a local group with User Manager**
- **Reviewing Windows NT Diagnostics**

NT Workstation 4 ships with a whole raft of administrative tools, and you might wonder what these tools have to do with regular people (that is, non-system administrators).

It's true that most of the tools aren't even accessible unless you have an administrative account. However, some of the tools *are* yours to use, and others may turn out to be part of your job. (Let's hope not, but life does sometimes take you in unexpected directions.)

Backup

The proper use of this crucial administrative tool is covered in detail in Chapter 19, so check there if you're wondering how to protect your precious data against disasters great and small.

Disk Administrator

Although you may see a box promising you that "Disk Administrator is initializing," if you try to start up the Disk Administrator, don't get your hopes up—unless you're logged on using an account with administrative privileges, you won't get any further.

The reason for denying most users access to the Disk Administrator is simple—it's a dangerous tool in the wrong hands. Sometimes it's a dangerous tool even in the right hands.

It's the job of the system administrator to perform the kind of system maintenance the Disk Administrator handles, such as changing disk partitions, assigning drive letters, setting volume labels, and so forth. Be glad it's not your responsibility.

Event Viewer

The Event Viewer is used to monitor events on a computer or on networked computers. But what is an event, you may ask? An *event* is a significant occurrence in the system or in an application that requires users to be notified.

You've probably experienced an event if you've ever been happily using your word processor, and then you type some random key combination that causes the program to perform an illegal operation. Before the program shuts itself down (the usual remedy for such an error), it flashes a dialog box telling you it's closing because it has done something it shouldn't have. Well, whatever keys you hit caused an event, which in turn caused you to be notified before the program terminated. But so-called fatal errors are by no means the only kind of events out there—an event occurs each time someone logs on to a network, browses a network, or uses the Event Viewer, just to name a few examples.

NOTE	Computer programmers are inordinately fond of language that sounds catastrophic. Do not be alarmed by terms like *illegal operation* or *fatal error.* Neither of these messages is anything to worry about. It just means the program and the operating system have disagreed on some small matter. And with Windows NT Workstation, the operating system always emerges as the victor. Just close the program and start it up again—and hope that this time they can play together nicely.

The NT Workstation Event Viewer can provide you with access to three different event logs: System Logs, Security Logs, and Application Logs. Depending on your network privileges and the way the system administrator has things configured, you may have access to one or more of these logs for your computer and possibly also for other computers on the network. In most situations, there's no reason for you to concern yourself with the Event Viewer, but in case you're curious, follow these steps to have a look at the System Log for your computer:

1. Click on the Start button on the Taskbar and select Programs.
2. From the menu that appears, select Administrative Tools (Common) and then Event Viewer.
3. This should bring up the main Event Viewer window shown in Figure 15.1.

Event Viewer - System Log on \\RCISRV2

Log View Options Help

Date	Time	Source	Category	Event	User	Compu
6/30/96	12:22:32 PM	NetDDE	None	64	N/A	RCIS
6/30/96	11:46:49 AM	W3SVC	None	101	N/A	RCIS
6/30/96	11:46:08 AM	EventLog	None	6005	N/A	RCIS
6/30/96	11:46:48 AM	W3SVC	None	101	N/A	RCIS
6/29/96	10:04:51 PM	Rdr	None	3012	N/A	RCIS
6/29/96	9:41:21 PM	W3SVC	None	101	N/A	RCIS
6/29/96	9:40:29 PM	EventLog	None	6005	N/A	RCIS
6/29/96	9:41:21 PM	W3SVC	None	101	N/A	RCIS
6/29/96	8:55:13 PM	Rdr	None	3012	N/A	RCIS
6/29/96	8:35:51 PM	Rdr	None	3012	N/A	RCIS
6/29/96	8:10:04 PM	Rdr	None	3012	N/A	RCIS
6/29/96	7:58:56 PM	W3SVC	None	101	N/A	RCIS
6/29/96	7:58:17 PM	EventLog	None	6005	N/A	RCIS
6/29/96	7:58:56 PM	W3SVC	None	101	N/A	RCIS
6/29/96	7:14:31 PM	EventLog	None	6005	N/A	RCIS
6/29/96	7:18:28 PM	Print	None	20	SYSTEM	RCIS

FIGURE 15.1: The System Log for your computer displays various kinds of events.

The System Log for your computer can tell you lots of things, including when somebody last logged on to your computer and when the browser (the utility that lets you examine the network) was last invoked.

Each event is logged by date and time, each has an event code attached to it, and many other facts and figures as well. The Event Viewer provides far more information than most of us can ever use (assuming we're not the ones responsible for the overall health of the network).

Performance Monitor

The Performance Monitor, as its name implies, is a tool for measuring the performance of your computer or (privileges allowing) other computers on a network. Using the Performance Monitor on a given computer, you can view the performance of objects, such as processors, memory, cache, threads, and processes.

With the click of a few buttons, you can access the Performance Monitor's charting, alerting, or reporting capabilities, and you can make it create log files among other things. Most of these capabilities should interest no one except the system administrator, but in case you're curious, here's how to create a couple of basic charts so you can see how your machine is doing.

To start the Performance Monitor and create a chart that shows you what your computer's CPU is doing at the moment, follow these steps:

1. Click on the Start button on the Taskbar and select Programs.
2. From the menu that appears, select Administrative Tools (Common) and then Performance Monitor.
3. This should bring up the main Performance Monitor window shown in Figure 15.2.
4. Pull down the Edit menu and select Add to Chart.
5. On the Add to Chart dialog box, pull down the Object list and select Processor.
6. Highlight %Processor Time on the Counter box.
7. The other options on this dialog box pertain mostly to the style of the chart, so you shouldn't need to change them; however, to add your computer's CPU to the chart, click on the Add button and then click Done.
8. You should now see a chart that resembles Figure 15.3.

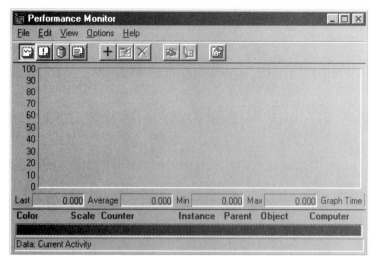

FIGURE 15.2:
The main Performance Monitor window is the blank slate on which you can chart your system's performance.

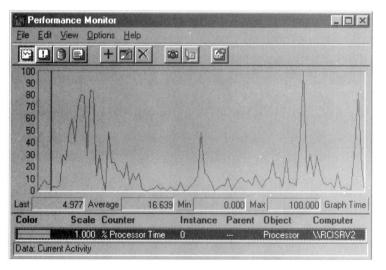

FIGURE 15.3:
Charting your computer's CPU time lets you see how you're using that processing power.

This chart shows you the fraction of time your computer's CPU spends doing useful work. Maybe it's a good thing your boss can't automatically create a chart like this for you; you never know what might happen if that were possible.

Now, if you'd like to get really fancy, you can add another element to your chart. Assuming you've already created a chart showing your computer's CPU, follow these steps to chart some memory information:

1. With the CPU chart on your screen, pull down the Edit menu and select Add to Chart.
2. On the Add to Chart dialog box, pull down the Object list and select Memory.
3. Highlight Pages/sec on the Counter box.
4. Again, the other options on this dialog box pertain mostly to the style of the chart, so you shouldn't need to change them; however, to add your computer's memory to the chart, click on the Add button and then click Done.

The chart in Figure 15.4 shows you the CPU information you added before, plus information about how fast this computer's memory is working. Specifically, the Pages/sec reading tells you how many *pages* (a unit of memory) are read from or written to the disk to resolve memory references to pages that were not in memory at the time of the references. Don't be concerned about what this means; once again, this is the kind of thing somebody is paying your system administrator to know.

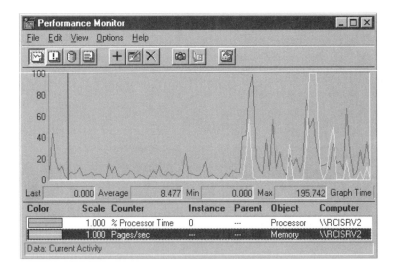

FIGURE 15.4:
Here's where you can see how your CPU and memory are doing.

> **NOTE** While these things are all great fun, they're probably not part of your job. So if you get caught, just blame this book. Your boss can't fire *me*.

Remote Access Admin

Depending on how NT Workstation is set up, you may or may not see this item on the Administrative Tools (Common) menu on your computer. If you need to set up Remote Access, Chapter 17 will tell you how.

User Manager

The User Manager in NT Workstation is sort of the junior version of the User Manager for Domains, which the system administrator uses to add new users and make password settings, among many other things. The version available to you is less powerful, but it does have uses.

Making a Group

You can definitely do one thing with User Manager: make and administer a local group. For example, you may be working with several people on a project, and you want to keep all the relevant files on your computer in a folder that all members of the project team can have access to. However, a whole bunch of other people on the network have access to various items on your computer but don't have any business in the project's folder.

Of course, the system administrator could take care of this for you, but if these things come up fairly often for a fairly large number of users, the administrator may turn surly. It's always better to take care of your own business when you can. With User Manager, you can make the team a group and grant everyone in the group permission to use the project's files.

Here's how to do it:

1. Click on the Start button and select Programs ➤ Administrative Tools (Common) ➤ User Manager.
2. In the dialog box that opens, select New Local Group from the User Menu.
3. On the next screen, you're prompted for the name of the group; type one in.
4. Then click the Add button to add members to the group.
5. In the Add Users and Groups dialog box (Figure 15. 5), click on the names of people or global groups and then the Add button. Those selected will appear in the window labeled Add Names.
6. When you have everyone you want, click the OK button and return to the New Local Group dialog box.

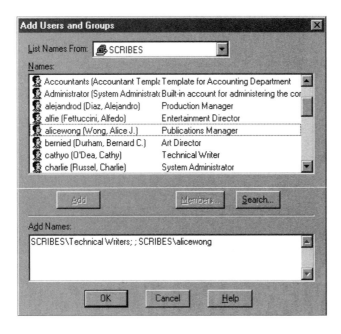

FIGURE 15.5:
Making a new local group

As you can see in Figure 15.6, the New Local Group consists of the Administrator, the Production Manager (Alice Wong), and all members of the Technical Writing group.

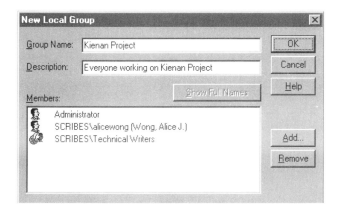

FIGURE 15.6:
The members of the new Kienan Project group

NOTE   If you want only some members of the Technical Writing group, you'll have to select them individually from the Add Users and Groups dialog box because there's no other way to select only part of a group.

To remove an individual or group from your group, just highlight the name in the New Local Group dialog box and select Remove.

Your group will still need permission to use the folder (and files) involved in the project. See Chapter 8 for information on how to grant permissions.

Windows NT Diagnostics

When you select NT Diagnostics from the Administrative Tools menu, you'll open the multiple-paged dialog box shown in Figure 15.7.

As you can see, the Windows NT Diagnostics page has nine tabs, each of which provides a different kind of information. Here's a rundown on what each tab shows you and an evaluation of what it's good for (or not).

FIGURE 15.7:
Diagnostics consists of several pages.

Version

The Version tab informs you which version of NT Workstation you're running, what kind of processor is inside your computer, and who this copy of NT Workstation is registered to. The most useful item here is probably the version number, which comes in handy if you're having problems and require tech support.

System

The System tab, shown in Figure 15.8, provides BIOS and CPU information about your computer. This tab falls into the "just in case you're curious" category because most of us don't need to worry about such matters (unless you're a harried system administrator trying to fix a BIOS problem—in which case you're reading the wrong book!).

Display

The Display tab, depicted in Figure 15.9, shows you video adapter, display, and driver information, including resolution settings, refresh speed, type of video card, and amount of video memory. You can also access this information through the Display icon in the Control Panel (see Chapters 3 or 14 for the details of how to do this), where you can actually change these settings should the need to do so ever arise.

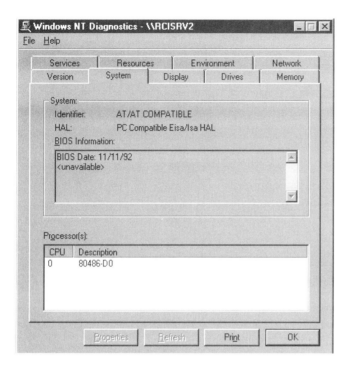

FIGURE 15.8:
The System tab displays BIOS and CPU information.

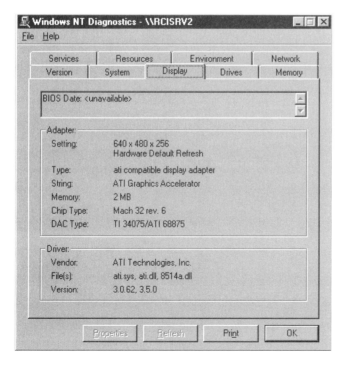

FIGURE 15.9:
The Display tab shows you more video information than you'll ever want to know.

Drives

The Drives tab (see Figure 15.10) provides information about floppy, hard, CD-ROM, and any other types of drives installed on your system. If you click on the plus sign (+) next to Local Hard Drives and then double-click on the hard drive you'd like to look at, you'll see a Properties dialog box with two tabs. The General tab displays the drive label, serial number, and free and used clusters and bytes, while the File System tab tells you what type of file system(s) is on this hard drive and the maximum number of characters that can be used in a filename.

Note that most of this information is also on the drive's Properties tab, which you can access by right-clicking on the relevant drive's icon once you've opened My Computer.

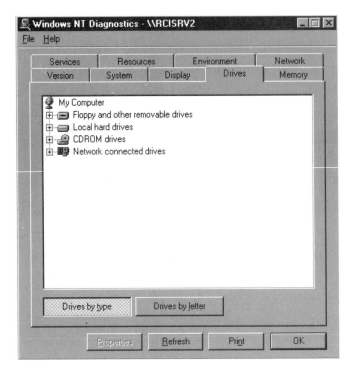

FIGURE 15.10:
The Drives tab tells you about the drives installed on your system.

Memory

The Memory tab, shown in Figure 15.11, definitely tells you more about various kinds of memory than you'll ever want to know. The only interesting thing is the

Physical Memory box. The number labeled Total is important if and when anyone asks you how much memory is in your computer.

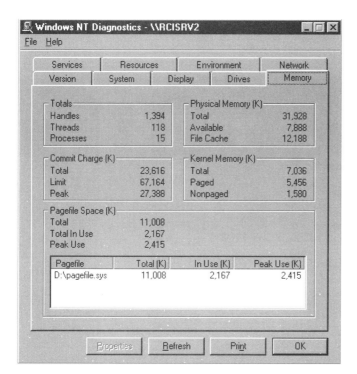

FIGURE 15.11:
The Memory tab provides an impressive array of facts and figures.

Services, Resources, Environment & Network

Feel free to take a look at these tabs. If you know what the information in them means, you are also free to modify what can be modified. But in general, avoid these unless you have a genuine system pro at your side.

Next Step

Now that you've seen that the administrative tools have little to do with your life, we're going to move on to some subjects that are a good deal more fun (and relevant), namely the communications within your network.

Chapter 16

COMMUNICATING WITHIN YOUR NETWORK

- **Using Peer Web Services**
- **Creating a Microsoft Mail postoffice**
- **Adminstering a Microsoft Mail postoffice**
- **Chatting with your colleagues using Chat**

Because the whole purpose of having a network operating system is to be able to communicate with other users, NT Workstation comes with a full complement of tools to assist in doing just that. In this chapter, you'll see how you can use NT Workstation to share information with users on your local network and, if the system is so configured, beyond and into the Internet.

The *Internet,* as you probably know by now, is the global network of computers everyone's been making such a fuss over. Many kinds of computers located almost anywhere in the world can connect to the Internet; what's important is that all these computers communicate using a common language.

By contrast, an *intranet* refers to a network that uses what's called *Web technology.* That means you can open Internet Explorer and see screens that look like those on the World Wide Web—except these screens are inside your network.

If you've never seen the World Wide Web, that's okay. The reason networks are starting to make themselves into intranets, is that Web pages are a very easy way for users to share information.

Internet Information Server

Microsoft's Internet Information Server, which runs under Windows NT Server 4, is in most cases the easiest way to create an intranet since it is the only Web server integrated into Windows NT. Its purpose is to provide WWW, FTP, and Gopher services, so users on a network can communicate with each other and potentially (provided the system administrator approves and has set network permissions accordingly) with the rest of the world.

You'll probably need to ask your system administrator some questions about network configuration to find out what is and isn't possible on your particular network, but with the Internet Information Server, achieving connectivity is certainly far less painful than it used to be.

Peer Web Services

With Microsoft's Peer Web Services you can not only create a personal Web site on your NT Workstation, you can also share information over your corporate intranet as easily as you share files or, network permissions allowing, publish your personal Web page to Internet users.

Other network users can access your files using Internet Explorer or their Web browser of choice because your workstation will use the *HyperText Transfer Protocol* (HTTP) to respond to browser requests. HTTP is the communications protocol used by the Internet's World Wide Web to allow users from anywhere in the world to view text, graphics, sound, and movies on their Desktop, even though the source of the text or graphics could be on the other side of the world. In addition, your workstation can be configured to provide FTP and Gopher services—but that's a story for another book. In this section, we'll keep things pretty simple: we'll tell you why you might want to consider using Peer Web Services, we'll show you how to install Peer Web Services, and we'll show you the basics of using Peer Web Services to set up a personal Web page.

What Can Peer Web Services Do for Me?

"But why might I want to use Peer Web Services?" you may ask. Some of the uses to which Peer Web Services can be put include publishing a personal home page; publishing project documents (schedules, memos, and reports, for example); publishing interactive programs; providing your remote sales force easy access to your sales database; and using an order-tracking database.

No doubt you can also think of other uses that haven't even occurred to anyone else yet. Essentially, Peer Web Services give you a more sophisticated way to share information than plain-old file-sharing or the clunky Clipbook (described in Chapter 18).

If you also plan to share information with people who aren't connected directly to your network, Peer Web Services gives you a means of doing so that won't compromise network security. That will definitely make your system administrator happy since he or she has worked so hard to get and keep the whole network running smoothly.

While you'll inevitably need to consult your trusty system administrator to get your personal Web page up and running, here, in short form, is what you need to do to prepare your workstation for using Peer Web Services to share information with your friends and colleagues.

Installing Peer Web Services

Installing Peer Web Services is simple once you've got your NT Workstation set up and your network connection configured. Here, in a series of steps, is exactly what you need to do:

1. Insert the NT Workstation 4 CD-ROM into the appropriate drive.
2. Click on the Start button on the Taskbar, select Settings, and then select Control Panel.
3. In the Control Panel, double-click the Network icon.
4. On the Network Properties sheet, click the Services tab and then click the Add button.
5. From the Network Services list, select Microsoft Peer Web Services and then click OK.
6. Type in the drive letter where your CD-ROM is located and click OK.
7. Follow the instructions on the screen. For information about any of the Setup dialog boxes, click the Help button.

That's all there is to installing Microsoft's Peer Web Services. Now let's move on to how to use it once you've got it.

How to Publish Information Using Peer Web Services

Assuming you've got Peer Web Services installed and running, you're all ready to create that personal Web page on your intranet. Providing information with Peer Web Services really couldn't be much easier; if the files you'd like to share are already in HTML format, just add them to the appropriate folder. The *HyperText Markup Language* is the document formatting language used to display Internet Web pages to people using a wide variety of different computers with as little difference and loss of information as the displaying computer will support.

For those of you who aren't as Web-savvy as some quite yet, it's handy to know you can use any text editor, such as Notepad or WordPad , to create and edit your HTML files. As the folks at Microsoft are quick to tell you, however, you'll probably find that using an HTML editor, such as Internet Assistant for Microsoft Word, *is* easier.

Suit yourself, but one way or another, you'll have to get those HTML tags into your files in order to make them look the way you want them to. Also, if you're planning to include images, sounds, or animation in your personal Web page, you'll need the appropriate software to create and edit those files, so be prepared. Once you've got your HTML files, put them in the folder mentioned above and you're ready to roll. Your friends and colleagues should have instant access to the information you've chosen to share.

Figure 16.1 shows an intranet page for a company's HR department. A page like this could also include links to a form for making your vacation request or links to pages showing internal job openings.

NOTE For those wanting to know a great deal more about how to create and publish a Web page, as well as the finer details of HTML, a good starting place would be *The ABC's of the Internet* (Sybex 1996) by Christian Crumlish. It's an excellent introduction to the subject.

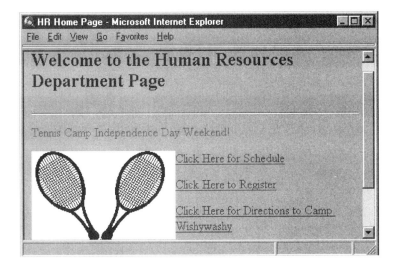

FIGURE 16.1:
A page on an intranet

Microsoft Mail

Although it's easy enough to communicate with colleagues on your LAN using a variety of e-mail packages, you may want to consider using Microsoft Mail instead because it was created specifically with Workgroups in mind. One significant advantage of Microsoft Mail is that if you create a post office for your workgroup, everyone will have easy access to messages, and you won't have to remember to cc: everybody in sight. In this section, you'll learn how to set up and administer a Microsoft Mail postoffice to help you work more efficiently.

Creating a New Microsoft Mail Postoffice

To begin setting up your Microsoft Mail postoffice, open the Control Panel and double-click on the Microsoft Mail Postoffice icon (if you've installed it with NT Setup). This should fire up the Microsoft Workgroup Postoffice Admin Wizard, shown in Figure 16.2. Like the other NT Workstation Wizards, this one will guide you through all the steps you need to take, so do what it says and soon your Microsoft Mail postoffice will be up and running.

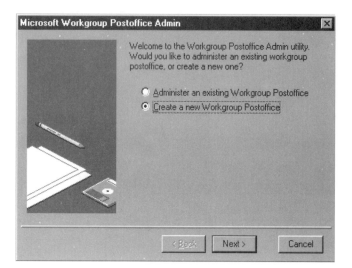

FIGURE 16.2:
The Microsoft Workgroup Postoffice Admin Wizard will show you what you need to do to set up and administer a Microsoft Mail postoffice.

Once you've specified the directory in which your post office will be located, you'll be confronted with the dialog box shown in Figure 16.3. Type your full name in the Name box, then type your mailbox name, password, and other information in the appropriate boxes. It's important to fill this dialog box in completely and correctly because this information will let other people know who's responsible for administering this particular Microsoft Mail postoffice and where he or she can be found.

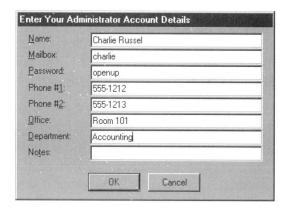

FIGURE 16.3:
Fill in the information on this dialog box completely so users will know who's in charge of this post office.

NOTE If you've just created a new Microsoft Mail postoffice, be sure the directory in which the post office is located is a shared directory; if it isn't, other users in your workgroup won't be able to access the post office. You'll also want to make sure you give users full access to the shared directory. If, for any reason, you want an additional layer of security in place, you can assign a password to this directory to ensure that only users with the proper permissions will be allowed to view its contents.

Administering a Microsoft Mail PostOffice

Now that you've got a post office, you need to specify who will be allowed to use it so start by adding yourself to the list of users in your workgroup post office. To do this, double-click on the Mail icon in the Control Panel. This should bring up the Mail Properties sheet shown in Figure 16.4.

FIGURE 16.4:
The Mail Property sheet is where you'll add users to your Microsoft Mail postoffice.

Then just follow these steps:

1. You'll notice that, at the moment, there's no profile in sight, so your first task will be to create one. Click on the Add button and you should see the Microsoft Exchange Setup Wizard, which will guide you through the process of configuring your profile (Figure 16. 5).

FIGURE 16.5:
Starting the Exchange Setup Wizard

2. Make sure Microsoft Mail is checked and then click the Next button. The Wizard will automatically find the Microsoft Mail postoffice you just created; if it doesn't, you may need to click the Browse button and point it to the proper place.

3. Since you just created this post office, your name will be the only one on the list, so select it, click Next, and be prepared to enter your Microsoft Mail password (the one you entered in the dialog box shown in Figure 16.3) to prove that you really are who you say you are.

4. Once you've successfully cleared that hurdle, you'll need to enter the path to your personal address book and your personal folders. You'll be asked if you'd like to add Microsoft Exchange to your Startup Group. With that, you're almost ready to start using Microsoft Mail to communicate with your colleagues.

NOTE If you put Exchange in your Startup Group, it means that whenever you log on to your workstation, Exchange (and thus Microsoft Mail) will start automatically.

5. Your last task before putting your Microsoft Mail postoffice into service is to add the names of the people in your workgroup to the list of users with permission to access it. To do this, return to the Control Panel and double-click on the Microsoft Mail Postoffice icon. This time, instead of opting to Create a New Workgroup Postoffice, you'll want to Administer an existing Workgroup Postoffice, as shown in Figure 16.6.

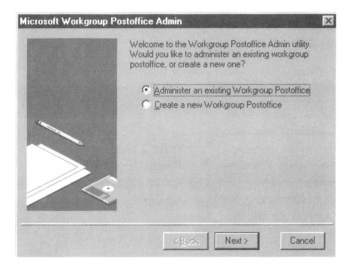

FIGURE 16.6:
Administering an existing Microsoft Mail postoffice is easy, thanks to the Microsoft Workgroup Postoffice Admin Wizard.

6. Once you've supplied your administrator's password, you should see the Postoffice Manager dialog box shown in Figure 16.7. This is where you'll add users to your post office workgroup.

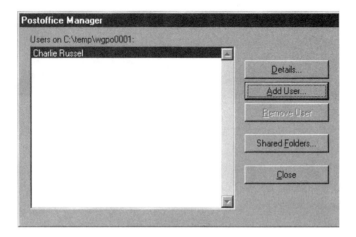

FIGURE 16.7:
The Postoffice Manager dialog box is the key to easy administration of your Microsoft Mail postoffice.

- To add a new user, click the Add User button, type in the appropriate information on the Add User dialog box (see Figure 16.8), and click OK. Your new user should now appear on the Postoffice Manager dialog box.

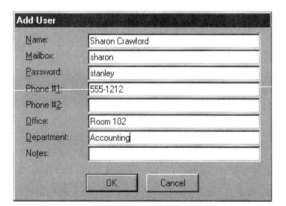

FIGURE 16.8:
The Add User dialog box lets you add users to your Microsoft Mail workgroup.

- To add another user, click the Add User button again and repeat the process.
- If you want to remove a user from your workgroup, highlight the name of the user in question and click the Remove User button.

7. When you're finished adding and removing users, click Close and you're through. Your workgroup is now ready to use its Microsoft Mail postoffice.

Chat

The Chat tool is another handy thing to know about, especially if you're in the habit of communicating with your colleagues over your network instead of by telephone. Using the Chat tool, you can "dial" someone at another computer on the network and they can accept your "call", so you can "talk" to each other by typing messages on the computer screen. Sound strange? Perhaps, but it's useful all the same.

To find the Chat tool, click on the Start button on the Taskbar, then select Programs ➤ Accessories ➤ Chat. This will open the Chat window shown in Figure 16.9.

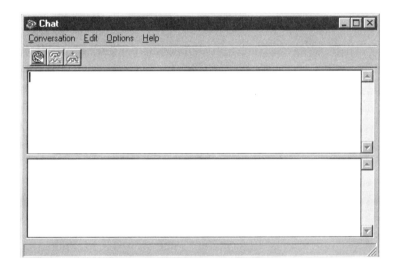

FIGURE 16.9:
The Chat tool lets you "talk" to other people on your network.

To call someone at another computer, you click the Make a Call button on the Chat tool's toolbar. This will open the window in Figure 16.10.

Highlight the name of the computer that the person you'd like to call is working on, click OK, and your call will be placed. On the receiving end, an icon will start flashing on the Toolbar that will include the name of the calling computer (not *your* name, just the computer's).

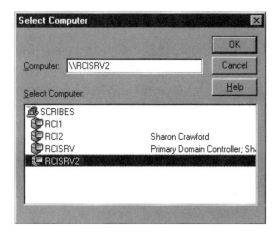

FIGURE 16.10:
Choose your victim on the Select Computer dialog box.

The receiving party has only to click on the icon, and the Chat window will open. The sender writes in the top of the window, and the receiver sees the text in the bottom of her window (Figure 16.11).

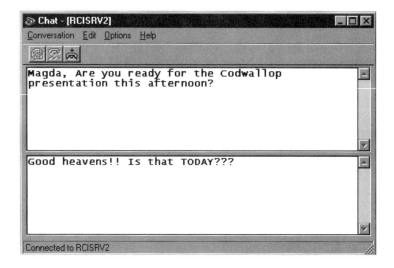

FIGURE 16.11:
A Chat in progress

 When you're finished, use either the Hang Up button on the toolbar or just close the window.

Although you can cut, copy, and paste text using the Edit menu and customize the Chat tool using the Options menu, you may find you don't use these functions very often. After all, if your communication needs to be more elaborate, chances are you'll use e-mail or Peer Web Services rather than the Chat tool. Still, there are times when the Chat tool comes in handy—if only to find out if your buddy is ready to go to lunch.

> **NOTE** As silly as the Chat tool is, people *love* it. So your not-so-fun-loving-system-administrator may not have installed it.

Next Step

In this chapter, you've seen how easy it is to communicate with people on your network. In the next chapter, we'll expand our horizons a bit and figure out how to communicate with the rest of the world.

Chapter 17

COMMUNICATING WITH THE WIDER WORLD

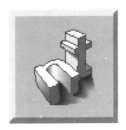

- Setting up Exchange
- Using Exchange to send and receive mail
- Setting up Remote Access
- Using Internet Explorer

During the first decade of PC history, most people who had computers—whether at work or at home—used them as independent, stand-alone machines. But now it's a rare computer that isn't connected to other computers in some way.

The most obvious types of connection are the networks that Windows NT Workstation machines operate so well on. Even in the absence of an ordinary network, computers also connect to the Internet, to mail services, and to commercial sites, such as America Online and CompuServe.

Now with Exchange and Internet Explorer coming as built-in operating system components, along with the concurrent rise in intranet Web publishing, it's becoming increasingly difficult to differentiate between internal and external connections. This raises plenty of security issues for your network administrator, but not for you. You just get to use and enjoy these new tools.

> **TIP**
> See "Internet Explorer" later in this chapter for more on the Internet and the intranet.

Exchange Basics

Exchange is a tool that made its debut in Windows 95 and is now part of the new NT Workstation interface. Exchange in its most basic form allows you to send and receive messages via the Internet or the Microsoft Mail program.

There are two versions of Exchange. The basic one that ships in the box with Windows NT Workstation 4 is what I'm describing in this chapter. When you double-click on the Inbox icon to open Exchange, you'll see an informational screen that announces Windows Messaging.

However, there's also a product called Exchange Server that may be installed somewhere on your network. If Exchange Server is installed, when you click on the Inbox icon, the opening screen is called Exchange. On a network with Exchange Server, your messaging will work as described here—except you'll have *additional* features to use.

> **NOTE**
> This chapter covers the basic Windows Messaging and Exchange functions—even when the screens look slightly different, everything works in the same way.

Setting Up Exchange

Double-click on the Inbox icon on your Desktop to start Exchange. The Microsoft Exchange Setup Wizard runs when you first opt to install the mail and/or messaging services. This usually happens when NT Workstation is installed, but it can always be done later by using Add/Remove Programs in the Control Panel.

Before You Go Further

There are a couple of terms used in Exchange that may not be familiar, so here are the definitions:

Services In NT Workstation, a service (also called an *information service*) is any of the various ways you connect to the outside world using Exchange. This includes

- Internet mail going by way of your Internet provider
- Microsoft Mail messages going to others on your network

Profiles Profiles are made up of combinations of services. You'll probably have only one profile on your computer. This profile will consist of the services you've installed and the configurations for each. The default profile is called MS Exchange Settings or Windows Messaging. You may need multiple profiles if more than one person uses the computer or you have more than one e-mail account with a particular provider. (Information on how to do this is in the section called "Creating Additional Profiles" later in this chapter.)

Running the Wizard

Even though getting everything set up requires a lot of steps, each step is quite easy, so don't be intimidated by the size of the list. With each item, I've also included an explanatory sentence or two. Here are the steps that you'll be presented with (you may not see every step, depending on what services you select) after double-clicking on the Inbox for the first time:

1. **You'll see a list of what the Wizard calls information services.** The list may be a very short one and consist of Internet Mail only, or it may include Microsoft Mail or other services (Figure 17.1). You check the boxes in front of the services you want to use and then click on Next.

2. **Microsoft Mail postoffice location.** If you're on a network that has Microsoft Mail, you'll need to supply the path to the post office. Ask your system administrator where the post office is.

3. **Select your MS Mail name from the list.** For an ongoing MS Mail system, you'll see a list of names. Select yours. If you don't see your name, ask your system administrator to add you to the list.

4. **Supply your mailbox (if necessary) and your password.** For an existing mail system (Figure 17.2), you'll already have a password. If you're installing Microsoft Mail for the first time, choose a new password.

FIGURE 17.1:
The Microsoft Exchange Setup Wizard starts with the information services available.

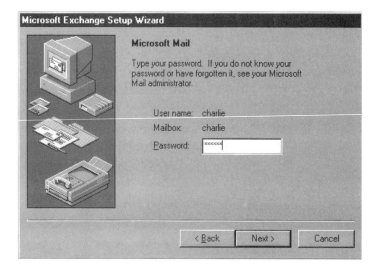

FIGURE 17.2:
If Microsoft Mail already exists on your network, the screen will ask only for your password.

5.   **Select Internet mail connection.** If you connect to an Internet provider using a modem and a phone line, select Modem. That means you have what's called a *dial-up connection.* If your connection is made through an adapter on your network, select Network.

6.   **Phone Connection for Internet mail.** For a dial-up connection, the next window asks for the name of the computer you're dialing. This isn't anything official, just a name you give to identify the service. (You may

have other dial-up services now or later—perhaps connecting from home to your work site—that will also require a name.)

7. **Phone number for Internet access.** Here you provide the phone number for a dial-up connection. The next window informs you of your success at creating a connection. This newly made connection will be placed in your Dial-Up Networking folder where you can later double-click on it to start the connection.

8. **Mail server name or IP address.** No matter how your Internet mail connection is made, you'll need to provide the name or IP address of the computer that receives your Internet mail (see Figure 17.3). Your Internet Service Provider supplies this information.

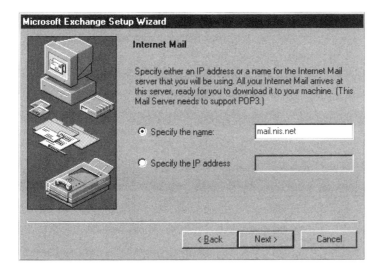

FIGURE 17.3:
Here's where you provide the Internet address for your mail server.

9. **Selective or automatic mail transfer.** How much Internet mail do you get? Use Selective if you want to use Remote Preview to filter out mail you don't want, Automatic if you want the system to automatically establish the connection and transfer all your mail whenever you open Exchange.

10. **E-mail address and full name.** Enter your Internet e-mail address in the format **name@domain** and your full name (as you want it to appear on your e-mail).

11. **Mailbox name and password.** Your mailbox name is provided by your Internet Service Provider. It's how the mail server identifies your mail location, and it's not the same as your e-mail address or the Microsoft Mail mailbox.

12. **The path to your personal address book.** The system will create a location for your address book. This is where you'll enter the e-mail addresses you use.

13. **The path to your personal folder file.** This is the storage spot for incoming and outgoing messages. More than one personal file (as well as address book) can be created if you have need for them.

14. **Want Exchange in the Startup group?** If Exchange is in the Startup Group, it will start itself whenever you log on to the computer. This can be handy in a minor sort of way—after all, you can get at Exchange anytime by double-clicking on the Inbox icon. But it's up to you which you prefer.

Looking at What You've Done

Now you get a list of the information services that are ready to use (see Figure 17.4). Most of the settings you choose during this installation are done without any real knowledge of how the choices will work out in actual practice. Fortunately, all of them can be changed—in fact, the whole next part of this chapter is about how to make those fine-tuning adjustments.

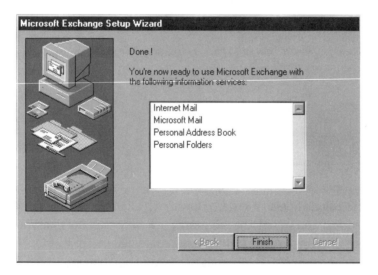

FIGURE 17.4:
Now you're ready to use any and all of the Exchange services.

Working with Messages

By default, the message addresses are kept in a file called MAILBOX.PAB in the Exchange directory. This file is referred to in and around Exchange as your Personal Address Book.

Adding Addresses

To add someone's address to the Personal Address Book, follow these steps:

1. Double-click on the Inbox icon on your Desktop.
2. Select Address Book from the Tools menu.
3. Select New Entry from the File menu. This will open the New Entry dialog box, shown in Figure 17.5. The entry types listed will depend on the types of information services you have installed.

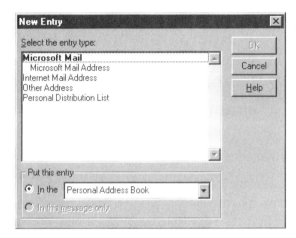

FIGURE 17.5:
Select the entry type from this list.

4. Select one of the address entry types and then click on OK.
5. Provide the information requested, and click on OK when you're done.

Now, whenever you select New Message from the Compose menu, you can click on the To button. This takes you to your Personal Address Book where you can select a recipient or add a new one.

The bad news is that if your old pal Bill has more than one e-mail address, you'll have to make a separate entry for each address. And when you click on the To button on a new message, you'll see your friend's name three times with no indication of which address is which.

Admittedly, this is not the smartest feature in NT Workstation, but you can bypass it somewhat. Plan ahead, and when you add a new name to the address book, include a notation to help you later (as shown in Figure 17.6).

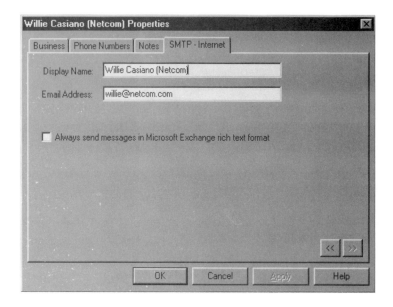

FIGURE 17.6:
Adding a notation to names that have more than one address can be of help later.

Sending Messages

To send a message, double-click on the Inbox on your Desktop to open Exchange. Select New Message from the Compose menu. Address and type your message (see Figure 17.7), and then select Send from the File menu.

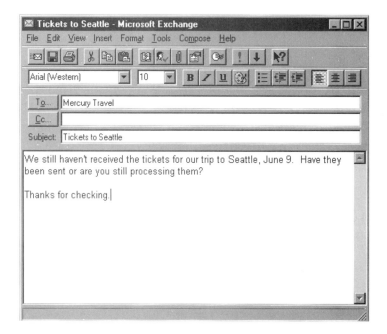

FIGURE 17.7:
When typing a message in Exchange, the subject line becomes the name of the message.

TIP   If you have Remote Mail enabled, you'll have to select Deliver Now from the Microsoft Exchange Tools menu to send mail.

Making a Distribution List

Sometimes you need to send a single message to a whole group of people. Of course, you can do the messages one at a time. But for the sake of efficiency (and your sanity), you can easily set up one or more of your own personal distribution lists. Just follow these steps:

1. Double-click the Inbox icon and click the Address Book button.
2. Select New Entry from the File menu.
3. In the New Entry dialog box, highlight Personal Distribution List and click OK.
4. Type in a name for the list, then click the Add/Remove Members button.
5. Your Address Book will open, as shown in Figure 17.8. Highlight the people you want to be on your distribution list and click Members. When the list is complete, click OK.

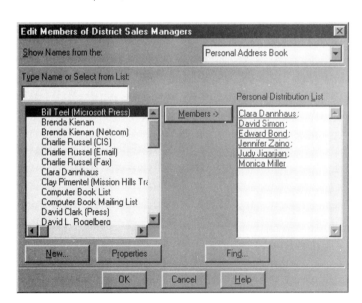

FIGURE 17.8:
Selecting the people to be on the distribution list

6. The window for the new distribution list opens (Figure 17.9). Click OK once again.

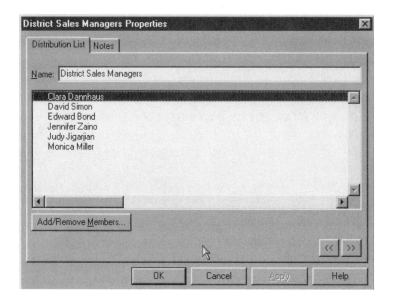

FIGURE 17.9:
The sales managers distribution list

The distribution list will show as an entry in your address book, and you can select it just as you'd select an individual recipient. You can make as many distribution lists as you need.

Receiving Messages

When you open Exchange, the way new mail will appear in your Inbox depends on the mail's source. The following sections describe these different ways.

> **TIP**
>
> Exchange is a little easier to understand if you select View ➤ Folders. This makes it easier to see what you've sent, what's been received, and so forth.

Internet Mail

How Internet mail is delivered to your Inbox depends on whether your Internet connection is a so-called *dial-up connection* (you use a modem and a phone line) or a *LAN connection* (the connecting device is somewhere on your network, and the connection is made there). Either way, you can go get your mail when you want it, or you can have it done automatically.

With an automatic connection, your Internet mail server is queried as soon as you open Exchange and thereafter as often as you specify. For a dial-up connection, that means Exchange will open the phone line, dial your Internet service provider, and connect to your mailbox.

To set up an automatic connection, follow these steps:

1. Open Exchange and select Services from the Tools menu.
2. Highlight Internet Mail and click on Properties.
3. Click on the Connection tab, make sure you have Work Offline and Use Remote Mail unchecked, and then click on Schedule Options.
4. Select how often you want the network to check for mail messages. You then select OK four times.
5. You will need to log off Exchange and then log back on again for your change to take effect.

Setting Up Remote Mail Preview

With Remote Mail Preview, Exchange will call your mail server, show you the headers for any messages waiting there, and then hang up. You can take your time selecting the ones you want to read and then have Exchange initiate a second call to transfer them to the Exchange Inbox.

To set up Remote Preview:

1. Open Exchange, select Services from the Tools menu, highlight Internet Mail, and click on Properties.
2. Click on the Connection tab. Make sure you have Work Offline and Use Remote Mail checked.
3. Click on OK three times (the second time is an alert saying the change will take effect next time you log on). Close and then restart the Exchange.

To check for mail, follow these steps:

1. When you want to check for mail, select Remote Mail from the Tools menu.

2. From the Tools menu for Remote Mail, choose to Connect. Mark the messages you want to move to your Inbox, the messages you want to copy to your Inbox, and the messages you want to delete.

3. Select Connect from the Tools menu, and the messages will be transferred, copied, or deleted.

Reading Messages

To read a message in your Inbox, just double-click on it. For a mail message, a window like the one in Figure 17.10 will open. If you want to know what any of the buttons mean, just position your pointer over one, and a descriptive box will pop open.

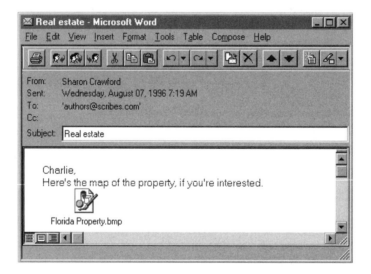

FIGURE 17.10:
Reading a new message

TIP

If you're used to getting Internet mail using other software, you'll notice the Exchange window shows only the name of the person sending you the mail with no clue as to the origins. Most of the time this doesn't matter, but if you need to see the entire Internet header, select Properties from the File menu, and then look at the Headers tab.

Forwarding a Message

When you receive a message, the Inbox window will have a button for forwarding the message on to another recipient. To forward a message, click on the Forward button.

This will open a window with the original message in it (Figure 17.11).

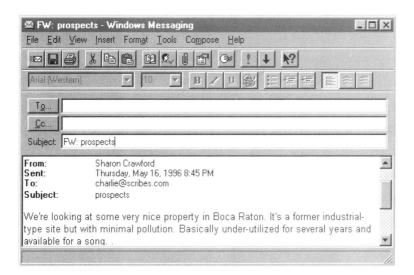

FIGURE 17.11:
Forwarding a message to someone is as easy as can be.

From here, you can send your forwarded message directly on its way by specifying the recipient in the To box and then selecting Send from the File menu. Alternatively, you can specify the recipient and then add your own text to the message by clicking in the text window and typing whatever it is you've got to say. When you're done, send the message as you usually would.

More on Profiles

As discussed earlier in this chapter, an *information service* is any of the various ways your computer connects to the outside world using Exchange. This includes local network mail and Internet mail. A *profile* is made up of a combination of information services you have installed and their configuration.

The following sections show you how to set up more than one profile on your computer, how to use multiple profiles, and how to customize them.

Creating Additional Profiles

The default profile for Exchange is MS Exchange Settings, but if you have multiple e-mail accounts at the same Internet provider or multiple people using the same computer, you'll need to set up one or more additional profiles. Here's how to do one:

1. Double-click on the Mail icon in the Control Panel, and then click on Show Profiles.
2. Click on the Add button to open the window shown in Figure 17.12.

FIGURE 17.12:
Select services for the new profile.

3. Select the information services you want to use in this profile, and then click on Next.
4. Enter a descriptive name for the profile (that is, something more memorable than MS Exchange Settings 1); click Next.
5. From here on, the Inbox Setup Wizard guides you through the same process you went through for the first Exchange setup. For a refresher course, consult the first part of this chapter.

NOTE On some computers running NT Workstation 4, the default profile may be called Windows Messaging. It matters not. You make new profiles in exactly the same way.

Selecting the One to Use

By default, the MS Exchange Settings profile will be the one loaded when you start Exchange. To use another profile on a regular basis, you'll have to open Mail in the Control Panel, click on Show Profiles, and select the one to start up with (see Figure 17.13).

FIGURE 17.13:
You can choose the profile you want to start Exchange with.

If you switch back and forth often enough for that to be a nuisance, you can set things up so you get a prompt each time you open Exchange. Just follow these steps:

1. Double-click on the Inbox icon on your Desktop.
2. Select Options from the Tool menu.
3. On the General page, select Prompt for a Profile to be Used.
4. Click on OK when you're done.

The next time you start Exchange you'll see a window like the one shown in Figure 17.14. Just click on the arrow next to the Profile Name box, and choose the profile you want to use.

Customizing Your Profiles

Unless you make some changes, all your profiles will use the same address book and the same set of folders for incoming and outgoing messages. This can be a bit of a problem if you don't want all your incoming (and outgoing) messages to be mixed together.

FIGURE 17.14:
Choose the profile that's best
for the job at hand.

To make separate sets of folders for your profiles, follow these steps:

1. Double-click on the Mail icon in the Control Panel. Click on the Show Profiles button.

2. Select the Profile you want to give the new folders to and click on Properties.

3. Highlight Personal Folders and click on the Remove button. After it's deleted from the profile, click on the Add button.

4. In the Add Service to Profile dialog box (Figure 17.15), highlight Personal Folders and click on OK.

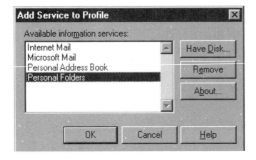

FIGURE 17.15:
You can add services to the
profile using this dialog box.

5. Personal folder files all have the extension .PST. You can make a new one for this profile using any name you want as long as the extension is .PST. Enter a name that you can identify as belonging to the profile, like **Antoinette's Mail.PST**.

6. In the Create Microsoft Personal Folders dialog box, you need to address several settings besides just giving a name to the Folders.

   Encryption Setting Even when password protected, .PST files can be opened and read in other applications (like word processors). If security is an issue, select Compressible Encryption, and if security is *very* important, select Best Encryption—the file can't be compressed, but there's greater protection with this option.

Password Whether or not the file is encrypted, you can add a password. If you check the box for saving the password to your password list, you won't be prompted for the password every time you connect to this set of personal folders.

Now this profile will have a completely separate set of Inbox, Outbox, Sent Items, and Deleted Items folders. To make a new address book for the profile, follow these same steps (except in step 5 the address book file has the .PAB extension).

Adding or Deleting Services

Although your Exchange services are initially configured when you run the Microsoft Exchange Setup Wizard, settings for services can be changed in several ways—the easiest being to double-click on the Mail icon in the Control Panel. From there, here's what to do:

- To remove a service, just highlight it and click on the Remove button.
- To add a service, click on Add, select one of the available information services, and then click on OK.

To configure a service, highlight it and click on Properties. The information you will need to supply varies depending on the service. (If it's Internet mail, for instance, you'll enter the name of your Internet mail service, account, and so forth.)

Most changes you make to Exchange don't take effect until you restart it. There's not always a dialog box to remind you of this fact. So, to be sure, shut down Exchange and restart it by double-clicking on the Inbox icon before trying to use any changed services or profiles.

It's TAPI Standard Time

TAPI is yet another in the never-ending series of cryptic computer acronyms. It stands for *Telephony Application Programming Interface* and is a standard for new communications programs. The idea is that you ought to be able to tell your *system* what kind of modem you have, where it's attached, and other settings just once.

All programs written to the TAPI standard will be able to detect the settings of your modem. If you change modems, you just go to the Modem icon in the Control Panel, delete the old modem, and install your new one, and all the TAPI-compliant programs will be instantly updated.

The communications capabilities built into NT Workstation—such as HyperTerminal and Phone Dialer—are all TAPI-compliant. Your legacy (that means *old*) software is probably not, though many newer programs have been adopting TAPI since it was built into Windows 95.

Installing Dial-Up Networking

Dial-Up Networking is the NT Workstation tool you'll need to use if you're planning to access your network remotely, that is, over phone lines using a modem. Thanks to NT Workstation's excellent connectivity features, installing Dial-Up Networking is a snap. Here's what you need to do:

1. To begin installing Dial-Up Networking, click on the Start button on the Taskbar, then select Programs, Accessories, and Dial-Up Networking. Provided you haven't already installed Dial-Up Networking, you should see a dialog box that gives you the opportunity to install the files you'll need to gain remote access to your network.

2. Click Install to begin copying the Dial-Up Networking files to your hard disk.

3. Insert your NT Workstation CD ROM into the appropriate drive, and specify the path to the Dial-Up Networking files. If necessary, use the Browse button to point the Remote Access Setup Utility to the files in question.

4. If you haven't installed a modem yet, the Remote Access setup utility will offer to invoke the Install New Modem Wizard for you. Otherwise, it will auto-detect the remote-enabled device in your computer and ask you to confirm its properties before clicking Continue to proceed.

5. At this point, the Remote Access Setup Utility will finish configuring everything, confirm the successful completion of the installation, and ask you to restart your computer.

6. After you've restarted your computer, open My Computer, then double-click on Dial-Up Networking to begin configuring the remote connection to your network.

7. When you see a dialog box telling you there are no entries in your phonebook, click OK to add a phonebook entry for your network.

> **TIP**
>
> **Every network is different, so consult your system administrator if you have questions about how to dial into your particular network.**

8. Test your remote connection by dialing into your network (see the following section for how to do this), and you're all set to go.

9. To hang up or check the status of your remote connection, right-click on the Dial-Up Networking Monitor on the right-hand side of the Taskbar.

If you haven't done so already, now would be a good time to install Exchange, Internet Mail, and/or Microsoft Mail. Once you've accomplished this, you can dial into your network and check your e-mail, regardless of whether you're in Boston or Bombay.

Using Dial-Up Networking for Remote Access

Once you've got your remote connection configured, using Dial-Up Networking couldn't be much easier. To dial in to your network, open up My Computer and double-click on Dial-Up Networking. Using the drop-down list in the Phonebook Entry to Dial dialog box, select the phonebook entry for your network and click Dial.

What happens next depends largely on how your network is configured; you may need to bring up a terminal window to type in your username and password, or your clever system administrator may be able to give you a script that will automate the whole logon process.

Internet Explorer

The Internet Explorer is installed on your Desktop by default. IE started out life as a Web browser that was part of the Windows 95 installation. Now with NT Workstation, the Internet Explorer is a remarkably sharp and powerful tool for navigating the World Wide Web on the Internet *and* for navigating what's recently become known as the *intranet*—Web pages published on your own network.

> **TIP** The version of Internet Explorer that comes with NTWS (2) is already outdated. The best use for version 2 is to use it to download version 3. Open the Go menu and select Internet Explorer Updates to download the newest version you can find. All the illustrations in this chapter are from version 3.

Some Clarification of Terms

The *Internet* is a global network of networks. Your network may be connected to the Internet by means of modems or by being one of the networks that make up the Internet. Or maybe you're not connected to the Internet at all.

In current usage, an *intranet* is a network that uses Internet technology (specifically Web technology) to share information. You can have an intranet that operates only within your network or both internally and with the Internet.

If you have an intranet, you'd use Internet Explorer to visit the Web pages on your network. Internet Explorer can also view Web pages on the Internet. If all this sounds potentially confusing—it is. The boundary between internal and external information can become blurred or even disappear. This, fortunately, is the problem of the system administrator and not yours. However, the administrator's solution may affect how Internet Explorer works for you and how it looks.

Internet Access with NT Workstation

If you already have an account with an ISP (*Internet Service Provider*), you can continue to use the e-mail software and Web browser that you had before. Just install them as you'd install any other software. (See the section "Add/Remove Programs" in Chapter 14.)

Using Internet Explorer

If you've been living in a cave for the past couple of years and haven't heard of "the Web" before, you're probably better off. That way you don't have to unlearn all the harder ways of using browsers and can just enjoy the easy Internet Explorer way.

Double-click on the Internet Explorer icon to start IE. Figure 17.16 shows the opening screen.

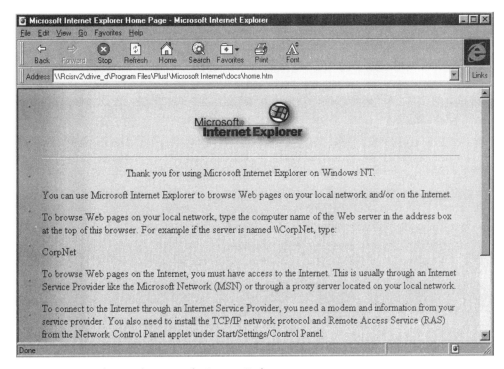

FIGURE 17.16: The opening screen for Internet Explorer

TIP If you're going to be using Internet Explorer for the Internet, you'll need a connection using a modem on your computer or a connection on your network. Whatever connection you use for Internet mail in Exchange (discussed earlier in this chapter) will be the one you use for IE. If you have questions about how to connect to the Internet, consult your system administrator.

The basic method for using the Internet Explorer is point-and-click; that is, you *point* Internet Explorer at a site you'd like to visit, *click* on the site, and you're off. To point the Internet Explorer at a particular site, click in the Address box and type the URL (*Uniform Resource Locator*) of the site to which you'd like to be transported.

For example, you could type **http://www.microsoft.com**, and you'd end up at the main Microsoft site on the World Wide Web.

If you're connecting to Web pages on your local network, you need only type in the name of a local Web server. Fortunately, once you've typed in one of those unwieldy URL addresses, you can open the Favorites menu and add the site. Thereafter, you need only select the site from the Favorites menu to return to it.

TIP If you were at a site recently but failed to add it to your Favorites list, you can find it again by clicking on the arrow next to the address field to open a drop-down list of recent URLs.

The buttons on the Internet Explorer toolbar are designed to help you navigate quickly and easily. Here's an overview of what each one does:

Button	Button Name	Function
Back	Back	Returns you to the document from which you just came. This button is grayed out if you've just started surfing, that is, if the document you're looking at is the first one you've visited during this session.
Forward	Forward	Takes you one document forward (to the next item) in the sequence of pages or sites you've already visited. This button is grayed out if you're on the last item on your *history list* (the list of pages and sites you've already visited).
Stop	Stop	Halts transmission of the document at which you've pointed the Internet Explorer. This button is especially useful if a connection is painfully slow, and you decide you'd rather bail out than wait.

Button	Button Name	Function
Refresh	Refresh	Refreshes the current document. You may want to do this if, for example, you believe the information on the displayed Web page may have been updated on the Web site since you last loaded it, or if you have a temporary communications problem with the Web server you're connected to, and the document you want to see is not completely displayed.
Home	Home	Returns you to the start-up home page. By default, this button will return you to the introduction page displayed in figure 17.16.
Search	Search	Connects you with a page full of Internet search engines on the Microsoft Network home page. Using one of these programs, you can search the Internet in a variety of ways.
Favorites	Favorites	Opens your own personal list of favorite documents. You can add a document to your Favorites folder by using the Add to Favorites option on the Favorites menu while you're viewing the document you'd like to bookmark.
Print	Print	Prints the current document.
Font	Font	Changes the display font used by Internet Explorer.
Links	Quick Links	Click here to display Quick Links to pages at `microsoft.com`. Click Quick Links again to see the Address window.

Using the Mouse

Internet Explorer has a multitude of handy features, the best being the use of the right mouse button. Come across a beautiful picture on a Web page? Just right-click, and copy it to your Clipboard, save it, or turn it into wallpaper for your Desktop.

Other right-click menus let you make a shortcut to the page or add it to your list of favorite pages or copy a link to your Desktop.

> **TIP**
>
> To see the *underpinnings*, click on a blank spot on the page and select View Source from the right-click menu and you'll see all the HTML source code used in building the page. If you're learning to build your own Web pages, you can use this tool to find out how others are achieving effects you want to copy.

More Internet Explorer Features

In addition to the features you can find using the mouse, more are found on the Internet Explorer's menus:

- Use the File menu to save a page as a file, or select Send and mail the page to someone through Exchange.
- On the Edit menu, you can cut, copy, paste, or find text on a page.
- The Go menu keeps a running list of sites you've visited during your current online session.
  - Select Open History Folder on the Go menu to see a list of the last 300 pages you've visited. To return to a particular page, highlight the page in question and double-click on it.
- To configure Internet Explorer for your own preferences, select Options from the View menu. On the General tab, you can change the look of Internet Explorer, and on the Navigation tab, select the page you want IE to start with. The settings on the Security and Advanced tabs should be left to the system administrator.

> **NOTE** Some of the tabs in the Options window may not even appear on your system, sparing you the anxiety of not knowing what you can change. In general, however, security options should be determined solely by the administrator.

Next Step

From communications in this chapter, we'll move on in the next chapter to some smaller programs that come with NT Workstation. This includes a word processor, a paint program, and several others that you'll undoubtedly find handy from time to time.

Chapter 18

A BUSHEL
OF APPLETS

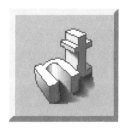

- **Briefcase**
- **Calculator**
- **Character Map**
- **Clipboard/ClipBook Viewer**
- **Clock**
- **HyperTerminal**
- **Imaging**
- **Notepad**
- **Object Packager**
- **Paint**
- **Phone Dialer**
- **Telnet**
- **WordPad**

From the first, graphical operating systems have come with a complement of smallish programs, such as calculators and paint programs. Because of their usually limited capabilities, these programs are called *applets* rather than applications.

In many cases, these programs are just as big as they need to be, so they actually *are* full applications. But the name applet has stuck and generally applies to programs that come as part of an operating system.

In this chapter, we'll discuss all the applets that aren't covered elsewhere. The basic use of many of these programs is very simple, so I'll make a point of mentioning the not-so-obvious functions (if there are any).

Packing a Briefcase

The Briefcase is not an applet in the usual sense. You won't find it listed under Accessories for one thing, but you can always right-click on the Desktop and select New ➤ Briefcase to create a new instance of it. Or a Briefcase may be on your Desktop from the original installation of NT Workstation.

Briefcase is a very handy tool for keeping files on different computers and sets of files on your Desktop and laptop synchronized. When keeping the same files on different computers, it's only a matter of time before things get confused as to which version of a memo or a report is the *current* version.

How It Works

When you open a Briefcase and copy a file into it, a link is made between the original and the copy in the Briefcase. This is called a *sync link*. After the link is made, you can work on the copy in the Briefcase or on the original file. Select Update (from inside Briefcase), and the latest version will be copied over the earlier version, keeping both in sync.

To move to the other computer, you copy the Briefcase to a floppy disk. At computer #2, open the Briefcase on the floppy. Copy the files from the Briefcase on the floppy (*not* the Briefcase itself) to the Desktop or another folder on computer #2. Work on the files and update the Briefcase when you're done. When you go back to computer #1, you can use the Briefcase on the floppy to update the files on computer #1.

Between a Desktop and a Laptop

Here's how to make use of Briefcase:

1. Open the Briefcase on the Desktop of computer #1. (Rename it if you wish.)
2. Copy the files you need to the Briefcase. Then move the Briefcase to a floppy disk.

3. Take the floppy to computer #2. Open drive A: either in the Explorer or My Computer.

4. Open the Briefcase. Work on the files inside the Briefcase on computer #2.

5. When you're finished, save and close the files in the usual way.

6. Return the floppy to computer #1. Open the Briefcase on the floppy disk, and select Update All from the Briefcase menu. That will open a dialog box like the one in Figure 18.1.

7. Click on the Update button.

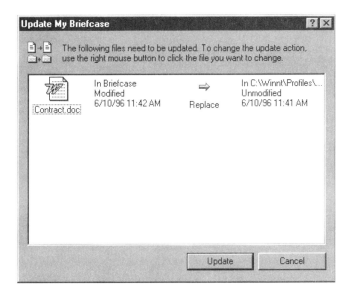

FIGURE 18.1:
Briefcase finds differences between the file on the hard disk and the file in the Briefcase.

Between Two Networked Computers

Briefcase is most useful when you're trying to keep two folders on different computers synchronized. Let's say your coworker has a folder that contains press releases. These press releases are updated by both of you at various times. Here's how to use Briefcase to make sure you always have the latest version:

1. Open My Briefcase, or make a new Briefcase by right-clicking on the Desktop and selecting New ➢ Briefcase.

2. Use Network Neighborhood to find the folder you want to stay current with.

3. Right-click on the folder and drag it to your new Briefcase. When you release the mouse button, you'll see a pop-up menu.

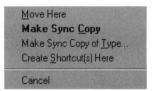

4. Select Make Sync Copy to copy everything in the folder. Choose Make Sync Copy of Type if there are only certain types of files you want updated.

5. To synchronize the files in your Briefcase with the files on the other computer, just open the Briefcase on your Desktop and select Update All from the Briefcase menu. After the files are checked, you'll see an Update My Briefcase dialog box, like the one in Figure 18.2, showing the differences found.

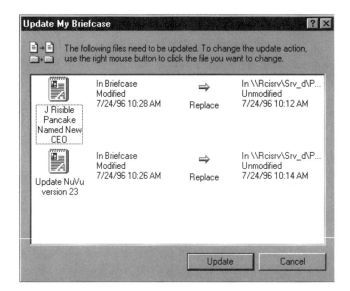

FIGURE 18.2:
The files in the Briefcase that are no longer identical

6. Accept all the updates, or right-click on the an individual file and change the action to be performed.

TIP

You can highlight individual files in the Briefcase and select Update Individual from the Briefcase menu. Or you can select Split from Original, and the file will no longer be connected with the original file on the other computer. A file that's been split from the original will no longer be updated.

Things to Remember about Briefcase

Briefcase is a handy tool as long as you bear in mind the following points:

- To synchronize your briefcase with a folder on another's computer, you must have *permission* to use the folder and its files. Similarly, you need to grant permission before anyone else can synchronize with your files. See Chapter 8 for the details of granting permissions.
- If you have more than one Briefcase in use, you'll probably want to right-click on the Briefcase icon and select Rename, so you're not trying to figure out what's in New Briefcase, New Briefcase (2), and so on.
- When synchronizing with a non-networked computer, such as a laptop, a Briefcase cannot be bigger than the size of the floppy disk you're copying to, and since you have to use copies and not shortcuts, the floppy fills up real fast.
- The floppy can be synchronized with the files on only one computer, not both. That's why you have to work *inside* the Briefcase on computer #2.
- Synchronization is not automatic. You must choose Update from the Briefcase menu.

Using the Calculators

You actually have two calculators in NT Workstation: a standard calculator, the likes of which you could buy for $4.95 at any drugstore counter, and a scientific calculator.

Just the Basics

To start the standard calculator, click on the Start button in the Taskbar, and then select Programs ➤ Accessories ➤ Calculator to display the calculator shown in Figure 18.3.

Using the mouse, click on the numbers and functions just as if you were pressing the keys on a hand-held calculator. Or if you have a numerical keypad on your keyboard, press NumLock, and you can use the keypad keys to enter numbers and basic math functions.

Or One Step Beyond

To access the scientific calculator, pull down the View menu on the Calculator and select Scientific. That displays the calculator in Figure 18.4.

FIGURE 8.3:
The standard calculator
is pretty basic.

NOTE If you're not sure what a particular function does, right-click on its button. You'll see a rectangle containing the words "What's This?". Click on the text to see a short explanation of the function.

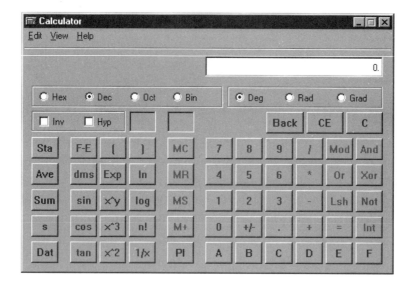

FIGURE 18.4:
The scientific
calculator is a
whole different
beast.

Getting Statistical

To see what the scientific calculator can do, let's enter a list of data for deriving statistical results:

1. Enter the first value in the series.
2. Click on the Sta button.
3. Click on the Dat button.
4. Enter the second value in the series.
5. Click on Dat.
6. Repeat steps 4 and 5 until you have entered the last value in the series.
7. Click on Sta.
8. Click on the function key that corresponds to the statistical command you want to enter.

Pasting in the Numbers

Both calculators can be used in conjunction with the Clipboard. Type a number in any application, and select it by dragging through it. Press Ctrl+C (for Copy), then Alt+Tab until the calculator is selected (or click on it in the Taskbar), and press Ctrl+V (for Paste). The number will appear in the number display of the calculator as if you had entered it from the calculator keypad.

Work your magic: adding, subtracting, multiplying, or deriving the inverse sine. You can pull down the Edit menu and select Copy, which places the contents of the display on the Clipboard—ready for you to paste into your document.

Making the Most of Character Map

The fonts that show up in your word processor are very nice, but they often don't go beyond the characters found on your keyboard. What about when you need a copyright sign (©) or an e with an umlaut (ë)? With the Character Map you have access to all kinds of symbols, including Greek letters and other special signs.

To start up the Character Map, click on the Start button in the Taskbar at the bottom of your Windows 95 screen. Select Programs ➢ Accessories ➢ Character Map to see the window in Figure 18.5.

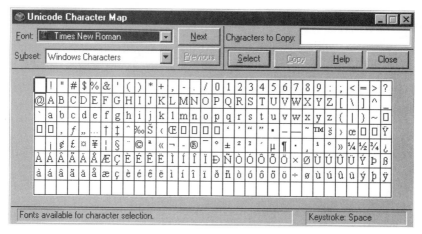

FIGURE 18.5: The Character Map shows all.

Entering Characters

Select the font you want to use by clicking on the downward-pointing arrow at the right-end of the Font list box. To enter a character, double-click on it in the window. It will appear in the text box at the top right of the window. Continue double-clicking until the entire string of characters you want is in the text box. When you have all the characters you want, click on the Copy button. Then return to your application by using the Taskbar or pressing Alt+Tab until your application is selected.

Position the cursor on the spot where you want to place the character, and select Paste from the Edit menu or just press Ctrl+V.

Chat

The Chat applet is covered in detail in Chapter 16, so look there if you want to find out how to "talk" to other people using this handy little tool.

What Clipboard Viewer Does

The Clipboard Viewer in NT Workstation 4 includes features that were not available in the one shipped with previous versions of NT Workstation. Although you'll have to experiment with using the Clipboard Viewer in order to judge how useful it will be for you, here's an overview of its basic features.

Taking a Look

To see the Clipboard Viewer, click on the Start button, and then select Programs ➣ Accessories ➣ Clipboard Viewer. You'll see a window like the one shown in Figure 18.6.

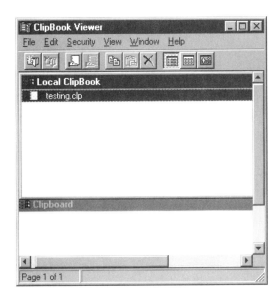

FIGURE 18.6:
The view of the Clipboard Viewer

Actually, you'll notice the Clipboard Viewer contains two smaller windows: the Clipboard and the Local ClipBook. When you first start the Clipboard Viewer, the Local ClipBook window opens on top, and the Clipboard window appears underneath it. But what do the Clipboard and ClipBook do anyway? Funny you should ask because that's just what the next section is all about.

Clipboard v. ClipBook

If you're clever, the Clipboard and the ClipBook can be used together to great advantage. But first you must understand what the function of each really is, so here's what you need to know about the tools you've got at your disposal.

Clipboard

The Clipboard is that magical place things disappear to whenever you remove something using the Cut option on the Edit menu of an application (or Shift+Delete or Ctrl+X, whichever happens to be your favorite method). Essentially, the Clipboard is useful for temporarily storing information if you're transferring it between documents and/or applications.

The contents of the Clipboard remain there until one of two things happens: either you clear the Clipboard or you cut or copy another piece of information there. If you'd like to save the contents of the Clipboard permanently, you can do that using the ClipBook (more on this in a moment), or you can paste them into any document as often as you'd like.

ClipBook

The ClipBook, by contrast, has two distinct but related uses: you can use it to permanently store information on your computer (this information usually comes from the Clipboard), or you can use it to share information you've stored in your Local ClipBook with other people on your network. In other words, the ClipBook can function as a kind of simple workgroup application.

Another thing that's nice to know is the ClipBook's contents can be copied to the Clipboard to use with NT Workstation applications. That is, if you've copied something from the ClipBook to the Clipboard, you can then insert it into any document by selecting Paste from an application's Edit menu.

Once information has been saved as a page in the ClipBook, it can be shared with other network users. Each computer has its own ClipBook, and (permissions allowing) it's possible to connect to the ClipBook on another computer and let others connect to your ClipBook, so they can see the information in your shared ClipBook pages.

Saving the Clipboard's Contents

To save the current contents of the Clipboard, make sure the Clipboard window is active, then pull down the File menu, and select Save As. You can save files under a proprietary format identified by the .CLP extension. These files are only used by the Windows Clipboard Viewer.

Once you've saved the contents, you can use the Clipboard to copy and paste other material, and later, you can reload what you saved by pulling down the File menu and selecting Open. Pull down the View menu to see all your options for viewing the data on the Clipboard.

Saving the ClipBook's Contents

To save the current contents of the ClipBook, make sure the ClipBook window is active, and then pull down the File menu and select Save As. As with the Clipboard, you can save files in the proprietary .CLP format.

Once you've saved the contents of the ClipBook, you can opt to make the contents of a page available to others. See "Sharing Your Clipbook with Others."

Copying, Pasting, and Deleting ClipBoard and ClipBook Information

These three buttons on the Clipboard Viewer's toolbar can help you make efficient use of the ClipBook and Clipboard.

The left-hand button copies the contents of the ClipBook page onto the Clipboard. Once you've done this, you can use the Paste option on the Edit menu in most NT Workstation applications to insert the contents of the ClipBook page into a document of your choice.

The center button pastes the contents of the Clipboard onto a ClipBook page. This is the fastest way to ensure the precious contents of your Clipboard will be preserved for all eternity.

Last but not least, the right-hand button deletes the ClipBook page or the contents of the Clipboard, depending on which window is active when you click on the button.

WARNING Be careful when deleting things in either the Clipboard Viewer or in the ClipBook Viewer because once you've deleted something, it won't come back.

Sharing Your ClipBook with Others

To make the information on a ClipBook page available to others, just click on the "Makes the Information in the Page Available to Others" button on the toolbar. To stop sharing the information on a ClipBook page with others, click on the "Makes the

Information No Longer Available to Others" button on the toolbar. These buttons are the second set from the left on the toolbar, the ones that look like this:

Makes Information in the Page Available to Others

Makes Information No Longer Available to Others

Using Someone Else's ClipBook

ClipBook Viewer is just a way of sharing information on your network. Anything you copy to the Clipboard can be copied to the ClipBook, and your ClipBook is available to anyone on the network (providing you're willing to share it).

More likely, there will be ClipBooks on other machines with information you want to see. To see if there's any fascinating reading on other computers, follow these steps:

1. Click on Clipboard Viewer in the list of programs that cascade out from the Accessories menu.
2. Click the File menu and select Connect. A window opens with a list of computers. Double-click on one.
3. The ClipBook on the computer in question will open and show you a list of what's available (see Figure 18. 7).
4. Double-click on your choice to see what's inside.

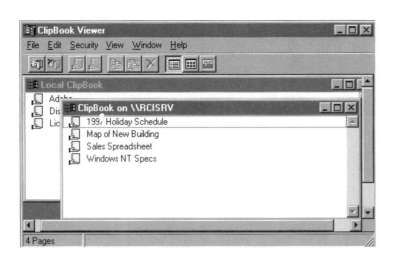

FIGURE 18.7:
Looking at the ClipBook on another machine

> **TIP** The list of items on a ClipBook can be shown as a table of contents (as in Figure 18.7) or as thumbnail-sized pages. Select either look from the View menu. Or highlight a particular item and select Full Page from the View menu.

When you're finished looking and want to close the ClipBook on another computer, select Disconnect from the File menu.

If you have problems viewing someone else's ClipBook, there are two possible reasons: first, network permissions won't allow this kind of access, or, secondly, the person whose ClipBook you're trying to see hasn't granted others access to it.

Clock

The Clock applet really couldn't be simpler. To try it out, follow these steps:

1. Click on the Start button on the Taskbar.
2. From the menu that appears, select Programs and then Accessories.
3. On the Accessories menu, select Clock, and you'll see a digital clock busily counting down the seconds until quitting time.

If you'd prefer an analog display, pull down the Settings menu and select Analog. You can also have your clock display Greenwich Mean Time, you can display the clock without a title bar, and you can have a second hand or not, as you prefer. All of these features are conveniently located on the Settings menu, so experiment a bit and see what you like.

Communicating with HyperTerminal

HyperTerminal provides the same functions as the former NT Desktop applet called Terminal by providing access through your modem to other computers, bulletin boards, and online services. The difference HyperTerminal offers is that it automates most of the process.

Where to Find It

Here's how to find HyperTerminal:

1. Click on the Start button on the Taskbar.
2. From the menu that appears, select Programs and then Accessories.
3. On the Accessories menu, select HyperTerminal. You'll see the HyperTerminal menu.
4. Click on the HyperTerminal icon. You will see something like the dialog box shown in Figure 18.8.

How to Use It

When you use HyperTerminal, each connection you make can be named and provided with an icon. That allows you to quickly identify connections so you can make them again.

FIGURE 18.8: The HyperTerminal window and the Connection Description dialog box are where you get started.

Let's create a fictional connection that will allow us to fill out the dialog box. Imagine you're a journalist working for a newspaper called *The Past Times,* and you need to log on to the paper's BBS to file stories and columns.

1. Type Past Times in the Name text box.
2. Scroll through the icons until you locate an icon that resembles a briefcase and umbrella—what better icon for a reporter? Click on it.
3. Click on the OK button. You will see the Connect To dialog box shown in Figure 18.9.

FIGURE 18.9:
The Connect To dialog box asks you where you want to connect to.

4. If the number you want to dial is located in a country other than the one listed in the Country Code list, click on the downward-pointing arrow at the right-end of the list box and select the correct country.
5. Enter the area code and phone number of the BBS in the appropriate text boxes. (For our example, enter 555-1212 as the number and click on the OK button.)
6. The Connect dialog box opens. If you'd like to make sure your connection is made properly, click on the Dialing Properties button to bring up the Dialing Properties dialog box (Figure 18.10).
7. If you click on the check box next to Dial Using Calling Card and then click on the Change button, a dialog box will open in which you can enter your telephone credit card number.

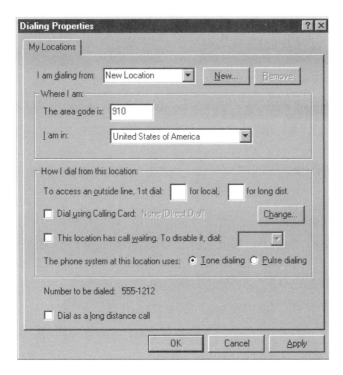

FIGURE 18.10:
The Dialing Properties dialog box lets you check your options.

8. If you have to dial a number to get out of your business or hotel phone system (typically 9 or 7), locate the text that reads "To Access an Outside Line, First Dial," and enter the number (or numbers) you dial for local and/or long distance access in the text boxes next to it.

9. If this is a long-distance call, click on the check box next to Dial as a Long-distance Call.

10. When you are through filling out this dialog box, click on OK to return to the Connect dialog box.

11. At this point, all you need to do is click on Dial to make the connection. If all the settings you made in the previous dialog boxes are correct, the call will go through, and you can use the BBS software to upload your story to the newspaper.

12. When you're through placing your call, pull down the Call menu and select Disconnect, or click on the icon that looks like a handset being hung up, and the connection will be broken.

13. When you close the window, you will be prompted to save the session.

Sending Files

Once you have connected with a remote computer, you will probably want to upload or download files. This is the principal reason for making this sort of connection. The file transfer protocols supported by HyperTerminal are

- 1K Xmodem
- Kermit
- Xmodem
- Ymodem
- Ymodem-G
- Zmodem
- Zmodem with Crash Recovery

Binary Files

To send a binary file, follow these steps:

1. After the connection is made, pull down the Transfer menu.
2. Select Send File. A dialog box will open.
3. Using the options in this dialog box (see Figure 18.11), specify the file to send. (Click on the Browse button to locate and identify the file to be sent.)
4. Select the protocol for file transfer. Zmodem is the best choice because it combines speed and good error correction.
5. Click on the Send button. The file will be transferred.

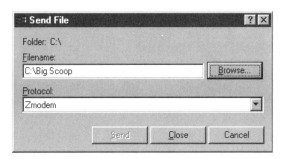

FIGURE 18.11:
Here's where you select a file and the protocol to send it.

Text Files

Text files are a little different from binary files. Most file transfer software distinguishes between binary files and text files—sending one in Binary mode and the other in ASCII mode or Text mode. HyperTerminal is no different.

To send a text file, follow the steps for a binary file, except choose Send Text File from the Transfer menu. When you specify the file to send and click on the Open button, the file will be sent as if you had typed it into the terminal program.

> **TIP**
>
> Unless you're transferring files to a UNIX system, send every file as a binary file. Even a little bit of formatting in the file can cause a text file transfer to fail, while *any* file can be sent as a binary transfer.

And Receiving Them Too

To receive a file being sent from another computer, follow these steps:

1. Pull down the Transfer menu and select Receive File. That will open a dialog box that looks like the Send File dialog box shown in Figure 18.11.
2. Click on the Browse button to specify a file name and location for the received file.
3. Select a file transfer protocol.
4. Click on the Receive button to start receiving the file from the remote location.

> **NOTE**
>
> You can set your modem to auto-detect through HyperTerminal, but do so only if there's no conflict with your Remote Access setup. In general, it's not a good idea to have an automatic answer setup on a network.

Saving a Session

To help you remember how to navigate the complexities of a service you don't use very often, terminal programs provide *logging*—a way to save everything you do in a particular session to disk and/or to print it on paper.

To save everything to disk:

1. Pull down the Transfer menu and select Capture Text.

2. By default, all the screen information in a session will be saved in a file called CAPTURE.TXT in the Windows NT folder inside the Profiles *username* \Start Menu\Programs\Accessories\Hyperterminal folder. Of course, you can use the Browse button to save the file in a different location. Click on Start when you're ready.

3. Pull down the Transfer menu again. Now you will note that there is a tiny triangle next to the Capture Text option. Select it, and you will see a submenu with Stop, Pause, and Resume options to give you control over the capture.

If you prefer to send the session to the printer rather than to a file on your disk, pull down the Transfer menu and select Capture to Printer.

Using a Connection

As you recall, when we started using HyperTerminal, we created a connection with a name and an icon. This connection appears in the HyperTerminal menu. Any time you want to use this connection in the future, simply click on its icon, and all the settings (telephone number and so forth) will be in place for you.

Any time you want to change the settings in a particular connection, open the connection, pull down the File menu, and select Properties.

Imaging

The Imaging applet is a scaled-down version of some of the full-fledged imaging applications that ship with scanners. You can either use it to scan and then manipulate images of various kinds, or you can import an image in one of a variety of common formats.

Only images in the .BMP (*Windows Bitmap*) and .TIF (*Tagged Image File*) formats can be modified; other formats are read-only. However, you can open a file in another format, save it as a .BMP or .TIF file, and then operate on it at will.

The Annotation menu is where you'll find the most fun. (To get there, select Start ➢ Programs ➢ Accessories ➢ Imaging.) Open a .BMP or .TIF file and add notes, draw on it, or mark it with a rubber stamp—either one of your own devising (Figure 18.12) or one that comes with the program.

FIGURE 18.12: Go ahead, add your opinion with a custom rubber stamp.

Scanning an Image

Scanning an image is very simple. You can either click on the Scan New button on Imaging's toolbar (it's the leftmost button, the one with the picture of a scanner on it), or you can pull down the File menu and select Scan New. Before scanning anything, you may need to have a look at the Select Scanner and Scan Preferences options on the File menu because this is where you'll make sure your scanner's all set up to go.

Using Notepad

Notepad is a simple text editor with very few charms except speed. Double-click on any text file, and it will immediately load into Notepad (unless, of course, it's bigger than 64K, in which case you'll be asked if you want to load it into WordPad instead).

What It's Got

Notepad has the bare minimum of facilities on its menus. You can

- Search for characters or words
- Use Page Setup to set margins, paper orientation, customize the header and footer, and select a printer

- Copy, cut, and paste text
- Insert the time and date into a document

> **NOTE** For some unfathomable reason, word-wrap is not on by default in Notepad. You have to select it from the Edit menu. Otherwise, text you type in stays on one line forever and ever. . . .

Object Packager

The Object Packager applet is a tool you can use to create what's called a *package* to insert it into a document. A package can include sound or animation files, pictures, text, or spreadsheets. It's probably good to know before you go too far, however, that you can only insert a package into Windows-based programs that support drag-and-drop functions for OLE, so now that's been said for the record.

As you'll see if you open the Object Packager, its window is split into two smaller windows: the Appearance window, which displays the icon that will represent the package you'll insert, and the Content window, which displays the name of the file containing the information you want to insert. To create a package, copy the contents of the Appearance and Content windows by selecting Copy Package from the Edit menu, then use the Paste command to insert the information into a document. The package appears in the document as an icon.

But what happens when you activate a package icon? That depends on what's in the package. To activate a package, double-click on its icon. Then, if the package contains a sound or animation file, the sound or animation will play. If the package contains a picture, text, or spreadsheet, the program associated with that file type will open, displaying the information. Neat, huh? No doubt you can use this one to amaze and amuse your colleagues, and perhaps even your boss.

Painting a Picture

As a drawing and painting program, Paint has its limitations, but it's nevertheless much improved over the Paintbrush included with NT Workstation 3.5. To find Paint, look under the Accessories menu. If you don't see it, use the Add/Remove Programs function in the Control Panel. (It's under Accessories on the Windows NT Setup page.)

What's New in Paint

If you've used the Paint program in previous versions of NT Workstation, there are some improvements in this version:

- Much better zooming capability, from 100 percent up to 800 percent.
- Opaque as well as transparent drawing. With opaque drawing, your additions cover the existing picture; transparent drawing lets the existing object show through your additions.
- More options for manipulation. The new Paint has more choices for stretching, skewing, flipping, and rotating the object being drawn.

Committing Original Art

Open Paint and, using the tools down the left side of the window, make a drawing and/or painting. When you're done, you can choose one of the following:

- Select File ➢ Save and give the picture a name. You can save it as one of several different kinds of bitmaps (see the Save as Type list).
- Select File ➢ Send, which will open Exchange, and let you select an e-mail recipient worthy of receiving your work.
- Select File ➢ Set as Wallpaper. This will let you tile or center your work of art as the wallpaper on your screen.

Modifying the Work of Others

Any file with the extension .BMP or .PCX or .DIB can be opened in Paint. Use the tools to make any modifications you want and then do any of the things listed in the section above.

Modified files are all saved as bitmaps (.BMP).

TIP

For a really good painting program at a very reasonable price, check out the excellent shareware program Paint Shop Pro. It's available for download on the major online services, as well as on the Web site http://www.jasc.com/. Or you can call JASC, Inc. at (612) 930-9171.

Getting Your Phone Dialed

Do you frequently have to make a lot of telephone calls? Has your dialing finger ever felt as if it were going to fall off? With NT Workstation, you can turn over the grief of dialing to its capable, if virtual, hands. Phone Dialer is a handy little program that doesn't do a lot, but if you need it, it's terrific to have.

> **NOTE** Essentially, NT Workstation uses your installed modem to dial your telephone. In order for this scheme to work, you need to have a telephone on the same line you're using for your modem. If you have a separate phone line for data, you'll need an actual telephone on that line to use Phone Dialer.

Here's how to access Phone Dialer:

1. Click on the Start button at the left end of the Taskbar.
2. Select Programs from the resulting menu.
3. Select Accessories from the Programs menu and click on Phone Dialer. You'll see the window shown in Figure 18.13

FIGURE 18.13:
The Phone Dialer can help you put an end to the heartbreak of *Digititis*.

Speed Dialing

To create a speed dial number, pull down the Edit menu and select Speed Dial. You will see the dialog box shown in Figure 18.14.

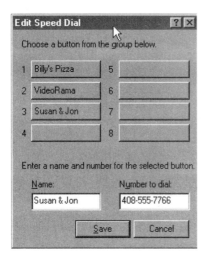

FIGURE 18.14:
The Edit Speed Dial dialog box puts you on the telephone fast track.

Here's how to set it up:

1. Click on the speed dial button you want to assign.
2. In the Name text box, type the name of the person or place that you will dial with that button.
3. Type the number to dial in the Number to Dial text box.
4. Click on Save. (You'll be returned to the Phone Dialer window, and the name you entered in the Edit Speed Dial dialog box will appear on the Speed Dial button you selected.)
5. To speed dial the number, just click on the button and lift your telephone handset.

Telnet

Telnet is a graphical version of the basic Telnet application that's been in use on the Internet for a long time. Essentially, NT Workstation's Telnet applet lets you (permissions allowing, of course) connect to a remote system, use the remote computer, create a log of your Telnet session (if you wish), and then disconnect from the remote system. Here's how to access Telnet:

1. Click on the Start button on the Taskbar.
2. Select Programs from the resulting menu.
3. Select Accessories from the Programs menu, and click on Telnet to open the basic, if uninformative, window.

> **TIP** This version of Telnet is about as bare-bones as an applet can get and still exist. It is not the preferred method for accessing other computers, so you're unlikely to use it unless you have a very specific job-function that requires it. In that case, someone will teach you the ins and outs.

Connecting to a Remote System

Connecting to a remote system is simple provided you've got the appropriate IP address or the name of the host computer on hand.

1. Pull down the Connect menu and select Remote System.
2. On the dialog box that appears (see Figure 18.15), type the IP address or the host name of the remote system in the Host Name box.
3. Change any of the other selections in the drop-down boxes and click Connect.

If your connection is successful, you'll see prompts for whatever logon information the remote system requires. If your connection is not successful, you'll see a Connect Failed dialog box.

The most common reason a connection fails is that you've made a typo, so try retyping the host name, and see if that makes a difference. If you still don't have any luck, the problem might be with the remote system, so wait a while and try again.

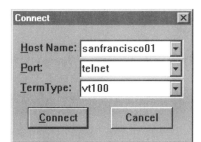

FIGURE 18.15:
The Connect dialog box is where you'll tell Telnet the IP address of the remote system you'd like to connect to.

Disconnecting from a Remote System

Disconnecting yourself from a remote system is even easier than getting yourself connected in the first place; just pull down the Connect menu and select Disconnect. That's all there is to it.

Logging a Telnet Session

Logging a Telnet session is pretty simple too. To start logging, pull down the Terminal menu, select Start Logging, and enter a file name to log to; to stop logging, pull down the Terminal menu and select Stop Logging. If you'd like, you can even (permissions allowing) save your log file on a remote computer. Ask your system administrator if you have questions about how to do this.

Terminal Preferences

Last but not least, if you're planning to use Telnet a lot, you may want to change your terminal preferences. To do this, pull down the Terminal menu and select Preferences.

Working with WordPad

WordPad is the successor to the Write program in previous versions of NT Workstation, and how you felt about Write may determine how you feel about WordPad. WordPad is an odd duck. It's more elaborate than Notepad but still falls way short of being a real word processing program.

To open WordPad, click on the Start button and follow the cascading menus from Programs to Accessories. At the bottom of the Accessories menu, you'll find WordPad.

Opening It Up

When you open WordPad (see Figure 18.16), it looks like most other editors, and on the menus, you'll find the usual things one associates with text editors. Pull down the menus to see the various options.

WordPad is different because it's completely integrated into NT Workstation. You can write messages in color and send them to Exchange recipients who will see your messages just as you wrote them—fonts, colors, embedded objects, and all. WordPad also has the distinct advantage of being able to load really big files.

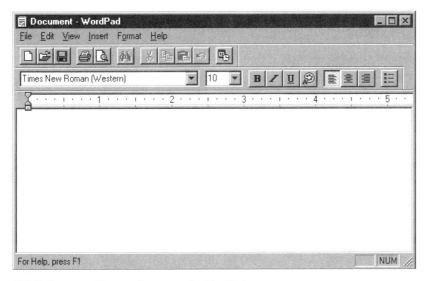

FIGURE 18.16: The opening screen for WordPad

Making and Formatting Documents

Most documents can be read in WordPad, just drag them onto a WordPad icon (or shortcut) and drop. Or use the WordPad File menu. Documents made by Microsoft Word (.DOC) and Windows Write (.WRI), as well as text (.TXT) and Rich Text format (.RTF) documents, are all instantly recognized by WordPad. You can also just start typing in the new document that WordPad opens when it's launched.

Formatting Tools

The toolbar (Figure 18.17) and format bar (Figure 18.18) are displayed by default. You can turn either of them off by deselecting it from the list under the View menu.

Tabs are set using the ruler. Click on the ruler at the spot where you want a tab. To remove a tab, just click on it and drag it off the ruler.

FIGURE 18.17: The various functions on the WordPad toolbar

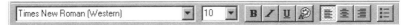

FIGURE 18.18: The WordPad format bar lets you manipulate text in all the basic ways.

Other Options

Other formatting tools are under Options on the View menu. This is where you can set measurement units as well as word-wrap and choose toolbars for each of the different file types that WordPad recognizes.

Page Setup and Printing

The File menu has the usual Print command, but there's also a Page Setup item that you can use to set margins as well as paper size and orientation. Unlike its predecessor, WordPad can print envelopes along with varying sizes of paper.

It may take some fooling around to get envelopes lined up correctly, but fortunately there's a Print Preview choice (also on the File menu). There you can see how the envelope or paper is lining up with your text. Adjust the margin in the Page Setup dialog box until you get it the way you want.

TIP	To change printers, select Page Setup from the File menu. Click on the Printer button to select any printer currently available to you.

Next Step

As you can see, some applets are valuable, and others you may never use. In the next chapter, we'll show you how to do what most of us hate doing—backing up your data. Backups may seem painful while you're doing them, but come the time something goes wrong with your hard disk, you'll be very glad you have them.

Chapter 19

PROTECTING YOUR DATA AND WORKSTATION

- **Selecting a backup strategy**
- **Backing up and restoring files**
- **Installing an uninterruptible power supply**
- **Virus protection**
- **Making an Emergency Repair Disk**

Now that you've got your NT Workstation set up exactly as you want it, it pays to protect your investment as best you can. Although backups are no one's favorite activity, they are a necessity. When you experience hardware failure or some other catastrophic event that gobbles up some or all of the precious data on your hard drive (notice that I didn't say *if*!), you'll be really, really glad if you've taken the time to back up your data.

Luckily for all of us, and particularly for those of you who have been living in denial about the importance of regular backups, NT Workstation comes complete with a nifty graphical backup tool that can ease backup pain.

There are also several other things you can do to protect your computer and the data on it: you can install a special kind of power supply that will keep it running even in case of a power failure, you can scan for viruses periodically, and you can keep an up-to-date emergency repair disk on hand. In this chapter, you'll learn how to use NT Backup and some of the system administrator's safety tricks.

Backing Up Your System

NT Backup helps protect your data from accidental loss and hardware or media failures by backing up specified files, directories, and/or drives to a tape drive attached to your computer. NT Backup works on NTFS and FAT file systems, and its many options let you customize your backup to make the process of protecting your investment as painless and foolproof as possible. Without further ado, here's what you need to know about backing up your NT Workstation.

Backing Up to a Tape

Using NT Backup to create a set of backup tapes for your computer is simple—provided you've installed your tape drive correctly. So first things first.

Checking Your Tape Device

If you'd like to check and see whether your tape drive is in good working order, follow these steps:

1. Open the Tape Devices icon on the Control Panel by double-clicking on it.

> **TIP** My favorite way to get to the Tape Devices icon is to click on the Start button on the Taskbar, then select Settings, and then Control Panel, but suit yourself.

2. On the Devices tab, shown in Figure 19.1, you'll see an entry for your tape drive if NT Workstation has already recognized its existence. If your tape drive is listed and you'd like to view its properties, you can either double-click on its entry or highlight the entry and then click the Properties button.

TIP

If there's no entry for your tape drive, click the Detect button to let NT Workstation search for the hardware. If the search is unsuccessful, the problem probably lies with the way the tape drive is connected to your computer. Check your setup and try again.

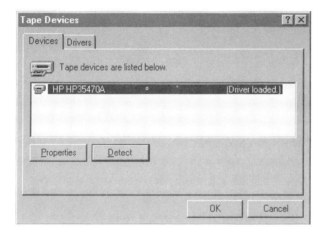

FIGURE 19.1:
The Devices tab on the Tape Devices dialog box tells you about tape device(s) installed on your system.

3. On the Drivers tab, shown in Figure 19.2, you'll see an entry for your tape device driver if NT Workstation has already recognized its existence. Click OK when you've confirmed everything.

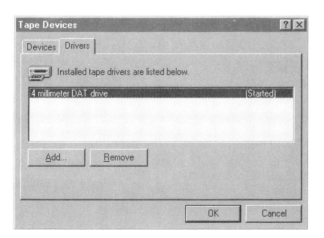

FIGURE 19.2:
The Drivers tab on the Tape Devices dialog box tells you about the tape device driver(s) installed on your system.

> **TIP**
>
> If you'd like to add a driver for a tape device, click the **Add** button in the **Tape Devices** dialog box. This will produce a list of the tape device drivers the operating system knows about. At this point, you can either select the applicable manufacturer and model from the lists on the **Install Driver** dialog box, or click the **Have Disk** button and specify where the disk with the new driver on it is located.

Now that you know your hardware is OK, you need to settle on a backup strategy.

Selecting a Strategy

In general, there are two types of backup strategies that make sense. The first is a full backup with incremental updates, and the second is a full backup with differential updates. How often you do your full backups will vary, depending on your circumstances, needs, paranoia level, and so forth.

I can't emphasis enough the importance of having a full *verified* backup as the starting point for any backup strategy. Once you've got your verified full backups and have decided how often you will be doing full backups, you need to decide how often you'll be doing interim backups and what kind they should be.

Types of Backups

The two basic types of interim backups supported by NT are *incremental* and *differential*.

- An incremental backup only backs up the data that has changed since the last time you performed a backup.
- A differential backup backs up everything that has changed since the last full backup.

If you're using incremental backups, you need *all* the incremental backups since the last full backup in order to restore everything in the event of a crash. But with a differential strategy, you need only the most recent differential backup tape (plus the full backup tape, of course) to restore your system to the point it was at when you did that last backup.

Pros and Cons of Each

The biggest advantage of using the incremental backup is speed. You need very little time to back up each day's work, since the only thing you're actually backing up is the stuff that's changed that day. But with a differential strategy, the time it takes to back up gets substantially longer each day between one full backup and the next.

The biggest advantage to using the differential strategy is that you reduce the chances of failure. Since each differential tape contains all the changes up to that point, it's easier to restore. You only need a pair of tapes—the full backup and the latest differential backup. If the differential is defective or can't be restored, you use the differential before it, and the worst that happens is you lose the changes made that last day—you know exactly where you are at all times.

A Solution That Combines the Types

Probably the best all-around solution is a single, weekly, full backup with daily differentials. I use two differential tapes for each week's backup set and rotate them. So, Friday night, before I quit, I start a full backup going, including verification. Then on Monday night, I fire off differential tape #1 at the end of the day. Differential #2 gets used on Tuesday, back to differential #1 on Wednesday, and so on.

Ultimately, you'll need to decide what level of exposure to disaster you're comfortable with. Today's modern hard drives are remarkably stable and dependable, but they still don't do well in a fire or volcanic eruption.

Another factor is whether you're on a network or not. If you're part of a large network with a reliable system administrator, you don't need to worry about backups, because you can reasonably expect that the entire network will be regularly and dependably backed up. But personally, I'd rather restore a local tape backup than have to go lay offerings on the altar of the system administrator gods when the mistake is mine.

How to Do a Backup

Now that you've got a sound backup strategy, it's time to get down to business. Here are the steps you'll need to follow to perform a tape backup on your NT Workstation:

1. Start the Backup application, which will look something like Figure 19.3. You'll find it located in the Administrative Tools section of the Programs menu.
2. Make sure you have a tape in the tape drive. Sounds obvious, but nonetheless necessary.
3. Select the drives you'll be backing up by checking the box next to the little drive icons.

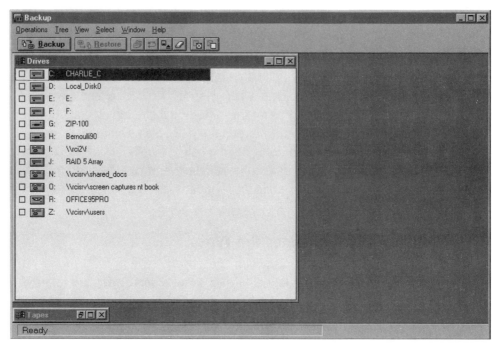

FIGURE 19.3: The NT Workstation Backup program

4. If you only want to back up part of the drive, double-click on the drive icon, and you'll open an additional window that will let you check or uncheck the folders and files on the drive, as shown in Figure 19.4.

5. When you have checked everything you want to back up click on the Backup button.

6. In the Backup Information dialog box (Figure 19.5), you can give the tape a name, as well as add descriptions in the Backup Set Information area for each backup set that will be created. (Use the scroll bar to see additional backup sets.) You'll get a different backup set for each drive selected.

7. Make sure you check the Verify after Backup box. While it'll double the amount of time it takes to do the backup, without it you'll never be able to trust the backup.

8. If you're backing up your system drive, make sure you check the Backup Local Registry box.

9. Select the type of backup. You'll use Normal for full backups and Differential or Incremental for interim backups.

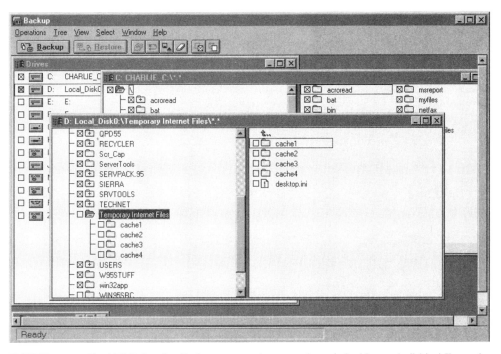

FIGURE 19.4: The NT Workstation Backup program lets you select whole drives or individual files and folders for backup.

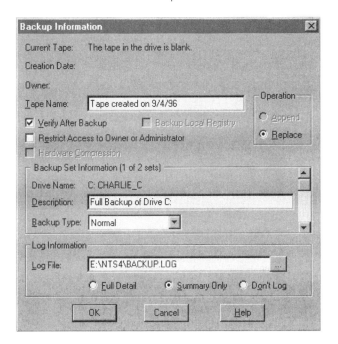

FIGURE 19.5:
Setting the options for your backup sets. Each drive gets its own set, but they will all be on the same tape.

10. When you have everything as you want it, click OK to begin the actual backup.

11. While the backup is going on, you'll see a progress report dialog box like the one in Figure 19.6. The amount of information it contains depends on what sort of logging you have opted for.

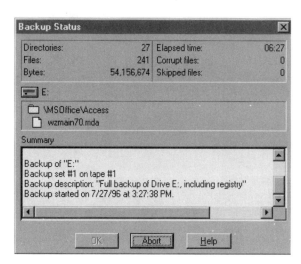

FIGURE 19.6:
NT Workstation's Backup keeps you informed about how well it's doing and how much it has done.

12. Finally, when you're done and the tape has been verified, you'll get a process report like that shown in Figure 19.7. Additional information will be available in the log file, if you created one.

13. Remove the tape from the drive, flick the little tab (if your tape has one) to write protect the tape so you don't accidentally overwrite it, and store it in a safe place.

Storing Your Backup Tapes

Tapes are a fairly delicate magnetic recording media. They do not respond well to heat, moisture, dust, or electrical or magnetic fields. This means you shouldn't put them on top of a monitor, next to the sink, or near the speakers of your sound card.

If you can possibly manage it, keep one set in a completely different location. The point here is that *if* there's a major catastrophe—say your office burns down—all the tapes stored in your office will suffer the same fate as the computer they're supposed to be backing up. So keep a set far, far away.

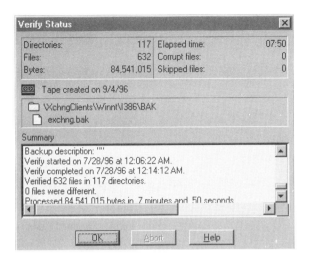

FIGURE 19.7:
When it's done, Backup will
give you a report on the results.

Restoring a Tape Backup

You can sincerely hope you'll never need those backups you've done so carefully, but if and when you do, it's nice to know how to restore a file, folder, or (perish the thought!) an entire drive. Here, in a nutshell, is how to do it:

1. Start the Backup application, which will look something like Figure 19.8. You'll find it located in the Administrative Tools section of the Programs menu.

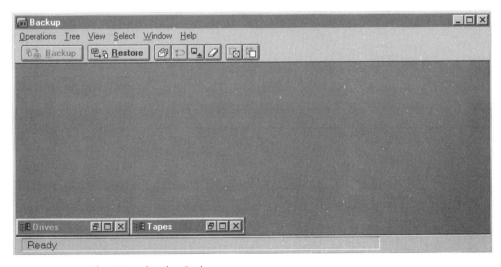

FIGURE 19.8: The NT Workstation Backup program

2. Put the tape you will be restoring from in the drive. Sounds obvious, but nonetheless necessary. Double click on the Tapes window title bar, located at the bottom of the Backup window, to open it.

3. Select Catalog from the Operations menu to find out what's on the tape. The Catalog Status dialog box, shown in Figure 19.9, will appear as it scans the tape for information about what's on it.

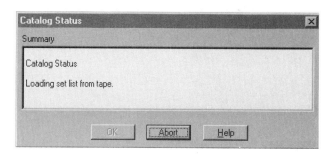

FIGURE 19.9:
The NT Workstation Backup program will load a catalog of your backup from the tape.

4. Select the drive(s) you want to restore by checking the box next to the little folder icon for that drive.

5. If you only want to restore part of the drive, double-click on the folder icon, and the backup program will read the tape to get additional information about what files and directories were backed up, and then you'll get an additional window where you can check or uncheck the folders and files on the drive, as shown in Figure 19.10.

6. When you have everything you want to restore selected, click on the Restore button.

7. In the Restore Information dialog box (Figure 19.11), you can set a variety of options, including where to restore to—the default is where the backup originated, but you can change both the drive and the directory here—whether to restore the permissions the files had before, and whether to verify the restored files against what's on the tape.

8. If you do not check the Restore File Permissions box, the files will inherit the permissions of the directory to which they are being restored. If it's checked, they will be restored with the exact permissions they had when they were backed up.

9. Make sure you check the Verify after Restore box. It'll double the amount of time it takes to restore your data, but I think the additional confidence is worth it.

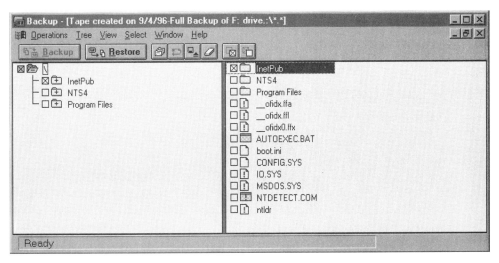

FIGURE 19.10: The NT Workstation Backup program lets you select whole drives or individual files and folders to restore.

10. If you're restoring your system drive and you want to restore the registry information, check the Restore Local Registry box. If you do, however, you will overwrite any changes to the registry since the backup was performed.

11. When you have everything as you want it, click OK to begin the actual restoration.

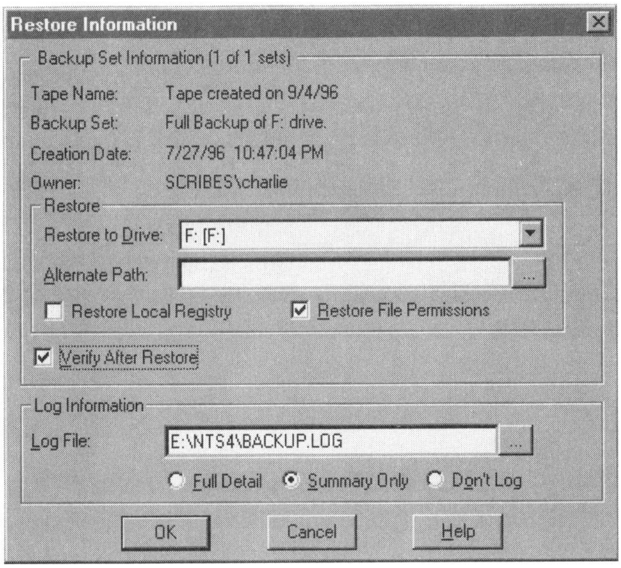

FIGURE 19.11:
Setting the options for the restoration of your files

12. While the restore operation is going on, you'll see a progress report box like the one in Figure 19.12. The amount of information it contains depends on what sort of logging you have opted for.

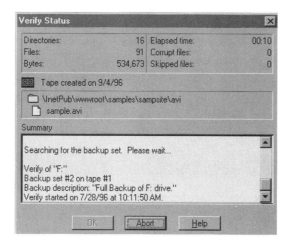

FIGURE 19.12:
NT Workstation's Backup keeps you informed about how well the restore is doing and how much it has done.

13. Finally, when you're done and the restored files have been verified against the tape (if you selected that option), you'll get a process report like the one shown in Figure 19.13. Additional information will be stored in the log file if you created one.

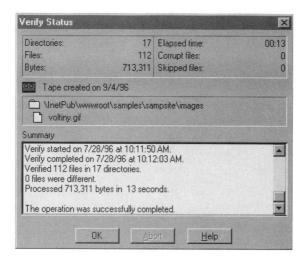

FIGURE 19.13:
When it's done, the NT Workstation Backup program will report on the results of the restoration.

14. Now if you have additional incremental or differential backup tapes to restore, insert them into the tape drive and repeat the process. Remember with an incremental backup schema, you will need to restore *all* of the incremental backups to get back to your most recent state. With a differential schema, you only need to restore the most recent differential tape.

One of the biggest weaknesses of the NT Workstation Backup program is you need NT up and running to restore files from tape. This means that in the event of a complete failure, you'll have to first re-install NT before you can restore the rest of your files. This is really the job of the system administrator, and you should not hesitate to call for help in that situation. But if all you need to do is restore a couple of files that got accidentally deleted or damaged, by all means, have at it.

Miscellaneous Tape Functions

Depending on the type of tape drive you have, you can erase the tape, format the tape, rewind or retension the tape, or eject it from the drive. When you are erasing the tape, you may also have a choice about whether to use a quick erase method, which takes a few seconds, or a secure method, which completely overwrites the entire tape. This can take several hours, so don't bother unless you are seriously concerned about someone with very expensive consultants getting at something on that tape.

With some tape technologies, the tape must be formatted before you can use it. This takes quite a bit of time, so it's kind of nice to do it when you have a spare couple of hours. Or better yet, buy the tapes pre-formatted. It's not that much more expensive and more than worth the cost.

Retensioning of tapes is left over from the bad old days, but it may still be a good idea with brand new tapes of some technologies. While it takes a few minutes, it insures that the tape is uniformly tensioned and will move through the drive at a uniform speed.

Finally, a word about cleanliness. Tape drives are notoriously prone to getting dirty over time. You don't notice the problem since it happens gradually, until suddenly you really, really need to read a tape and discover that it's no good. And you weren't verifying each and every backup tape because it took too long. Develop a cleaning schedule and stick to it. Each drive has different requirements, but follow the manufacturer's recommendations. They're usually pretty conservative, but so should you be. The cost of tape drive cleaning tapes is minimal compared to the cost of a failed restoration.

Installing a UPS (Uninterruptible Power Supply)

Another excellent way to protect your NT Workstation against disaster is to install a special kind of power supply, called a UPS (short for *Uninterruptible Power Supply*), that will continue to supply power to your computer even in case of a power failure. Although not everyone will have the hardware budget to do this, it is a good idea, especially if you've got a standalone workstation whose data is not accessible elsewhere (except on those backup tapes, of course!).

Although the UPS configuration dialog boxes look a bit daunting at first, they really aren't all that difficult to understand. Here are the steps you'll need to follow to install a UPS on your NT Workstation:

1. After you've connected the UPS to your computer, the first thing you'll need to do is find the UPS element in the Control Panel. To do this, click on the Start button on the Taskbar, then select Settings, and then Control Panel. When you've located the UPS icon, double-click on it and you should see a dialog box that looks like Figure 19.14.

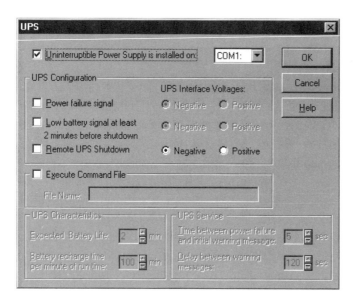

FIGURE 19.14:
The UPS dialog box lets you configure options for your Uninterruptible Power Supply.

2. To start configuring your UPS, you'll need to let NT Workstation know two things: that it's attached and which port it's attached to.
   - Single-click in the box next to "Uninterruptible Power Supply Is Installed On" to place a check mark in it. This lets NT Workstation know that you'll be using a UPS.
   - Use the drop-down list to the right of the checked box to specify the relevant serial port.
3. In the UPS Configuration area, select the options you want. Check your UPS documentation to determine whether the UPS interface voltage is positive or negative.

   Power Failure Signal Select this option, and you'll also need to specify the expected battery life of your UPS, how long it takes to recharge, and particulars about message timing.

   Low Battery Signal Select this option to get a warning when the battery power is low.

   Remote UPS Shutdown Select this option to enable shutdown from a remote location.

4. After making all the selections, click the OK button.

Protecting against Viruses

What, we need to worry about viruses? I though NT Workstation was totally secure and would protect itself?

Well, yes and no. In a discussion I had with a Microsoft support engineer, he stated that the single biggest cause of installation failure was a pre-existing virus on the user's hard drive. And all reports they'd had of boot sector viruses could be traced to someone booting the machine off an infected floppy.

An anti-virus product is only as good as you let it be. You *must* update it regularly. At a minimum, every couple of months. In many ways, an outdated anti-virus program is worse than no anti-virus protection at all because it will give you a false sense of security.

If you're on a network, the chances are good that your network's system administrator is already protecting the network against viruses, but this may or may not be sufficient to protect your workstation. If you regularly work on more than one machine, download files from an online service or the Internet, or if your machine is shared amongst several users, you need to have a heart-to-heart talk with your system administrator about whether you need specific protection on your machine. If you do, the system administrator will have specific recommendations for the program and may well have an automated way to ensure that it is regularly updated.

Updating the Emergency Repair Disk

When NT Workstation was installed, you (or someone else) made an Emergency Repair Disk. This disk contains all of your current system settings and can restore your computer if system files become damaged, so it's always a good idea to have it on hand. Each time you make a significant change to your hardware or software setup, you should update your Emergency Repair Disk. NT Workstation's Repair Disk utility is the tool you'll use to do this.

To make a current Emergency Repair Disk, follow these steps:

1. Click Start ➤ Help.
2. Click the Index tab on the Help Topics window and type Repair Disk.
3. Click the Display button to open the window shown in Figure 19.15.

FIGURE 19.15:
The NT Help file provides the most convenient access to the Repair Disk utility.

4. At the bottom of the window is a button marked Click Here, so just do it. This action opens the Repair Disk Utility dialog box, as seen in Figure 19.16.

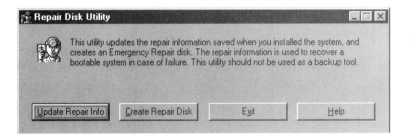

FIGURE 19.16:
The Repair Disk utility is the key to keeping your Emergency Repair Disk up-to-date.

5. Click Update Repair Info. A slightly alarming dialog box (shown in Figure 19.17) opens. It's harmless though, so just click Yes.

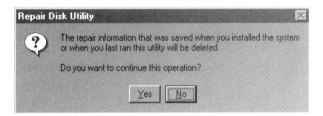

FIGURE 19.17:
The text in this confirmation box isn't as reassuring as it should be.

6. First the configuration information stored on your hard disk is updated. Then you are prompted as to whether you want to create an Emergency Repair Disk. Choose Yes. The floppy is formatted, and the configuration files are copied to it. When the progress bar disappears, the disk is complete. Click the Exit button to close the utility.

7. Label the disk and put it in a safe place.

Don't forget to update your Emergency Repair Disk regularly. If you back up your important files often, scan your machine regularly for viruses, and have a recent Repair Disk, you're as ready as you can possibly be for any computer unpleasantness.

NOTE When running the Repair Disk utility, you can also select Create Repair Disk. You normally wouldn't use this because the hard drive isn't updated when you choose this option.

Next Step

In this chapter, you've learned how to protect your data and your workstation. You're now pretty familiar with the basics of NT Workstation 4. If you still have questions, try using the Help files or consult your friendly neighborhood system administrator.

Arcane acronyms and weird words spring up around networks like toadstools after a rain, so take a look at the Glossary after this chapter for the definitions (in plain language) of many mysterious terms.

Glossary

16-bit, 32-bit   Refers to how certain programs address memory and other technical details. In general, 16-bit programs refer to those written for DOS or earlier versions of Windows. NT Workstation 4 allows the use of 32-bit programs, which can do true *multitasking* (as opposed to *task switching*). If designed correctly, 32-bit programs can be faster than 16-bit programs, but they are not inherently so.

Active window   The window that keyboard or mouse movements act on. Many windows can be open, but only one is active at a time. You can spot the active window by its title bar, which is a different color than the title bar of other windows.

Administrator/System administrator   The individual in charge of planning, setting up, and maintaining a network. This person is responsible for making sure that system resources are made available to users in an orderly and secure manner, and he or she is the one to whom you'll inevitably go running whenever there's a problem.

Application   An application is a program designed to accomplish a particular set of tasks. The program may consist of several supporting files and may include numerous components. WordPerfect, Excel, and PowerPoint are examples of applications. Applications are normally grouped by type, such as word processing, spreadsheet, database, and so forth.

ASCII   Stands for the *American Standard Code for Information Interchange*. Developed back in the '60s as a standard numerical code for characters used on all computers. Today, ASCII usually means normal text as opposed to code unreadable by regular folk. (Pronounced *AS-key.*)

Associate   To connect files having a particular extension to a specific program. When you double-click on a file with the extension, the associated program is opened, and the file you clicked on is opened. In NT Workstation, associated file extensions are usually called *registered* file types.

Attribute   A bit of code in a file that determines an aspect of the file's status. The four file attributes are read-only, hidden, archive, and system. A file can have none or any number of the attributes set. You can modify these but only if you have a good reason. (This is a noun, pronounced with the accent on the first syllable, not the second.)

Background   The screen area behind the active window. Can also mean a process that is going on somewhere other than in the active window.

Backup domain controller   A computer that stores a copy of a domain's account database. Many system administrators believe (and rightly too!) that there should be a backup domain controller in each domain on a network; this way, users may continue to log on and work even if the primary domain controller must be taken out of service.

Baud   The speed at which data is transmitted over a communications line or cable. This is not *really* the same as *BPS* (bits per second) but the terms are used interchangeably.

Bit   Represents a single switch inside a computer set to 0 or 1. There are millions of them in every computer. Short for binary digit, 8 bits make up a *byte,* the basic unit of data storage.

Bitmaps   Picture or image files that are made up of pixels. Pictures made in Paint are automatically saved as bitmaps (with a .BMP extension).

Boot   A simple name for the complicated process your computer goes through when starting up.

Bootable disk   A disk containing the system files needed to start the computer. When your system starts up, it looks for a disk first in drive A:; if it doesn't find one there, it goes to drive C:. When a disk is found, the computer examines the disk to see if it contains the system files. When a disk with system files is found, the computer uses that disk's information to start the system running. If a disk with system files is in drive A:, information on that disk will be used to tell the computer about itself. Computers can normally be booted only from drive A: or drive C:.

BPS   *Bits per second.* A unit of measurement for the communication speed of modems and fax modems.

Browse   To examine a list of computers on a network or files on a disk. When you use Network Neighborhood and/or the Entire Network icons, you're browsing the network. When you use the Explorer or My Computer, you are browsing your local disks.

Byte   The basic unit of data storage. A byte is 8 bits. For all intents and purposes, a byte equals a single character.

Client   In a client/server network environment, a client is a computer that says, "You've got it, give it to me." In other words, a client accesses shared network resources (be they files, printers, or whatever) provided by a *server*.

Client/Server network   A network that consists of at least one server and one client, though usually many more. Client/server networking has many advantages, not the least of which is that it allows users to share system resources in an efficient, secure manner.

Computer name   A unique name of up to 15 characters that identifies a computer to the network. An NT Workstation computer name can't contain any blank spaces.

Configuration   A set of values in a program or for a device such as a printer. The values determine how menu options work or tell the printer a particular size of paper to use.

DDE   Stands for *Dynamic Data Exchange.* An older standard for communication between programs. It has largely been replaced by *OLE.*

Default   The configuration settings that a device or program will have without any intervention from you. Usually you can change the default settings, but care should be taken.

Desktop   In Windows NT, the Desktop is your entire screen. The files and folders on your screen are in a folder called Desktop, but you have to delve pretty deep to find your own Desktop folder. Start with your Windows NT Workstation folder and then go to Profiles. Inside Profiles should be a folder with your username on it and inside *that,* will be your Desktop (unless of course, the administrator has made other settings).

Dialog box   A window that opens to ask you impertinent questions or to request input. Windows and Windows NT programs are knee-deep in dialog boxes.

DLL Short for *Dynamic Link Library.* A file with information needed by one or more programs. Don't delete files with this extension willy-nilly because your programs will be dysfunctional without the .DLL files they need.

Domain The basic unit of a client/server network. In its simplest form, this is a server and a couple of workstations. To put it as generally as possible, a collection of computers that share a common domain database and security policy.

Driver A program made up of instructions to operate things added on to your computer, such as a printer, modem, or mouse. NT Workstation includes most drivers you're likely to need, but there are rare times when you need to acquire a newer driver (and instructions on installing it) from the manufacturer of the device.

Entire Network An NT Workstation icon that you'll see if you double-click on the Network Neighborhood icon on your Desktop. Sometimes, to see all the computers on a particular network, you'll need to double-click the Entire Network icon.

Exchange Microsoft's new messaging application, which you can access by double-clicking on the Inbox icon on your Desktop. With Microsoft Exchange, you can send and receive electronic mail using various services, including Microsoft Mail and Internet Mail, but you send messages from and store all messages in Microsoft Exchange, so you can find all your messages in one convenient place.

FAT An acronym for *File Allocation Table*, the file system type used by DOS, Windows 3.*x* and Windows 95, and one of the two file system types recognized by Windows NT.

File system A method used by the operating system to manage the files stored on a disk or one partition of a disk. NT Workstation recognizes both *FAT* and *NTFS* file systems.

Folder A means of organizing files. Each installed program will make its own folder and perhaps several subfolders. The user can likewise make folders to organize programs and files. Folders are analogous to Directories in Windows 3.1, DOS, and earlier versions of Windows NT.

Gateway/Hub A computer that connects two or more networks and relays messages and other communications from one network to another.

Home directory A directory that is accessible to a user and contains files and programs belonging to him or her. In Windows NT, a home directory is by default assigned to an individual user, but if permissions are set properly, it can be shared by many users.

Initialize To prepare for use. With disks, this means to format the disk so it can be read. Programmers use this term to mean to get everything in the program to a known, beginning state.

Kilobyte One thousand bytes (actually 1,024); abbreviated as *K* and *KB*.

Landscape A printer setting in which the characters are printed sideways along the length of the page. The opposite setting is *portrait.*

Log off To leave the operating system you're currently in and (in some instances) shut down the computer. Logging off an NT Workstation computer is simple; click the Start button on the Taskbar and select Shut Down. At this point, you've got three options: you can log off and shut down the computer, log off and restart the computer, or shut down all programs and log on as a different user. Click the circle next to the option that suits your present needs, then click Yes, and you'll be logged off.

Log on To sign on to a computer so you can use it. When you log on to most kinds of computers, you'll be asked to provide a username and password. NT Workstation is no exception to this rule. To log on to an NT Workstation computer, turn on the computer, and, when prompted to do so, press Ctrl+Alt+Delete and supply your username and password. Provided you've typed everything correctly, you should see the familiar NT Workstation Desktop. If you've made a typo, try reentering your username and password in the appropriate boxes on the logon screen. If you're still having problems after that, contact your system administrator.

Mapped drive A network drive that has been assigned a drive letter on your computer.

Megabyte One million bytes (actually 1,048,576); abbreviated as *M* or *MB.*

Modem A contraction for *modulator-demodulator.* A device that hooks up to phone lines so your computer can communicate with other computers, either individually or through an online service.

Multitasking   Using more than one application at a time. In Windows 3.1, you were *task switching,* moving back and forth between applications, but not actually using more than one at the same time. NT Workstation 4 makes true multitasking possible, but to get the full effect, you need to be running 32-bit programs.

Network   A series of two or more computers that are linked together. In a LAN (*Local Area Network*), the computers are physically connected by means of network adapter cards and cables. In a WAN (*Wide Area Network*), computers may be connected in a variety of ways, using modems and telephone lines or satellite connections, just to name two examples.

Network adapter   Also known as a network card, the piece of hardware that physically connects a server or workstation to a network.

Network Neighborhood   An NT Workstation icon that you'll see on your Desktop. Network Neighborhood is your key to sharing files, folders, and printers with other people. If you double-click on the Network Neighborhood icon, you should see icons for all the computers currently connected to your network. See Chapter 8 for complete details on how to use Network Neighborhood to your best advantage.

Network protocol/Network protocol stack   The agreed-upon language that computers on a network use to communicate with one another. Three of the most common network protocols are IPX/SPX, NetBEUI, and TCP/IP.

NTFS   An acronym for *New Technology File System.* A file system type recognized by Windows NT.

OLE   Short for *Object Linking and Embedding.* An automatic way for Windows programs to share data. (Pronounced *O-lay.*)

Online   To be in a state of readiness. A printer is said to be online when it's ready to print. These days, online mostly means being connected to another computer via a modem. The connection can be to a commercial service, an Internet provider, and so forth.

Optimize   Computer jargon for "improve the performance of."

Parallel A port on your computer usually used to connect a cable to a printer. Can also be used to connect other devices, such as an external drive or network adapter, to your computer. Information transmitted through a parallel port travels through multiple side-by-side paths inside the cable.

Password A sequence of characters that a user types when logging in to verify his or her identity.

Peer-to-peer network A network scheme that is often contrasted with client/server networking. On a peer-to-peer network, there is no hierarchy of server vs. client; all the computers are equal, and each may provide services to others, provided the appropriate permissions have been granted.

Peripheral A device attached to the outside of your computer. This includes the monitor, keyboard, mouse, and printer.

Permission A rule associated with an object (usually a directory, file, or printer) that regulates which users can have access to the object and in what manner.

Port A connecting point on your computer for plugging in external devices. At a minimum, most computers have two serial ports and one parallel (printer) port. Computers also have a specialized port for the keyboard; some have a special mouse port, too.

Portrait The usual way a page of text is printed with characters running across the width of the page. The opposite setting is *landscape.*

Primary domain controller The main server in a domain that stores the master copy of that domain's account database.

Protocol A set of rules that determine the flow of data and how it's used. The modems at either end of a communication line have to use the same protocol to talk to each other. Likewise, computers on a network need to be speaking the same protocol in order to connect.

RAM   Short for *Random Access Memory*. In a nutshell, RAM is where things happen in your computer. The processor (CPU) does the work, but it can hold only so much information. Programs and files are retrieved from the hard disk and stored in RAM so operations can proceed rapidly.

Register   To tell NT Workstation what program to use to open files of a certain type (that is, files with a particular extension). If a file type is registered, a double-click on a file of that type will start the necessary application and open the file. For example, a file with the .DOC extension will automatically be opened in WordPad or Word if you have it installed. A file with a .TXT extension will be opened in Notepad. Same as *associate*.

Registry   A database that keeps track of the configuration for a Windows NT computer. It is accessible only by using the Regedit program and is for experts only.

Remote Access   Something most of us who aren't system administrators probably don't have. Remote Access enables a user with the proper network permissions to log into a network using a dial-up (modem) connection. The reason most of us don't have Remote Access is that it can pose a serious network security risk.

Resources   A general term for some of the items commonly shared over a network: disk space, printers, network fax modems, and so forth.

Serial   A particular type of port that transmits information one bit at a time. Mostly used by a modem or a mouse and occasionally by a scanner.

Server   In a client/server network environment, a server is a computer that says, "You want it, I've got it." In other words, a server is the machine that provides *clients* with access to shared network resources, be they files, printers, or whatever.

Sharing   The process of making a resource (be it a file, directory, printer, fax modem, or whatever) available to network users.

Shortcut   A file that acts as a pointer to a file, folder, application, or device. Shortcuts are very small files that you can place almost anywhere. When you double-click on a shortcut, the object it points to will be opened, so you can have a shortcut to an object in various places without having to physically move or copy files.

Swap file   Space on the hard disk that NT Workstation uses to increase the amount of memory available to Windows NT programs. The swap file in NT Workstation 4 is dynamic, so it automatically grows larger or smaller based on current activity on the computer.

System resources   A finite portion of memory set aside for Windows NT to keep track of all its pieces. In earlier versions of Windows, running out of resources is common even if you have a lot of memory because the amount available for system resources cannot get larger. NT Workstation 4 has more space for system resources and manages those resources much more intelligently, so you can have many more programs open at once.

TCP/IP   An abbreviation for *Transport Control Protocol/Internet Protocol.* The most widely used network protocol stack on the Internet and on many other networks, large and small. TCP/IP is currently used to link all kinds of computers worldwide over a variety of media, from high-speed optical network cabling to regular phone lines.

Topology   A fancy term for the way a network is designed.

Username/Login name   A unique name identifying a user account to a system.

Virtual memory   Simulated RAM created by taking advantage of free space on the hard drive. Also called a *swap file.* If you start more programs or processes than your RAM has room for, the programs actively doing something will be placed in RAM while the less active or inactive ones will be moved to the swap file space on the hard drive. NT Workstation will automatically swap programs back and forth as needed. The swap file is dynamic in NT Workstation, which means it will automatically grow and shrink as needed.

Workgroup   A logical grouping of several computers whose users or work are in some way connected and who need or want to share resources with one another.

Workstation   In Windows NT parlance, a computer running NT Workstation 4 or any earlier version of NT Workstation. Also used as a generic term referring to a user's desktop computer.

Index

Note to the Reader: Main level entries are in **bold**. **Boldfaced** page numbers indicate primary discussions of a topic. *Italicized* page numbers indicate illustrations.

Q